Second Edition
Skillful 4

Reading & Writing Student's Book

Authors: Lindsay Warwick and Louis Rogers
Series Consultant: Dorothy E. Zemach

SCOPE AND SEQUENCE

		Video	Reading	Vocabulary
1 GATHERING **PAGE 8** **Business** ▶ **Magazine interview:** The rise of crowdfunding **Psychology** ▶ **Magazine article:** Are online "friends" a threat to development?		A Lebanese start-up	Recognize and understand assumptions in questions Read to identify the writer's position	Practice and use synonyms to adapt the register of your text
2 GAMES **PAGE 26** **Sociology** ▶ **Newspaper article:** Instant satisfaction **Behavioral research** ▶ **Journal article:** Gaming, society, and the individual		Mobile gaming	Interpret graphs and charts to better understand academic texts Read to identify stance and distancing	Practice and vocabulary for the description of data
3 ENERGY **PAGE 44** **Science** ▶ **Newspaper article:** The oldest energy source **Environment** ▶ **Magazine article:** Fracking—the future?		The nuclear debate	Complete a flow chart to understand stages of a process Read to infer the meaning of technical vocabulary	Practice and use language for describing energy production
4 RISK **PAGE 62** **Finance** ▶ **Article:** The credit crunch: Whose fault was it anyway? **Psychology** ▶ **Magazine article:** Risk-takers: Who are they?		Greek austerity	Read to identify the sequence of past events Practice taking notes for summaries	Practice and use attributive language
5 SPRAWL **PAGE 80** **Industry** ▶ **Online news article:** Rust Belt dystopia **Suburbanization** ▶ **Magazine article:** Suburbs of the future		Slum renewal	Practice questioning while reading Read to identify similarities and differences between multiple viewpoints	Practice and use academic alternatives to phrasal verbs

SCOPE AND SEQUENCE

Grammar	Writing	Study skills	Unit outcomes
Use concessive clauses and contrastive structures	Practice analyzing essay questions Write an essay analyzing the social and economic impacts of social media	Proof-reading	Recognize and understand the use and effect of assumptions in questions Identify and understand the writer's position Brainstorm and compose an essay
Use inverted conditionals: real and unreal present	Practice using data to support opinions Write a report describing the changes in online multiplayer gaming	Questioning numbers and statistics	Understand and use graphs and charts to support reading Understand stance and distancing to recognize the writer's attitude Compose and edit a report describing changes
Use transitive and intransitive verbs	Practice writing definitions Write a technical description of how hydroelectric energy is produced	Stages of the memory process	Recognize and understand the different stages presented in a text Recognize and infer meaning of technical vocabulary Brainstorm and compose a technical description
Use infinitive phrases	Practice integrating sources in your writing Write a summary of an article	The Harvard system	Recognize and understand the sequence of past events Practice taking notes for summaries Compose and edit a summary of an article
Use parallel structures	Practice integrating direct quotations in your writing Write an argumentative essay on the topic of suburbanization	Reflective learning	Practice using questions to process and reflect on the content of a text Recognize and understand similarities and differences in authors' opinions Brainstorm and compose an argumentative essay

SCOPE AND SEQUENCE

	Video	Reading	Vocabulary
6 BEHAVIOR **PAGE 98** **Criminology** ➤ **Online magazine article:** Born criminal **Cognitive neuroscience** ➤ **Magazine article:** Is your brain ready yet?	Kitchen rehab	Read to identify in-text referencing Read to identify cause and effect	Practice and use consequence phrases
7 EXPANSE **PAGE 116** **Urbanization** ➤ **Evaluative essay:** The benefits of urbanization **Society** ➤ **Newspaper feature:** Overpopulation: A problem or a myth?	Cairo's new capital	Read to identify and infer connections Read to identify persuasion techniques	Practice and use adjective + noun collocations
8 CHANGE **PAGE 134** **Business** ➤ **Online magazine article:** Adapt or die **Business** ➤ **Book excerpt:** Leadership and change management	Joint ventures	Read to infer cause and effect Read to identify concepts and theories	Practice and use academic phrases
9 FLOW **PAGE 152** **Environment** ➤ **Newspaper article:** Climate change 101 **Environment** ➤ **Journal article:** Thirstier than ever	The CO_2 forest	Practice using headings to predict the content of an academic text Read to identify commentary on evidence	Practice and use verb and noun collocations
10 CONFLICT **PAGE 170** **Psychology** ➤ **Magazine article:** Groupthink **Business** ➤ **Magazine article:** Successful teams and conflict	Escape rooms	Read to identify the function of in-text references Read to prepare for a seminar	Practice and use adverbs of stance

SCOPE AND SEQUENCE

Grammar	Writing	Study skills	Unit outcomes
Use inverted conditionals: imagined past	Practice using anaphoric and cataphoric referencing Write a cause-and-effect essay evaluating the cause of delinquent behavior in teenagers	Aiming for clarity	Identify and understand in-text referencing to support opinions in a text Practice identifying cause and effect Compose and edit a cause-and-effect essay
Use nominal clauses	Practice paraphrasing Write a persuasive essay on the topic of education in the fight against overpopulation	Emotive language and persuader words	Practice identifying and inferring connections made by the writer Practice identifying persuasion techniques employed by the writer Brainstorm, compose, and edit a persuasive essay
Use participle clauses	Practice report writing Write the body and conclusion of a business report	Checking your reading speed	Practice inferring cause and effect in an academic text Practice identifying and understanding concepts and theories presented in a text Compose and edit part of a business report
Use verb patterns	Practice commenting on sources Write a problem-and-solution essay on the topic of global warming	Planning your writing assignments spatially	Practice using headings to make predictions about what you are going to read Recognize and understand commentary on evidence Brainstorm, compose, and edit a problem-and-solution essay
Use subordinating conjunctions: *whatever, whoever, whichever,* etc.	Practice writing a reference list Write an argumentative essay about cooperation and conflict on teams	Using material of suitable quality and content	Recognize and understand references in a text Prepare and discuss a topic in preparation for a seminar Compose and edit an argumentative essay

INTRODUCTION
To the student

Academic success requires so much more than memorizing facts. It takes skills. This means that a successful student can both learn and think critically.

Skillful gives you:

- Skills you need to succeed when reading and listening to academic texts
- Skills you need to succeed when writing for and speaking to different audiences
- Skills for critically examining the issues presented by a speaker or a writer
- Study skills for learning and remembering the English language and important information.

To successfully use this book, use these strategies:

Come to class prepared to learn. This means that you should show up well fed, well rested, and prepared with the proper materials. Watch the video online and look at the discussion point before starting each new unit.

Ask questions and interact. Learning a language is not passive. You need to actively participate. Help your classmates, and let them help you. It is easier to learn a language with other people.

Practice! Memorize and use your new language. Use the *Skillful* online practice to develop the skills presented in the Student's Book. Review vocabulary on the review page.

Review your work. Look over the skills, grammar, and vocabulary from previous units. Study a little bit each day, not just before tests.

Be an independent learner, too. Look for opportunities to study and practice English outside of class, such as reading for pleasure and using the Internet in English. Remember that learning skills, like learning a language, takes time and practice. Be patient with yourself, but do not forget to set goals.

I hope you enjoy using *Skillful*! Check your progress and be proud of your success!

Dorothy E. Zemach – Series Consultant

Opening page

Each unit starts with two opening pages. These pages get you ready to study the topic of the unit. There is a video to watch and activities to do before you start your class.

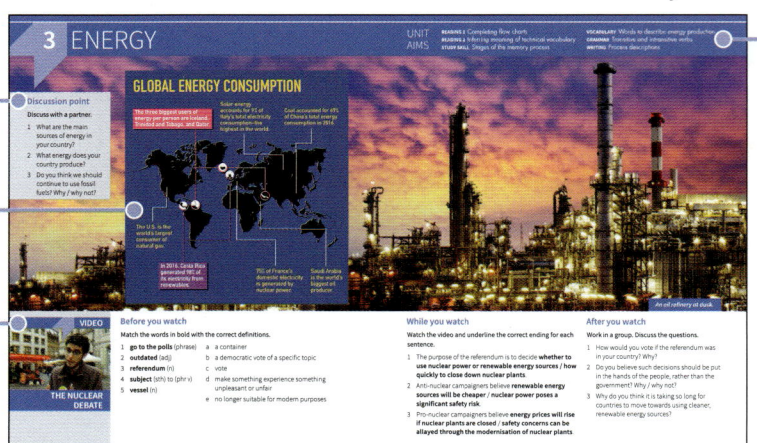

INTRODUCTION

Reading lessons

In every unit, there are two reading lessons and they present two different aspects of the unit topic and help you with ideas and language for your writing task.

Vocabulary to prepare you for the reading activities.

Every reading section helps you use a new reading skill.

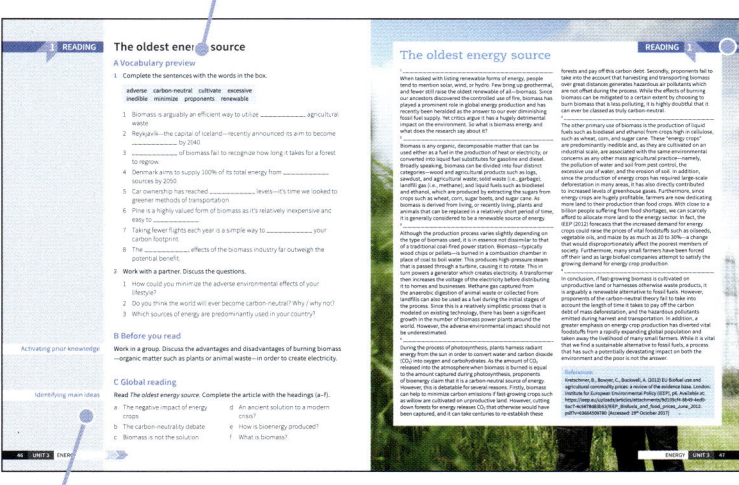

Develop your reading skills in each part of the reading lesson.

Writing lessons

After your reading lessons, there is a page for you to analyze a model answer to a writing task. This will help you organize your ideas and language and prepare for your final task at the end of the unit.

First, analyze the model answer.

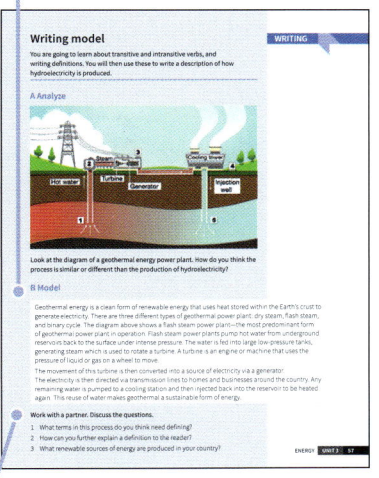

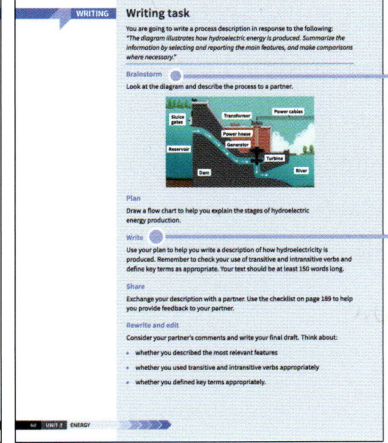

Brainstorm and plan your final writing task.

Finally, write your paragraph or essay.

Next, discuss your ideas.

INTRODUCTION

1 GATHERING

Discussion point

Discuss with a partner.

1 Which statistic in the infographic surprises you the most? Why?
2 How has social media influenced or changed shopping habits?
3 Do you find targeted advertising on social media useful or invasive? Why?

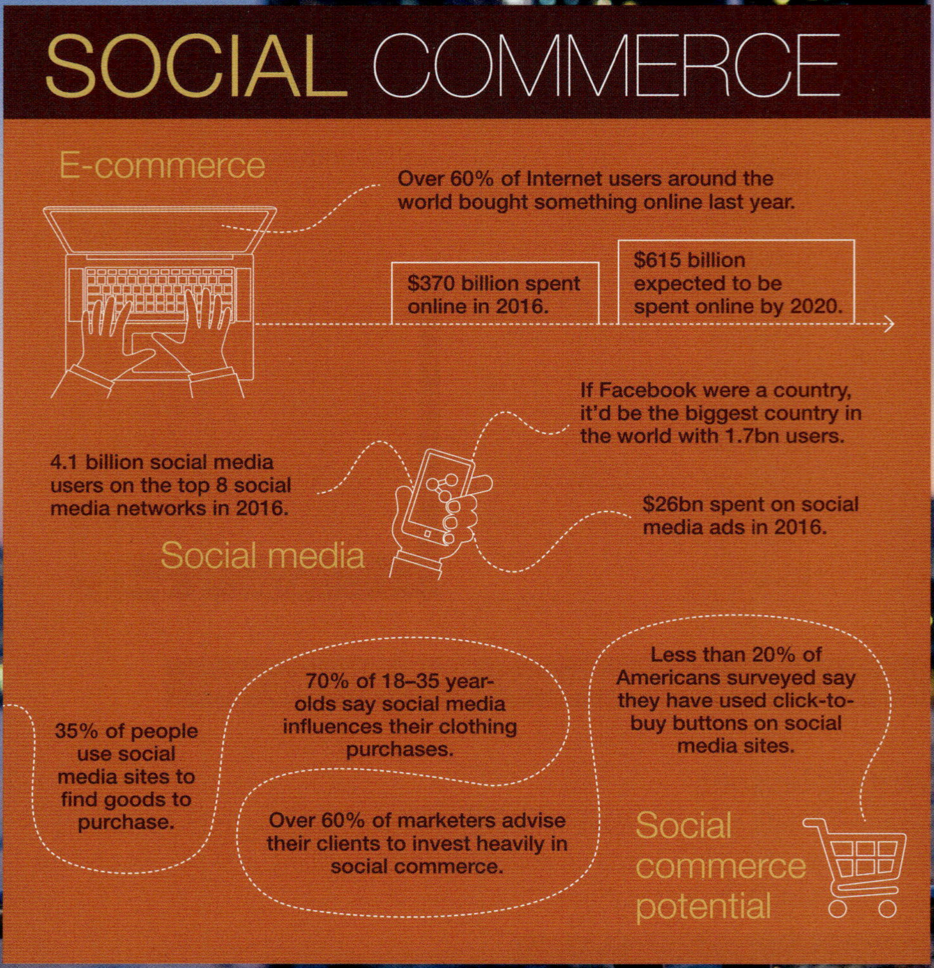

SOCIAL COMMERCE

E-commerce

Over 60% of Internet users around the world bought something online last year.

$370 billion spent online in 2016.

$615 billion expected to be spent online by 2020.

Social media

4.1 billion social media users on the top 8 social media networks in 2016.

If Facebook were a country, it'd be the biggest country in the world with 1.7bn users.

$26bn spent on social media ads in 2016.

Social commerce potential

35% of people use social media sites to find goods to purchase.

70% of 18–35 year-olds say social media influences their clothing purchases.

Less than 20% of Americans surveyed say they have used click-to-buy buttons on social media sites.

Over 60% of marketers advise their clients to invest heavily in social commerce.

VIDEO

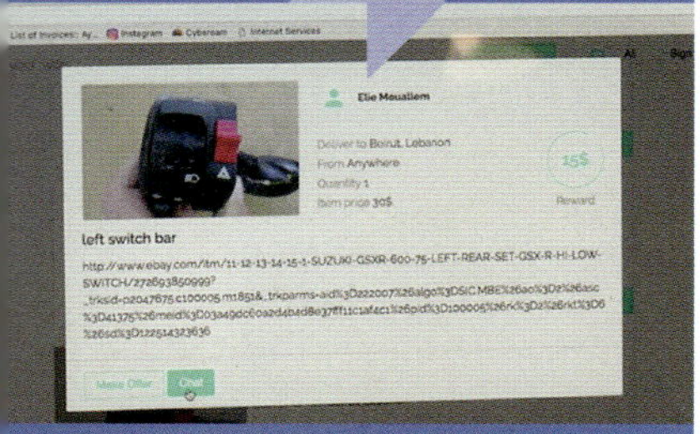

A LEBANESE START-UP

Before you watch

Match the words in bold with the correct definitions.

1 **anchor** (n)
2 **founder** (n)
3 **transaction** (n)
4 **viable** (adj)

a the process of buying and selling something
b a person who reads the news
c effective, able to succeed
d someone who starts an organization, business, etc.

UNIT AIMS

READING 1 Understanding assumptions in questions
READING 2 Identifying the writer's position
STUDY SKILL Editing your draft
VOCABULARY Synonyms and register
GRAMMAR Concessive clauses and contrastive structures
WRITING Analyzing essay questions

A young businesswoman using a smartphone in the city.

While you watch ✓

Watch the video and choose *T* (True) or *F* (False).

1 *On Your Way* helps people import Lebanese products. T / F
2 The majority of their customers are men. T / F
3 *On Your Way* offers its services for free. T / F
4 *On Your Way* is a great way for regular travelers to make money when they travel light. T / F

After you watch ✓

Work in a group. Discuss the questions.

1 Would a service like *On Your Way* be useful for you?
2 Would you be happy to fulfil an *On Your Way* request for somebody? Why / why not?
3 Can you foresee any issues a cross-border courier service like this may face?
4 What impact do you think a service like *On Your Way* could have on online retailers?

1 READING

The rise of crowdfunding

A Vocabulary preview

Complete the paragraph with the words in the box.

> backers   crowdfunding   entrepreneur   equity
> philanthropic   start-up   tangible   venture capital

Less than two decades ago, any [1] *entrepreneur* with a new idea would have had to go to a [2] *venture capital* company or similar to receive funding for their [3] *start-up* project, giving up a significant share of the [4] *equity* in exchange. These days, they have another option—[5] *crowdfunding*—a model that allows small businesses to attract online [6] *backers* who each invest small amounts of money in return for either a [7] *tangible* reward, such as a copy of the finished product, or a [8] *philanthropic* reward, such as helping someone in need.

B Before you read

Activating prior knowledge

Work with a partner. Discuss the questions.

1. Why do you think crowdfunding has become such a popular means of gaining investment?
2. What do you think makes a successful crowdfunding campaign?

C Global reading

Preparing to read

Read *The rise of crowdfunding*. Complete the interview with the questions (a–f).

a. What else, other than a lack of video and updates, can result in a failed campaign?
b. What should users do to give their start-up the best chance of achieving their targets?
c. Why is crowdfunding a more attractive way of getting investment these days?
d. The Keep-it-all model is clearly more beneficial, but does it work for all campaign types?
e. What type of reward should entrepreneurs offer potential investors?
f. How sure can I be that I'll get that large amount of funding I want?

The rise of crowdfunding

Journalist Sarah Finch interviews the economist Thomas Kerr about the rise of crowdfunding and how to run a successful campaign.

Sarah: 1 _____

Thomas: Crowdfunding allows entrepreneurs to bypass venture capital companies and reach a large number of potential investors online; where geography no longer matters. However, it's worth considering what level of investment you need. Last year, crowdfunding raised $4bn for entrepreneurs in the U.S., yet venture capital firms invested over $60bn. So, while crowdfunding may be an attractive option, investment from venture capitalists is still much higher. The latter is certainly something I'd recommend to entrepreneurs with large projects, or those who need expertise and support to help get their project off the ground.

Sarah: Let's imagine I decide to go down the crowdfunding route. 2 _____

Thomas: Firstly, you need to be realistic about how much money people will be willing to invest in your project. Kickstarter—one of the best-known crowdfunding sites—says that of the total projects that have been successfully funded on the site to date, 69% have raised less than $10,000. Only 3% of projects have raised over $100,000 and just 0.2% have raised $1 million. That suggests crowdfunding is more appropriate for smaller projects than large companies, even if it's the latter that get more attention in the media. It's also important to consider that Kickstarter campaigns currently have around a 35% success rate, meaning that 65% of projects fail to get the funding they need.

Sarah: 3 _____

Thomas: Research has shown that when it comes to more traditional types of investment, perception of quality is highly significant as investors use it to predict how much of a return they may get on their investment. Research carried out by Mollick at the University of Pennsylvania has indicated that the same is true of crowdfunding projects—those that were perceived to be of a higher quality were far more likely to hit their investment goals. Successful campaigns were also aided by videos explaining the product and frequent updates, particularly in the early stages. In fact, for many projects, a well-produced video pitch is a necessity. For example, I recently saw a campaign for a product called Flic—a small button in your house that allows you to wirelessly control apps on your phone. Now, read or hear that description and it means very little, but watch the video and within the first ten seconds you know exactly what it is and how it can benefit you. Of course, it's important to remember that not all campaigns involve start-ups—existing entrepreneurs have been known to turn to crowdfunding to get funding for new ideas. There are notable examples in gaming where designers wanted to pursue passion projects that publishers didn't want to make. There are also experienced scientists looking to fund research.

Sarah: 4 _____

Thomas: Mollick found that spelling errors, asking for too much investment, and having too long a deadline gave the perception that the project was low in quality and this reduced the success rate. However, it's not just quality that has an impact. Several studies have shown that without an effective network, an entrepreneur is likely to be unsuccessful in his or her campaign. This is true whether you're seeking venture capital or crowdfunding. With the latter, it's your social, online network that can make the difference. 30% of a crowdfunding campaign's investment comes from friends and family, showing just how vital they are. They start off the bidding and then tell others about it. If you don't know enough people to do that for you, your campaign won't develop much momentum.

Sarah: 5 _____

Thomas: There are four types of campaigns, not all of them offering a tangible benefit. Lending-based campaigns and donation-based campaigns are more philanthropic, especially the latter where the money goes towards scientific research or humanitarian projects. Equity-based campaigns, where investors get a share of the company in return for their investment, and reward-based campaigns are those which offer tangible rewards. The latter are the most common type and generally offer the investor a copy of the product they've backed or the opportunity to consume it; for example, to see the film that was produced. Researchers from the University of North Carolina have found that offering different tiers of rewards also helps to attract funding. Tiers give people the opportunity to decide how much money to invest and what they'd like to receive in exchange. For example, backers at higher tiers often receive limited editions of the product or promotional merchandise. Interestingly, a study in Asia found that people motivated by helping others tended to invest early, whereas those motivated by the promise of reward were late investors, so adding late rewards in the final days of the campaign can help projects get across that investment goal line.

Sarah: 6 _____

Thomas: With a Keep-it-all model, entrepreneurs keep any money invested, even if the target investment isn't reached. Although this sounds more beneficial to the entrepreneur, these campaigns are perceived as riskier and tend to be less successful as a result. Backers invest on the understanding that if the project doesn't reach its target, the product may never be made and they will lose their money. All-or-nothing campaigns are perceived as less risky as investors know that if the campaign doesn't achieve its target, they get their money back. I'd say that it's worth selecting the Keep-it-all model for small projects, but I would definitely recommend the All-or-nothing model for larger projects that are looking for greater investment.

1 READING

Understanding assumptions in questions

D Close reading

Interviewers often use assumptions in questions to encourage the interviewee to give a desired answer. Sometimes this works, and the interviewee confirms the assumption. However, sometimes the assumption is false and the interviewee corrects it. For example;

Q: *How can women compete successfully against men when running a crowdfunding campaign?*

(assumes that women are less able to run a successful campaign)

A: *Research shows women attract less venture capital funding. However, one study suggests they are around 10% more likely to achieve their target investment than men when crowdfunding.*

(interviewee corrects the false assumption using research and a statistic)

1 Read the questions in *The rise of crowdfunding* again. Identify the assumption the journalist makes in each. ✓

2 Read the economist's response to each question. ✓

   1 In which does he correct the journalist's assumptions?
   2 What evidence does he provide to support each correction?

3 Complete the sentences below with one word from the interview. ✓

   1 Crowdfunding makes _venture capital companies_ irrelevant when finding possible backers.
   2 Research indicates that crowdfunding best suits _high quality_ campaigns.
   3 Effective campaigns include video pitches and regular updates in the _early_ stages.
   4 An entrepreneur needs a good _network_ to help promote and invest in their campaign.
   5 Studies suggest that having reward _opportunities_ makes a campaign more attractive.
   6 Investors see Keep-it-all campaigns as _less risky_ than All-or-nothing campaigns.

E Critical thinking

In a group, discuss why you think women are less successful than men at attracting capital investment, but more successful at attracting crowdfunding.

Study skills: Proof-reading

When writing, you should edit your draft until you are happy with it. Then do some final proof-reading.
- Read it once again aloud—does it make sense?
- Look for mistakes such as typing and spelling errors. Look up doubtful spellings.
- If you used a spellchecker, check for words that are not misspellings but which are not the word you want to use (e.g., there/their).
- When proof-reading for grammar, punctuation and spelling, it can help to work backwards through your writing to avoid drifting into skim-reading.
- Note down certain errors you make regularly and be particularly careful in checking them.

© Stella Cottrell (2013)

1 Read the excerpt below aloud. Does it make sense? Does reading aloud help you to answer this question more easily?

> The rise of crowdfunding has positively contributed to the economy. Mollick (2016) surveyed 61,654 Kickstarter projects that had acheived their target investment of over $1,000 between 2009 and 2015. He found that, 5,135 full-time jobs has been created by these projects in addition to the creator's jobs. Furthermore, around 4,994 new companies or partnerships has been created with around 4,130 still in operation in 2016. While no further revenue was generated by 30.8% of projects once their campaign had finished, the other 59.2% generated a total revenue of $3.4bn outside of Kickstarter. This means that, for every dollar that was bid in Kickstarter, an average of $2.46 revenue were raised outside of the site. As these statistics represent just one of many crowdfunding sights and only 30% of the 61,654 projects responded to Mollick's survey, they demonstrate that crowdfunding has had a significant economic impact since it's inception.

2 Read the paragraph again and correct the eight errors. Categorize them into:
1 grammar errors
2 punctuation errors
3 spelling errors
4 words spelled correctly but incorrectly for the sentence context (e.g., *there / their*).

3 Work with a partner. Discuss the questions.
1 Did you find the strategies in the skills box useful when proof-reading the paragraph? Why / why not?
2 How can you approach this when proof-reading your own work?

2 READING

Are online "friends" a threat to development?

A Vocabulary preview

Complete the definitions with the words in bold.

1. I'd actually class him as more of an **acquaintance** than a friend.
2. Research links smartphone addiction to **anti-social** behavior in adolescents.
3. Critics are concerned that social media is turning us into **narcissists**.
4. **Ties** between families have strengthened in the social media age.
5. **Adolescents** are negatively influenced by their online peers.
6. It's important to **nurture** both our online and offline relationships.
7. Despite living in a **hyper-connected** society, we are more alone than ever.
8. I'd argue that social media actually promotes **empathy**.

a _____ (n) relationships or connections with a person or place
b _____ (v) to help someone or something to develop
c _____ (n) someone you know a little, who isn't a close friend
d _____ (adj) always linked to people via technology
e _____ (n) people who admire themselves too much
f _____ (n) children who are changing into young adults
g _____ (adj) showing a lack of care for others or society in general
h _____ (n) the ability to understand or imagine how someone feels

B Before you read

Activating prior knowledge

With a partner, discuss the advantages and disadvantages of young people using social media. Then decide whether the former outweigh the latter.

C Global reading

Identifying the writer's position

> To identify if the writer agrees or disagrees with a viewpoint, look for:
> - positive or negative adjectives or adverbs (e.g., *not credible*, *interestingly*)
> - opinion language (*agree*, *disagree*, *true*, *untrue*, *believe*, *view*)
> - linking phrases and signposts (*however*, *therefore*, *although*, *in fact*)

Read *Are online "friends" a threat to development?* Which two statements describe the writer's position on social networking?

1. Young people are losing their face-to-face friends.
2. There are advantages to having online friends.
3. People reveal too much information online.
4. Social networking is changing young people's personalities.

Are online "friends" a threat to development?

> An excerpt from *Nurturing a Child's Emotional Development* by psychologist Dr. Kristel Sharpe

[1]Chapter two comprised a discussion on how vital childhood friendships are for a person's emotional development. They help us to build trust with people outside of the family and learn how to compromise, share, and manage conflict. When growing up, our friends provide the support we need to allow us to experiment with who we are. They give us feedback which helps us to change our behavior, and the people we ultimately become.

[2]The impact of technology on the nature of our friendships has been a much-debated topic since the meteoric rise of social networks. Advancements in mobile technology and social networking sites mean we spend more time online than ever before. After all, if Facebook were a country, it would be the largest in the world by population (World Economic Forum, 2016). According to the Nielson Group (2016), 22% of our overall online media time is spent on social media. It is therefore not surprising that so many psychologists, sociologists, and others are eager to give their thoughts on how this is impacting negatively on our society. It is only now, however, that we are starting to see the kind of empirical evidence necessary to differentiate fact from fiction.

[3]The biggest criticism levelled at social networking is that our young people are losing their offline friends to online friends who are unable to provide the same level of emotional support and satisfaction. In fact, there is a lot of research that shows these criticisms are generally unfounded. Psychologist Kelly Allen believes that it is socially adjusted adolescents who are more likely to have a social networking profile than those who are not and that people are not substituting offline friends with online companions, but are instead using them to support their offline relationships. There is also evidence that social networks allow people to have a much more diverse set of friends. One study conducted by the Pew Internet and American Life Project (2009) found that people seek knowledge from, and share knowledge with, people from a wider variety of backgrounds online.

[4]It is certainly true that our definition of friendship is evolving. An acquaintance we saw twice a year is now a friend we regularly talk to online. Yes, this tie is weaker than a relationship in the real world, but there is evidence that young people still have a lot to gain from it. A study conducted by Michigan State University (2010) concluded that our virtual friendships provide social benefits and improve our psychological well-being. Our weaker ties contribute to this in particular. So, teenagers do not appear to be losing their face-to-face friends, and the additional connections provided by social networking have proven to be beneficial.

2 READING

[5]But there is one element of social networking that is deeply worrying and that is the fact that we find ourselves in a hyper-connected world: one where people access social media day and night, excited to make announcements about the tiniest details of their lives. Research is starting to show that this culture is negatively affecting not our friendships, but our character. Professor Larry D. Rosen, in his book *iDisorder*, presents evidence that social networking is turning us into narcissists. He says that young people who overuse social networking sites can become vain, aggressive, and display anti-social behavior in their offline lives. He says that sitting behind a screen makes them harsher and more mean-spirited. But perhaps an even more disturbing repercussion is that one of our most basic emotions seems to be disappearing—empathy. This is the emotion that bonds us together; it allows us to see the world from our friends' points of view. Without it, we are far less able to connect and form meaningful adult relationships. And yet a study has found that college students are actually 40% less empathetic than college students 30 years ago, with the largest decline occurring from the year 2000. In the 2010 study, fewer students described themselves as "soft-hearted" and more claimed that they are not affected when friends have bad fortune (O'Brien, 2010).

[6]Sherry Turkle, a professor of social sciences at MIT, has made a fascinating observation about the impact of being constantly plugged into your smartphone. She has noticed that these devices permit us to have complete control over our friendships. She has seen that young people determine who they communicate with, when, and how as social networks allow them to tidy up and manage friendships, even though in the real world they are unpredictable and difficult to deal with. She has observed teenagers eradicate the need for a lengthy, awkward conversation to resolve an issue by simply clicking a button and unfriending that person.

[7]It appears that people are no longer comfortable being alone and yet, Turkle asserts that being alone is a time when we self-reflect and get in touch with who we really are. It is only when we do this that we can make meaningful friendships with others. She believes, as is the title of her 2011 book, that we are simply *Alone Together*. The impact of being "alone together" is one that should concern parents. I have spoken to children who have expressed frustration at losing their parent's attention to a mobile phone. One child highlighted the fact that their mother would once stand and chat to other parents at the school gate, but now just stands and spends that time in the virtual world. This is teaching children how not to connect with others.

[8]These changes in both our behavior and character are rather disconcerting, so it is clear that we need to place our focus here when nurturing a child's development. Our young people may still have good offline relationships and may only use social networking for fostering face-to-face friendships. However, if they continue to develop the narcissistic tendencies outlined above, along with a reduction in empathy, a fear of the unpredictability of friendships, and an inability to self-reflect, our young people could well be in trouble. It is therefore here that I would like to move on to making suggestions about ways to encourage our young people to modify their online behavior so that they can develop the kinds of friendships that are required to grow into well-adjusted and happy adults.

D Close reading

Read the text again and choose the correct answer (a, b, c, or d).

1. According to the author, children modify their conduct when friends
   a. force them to give up things they want.
   b. provide comments on their actions.
   c. start arguments with them.
   d. demonstrate confidence in them.
2. According to 2009 research, one effect of social networking is that people
   a. replace offline friends with online acquaintances.
   b. become better able to manage friendships.
   c. expand their offline friendship network.
   d. learn from a wide range of other users.
3. Larry D. Rosen believes that social networking has
   a. a negative impact on our offline behavior.
   b. improved our emotional bonds.
   c. given us a better understanding of others.
   d. given away too much of our privacy.
4. Sherry Turkle believes that technology has resulted in people
   a. going online to solve relationship issues.
   b. thinking more carefully about their lives.
   c. interacting with friends in a less emotional manner.
   d. building more challenging friendships.

E Critical thinking

Work in a group. Discuss the questions.

1. Is social networking good for our emotional health? Why / why not?
2. Has social media had a negative impact on our offline character? Why / why not?
3. What can young people, parents, schools, and the government do to reduce the problems associated with social networking?

READING 2

Reading for detail

VOCABULARY

Vocabulary development

Synonyms and register

A large part of academic writing is choosing language that is appropriate to your intended reader. Vocabulary that is appropriate in one context may not be appropriate in another. Learning a broad range of synonyms will help you adapt the register of your text.

1 Skim read *Are online "friends" a threat to development?* Find more formal synonyms of the words in bold. Use the paragraph number in parentheses to help you.

1 **included** (1) _____ 7 **happening** (5) _____
2 **developments** (2) _____ 8 **let** (6) _____
3 **ask for** (3) _____ 9 **decide** (6) _____
4 **shown** (4) _____ 10 **remove** (6) _____
5 **part** (5) _____ 11 **states firmly** (7) _____
6 **effect** (5) _____ 12 **worrying** (8) _____

2 Replace the underlined words with the more formal synonyms in the box.

> are able to   asserts   comprehend   derived   disconcerting   distant   diverse
> element   establish   gravity   manage   permits ... to   repercussions   seek   strategy

1 Many sociologists find the negative <u>effects</u> of our hyper-connected world <u>worrying</u>.
2 Social media <u>lets</u> us connect, even when physically <u>far apart</u>.
3 A worrying <u>part</u> of social media is the ability to <u>start</u> friendships with people you have not met in person.
4 With social media, we <u>can</u> <u>look for</u> friendships among a more <u>varied</u> group of people.
5 It's difficult to <u>understand</u> the <u>seriousness</u> of social media's impact.

✓3 Replace repeated words in the text with suitable formal synonyms.

The human brain is constantly changing, and neuroscientist Gary Small says new technologies are changing it further. He also says that technology is improving our decision-making skills. One study carried out with people aged between 55 and 76 showed that the brains of those that could already use the Internet showed much greater activity than those who could not. As many older people find they are unable to keep the same level of brain function as they age, Gary believes using the Internet may help them keep good brain function throughout their lives. However, he is also aware of the danger of using the Internet, such as a fall in empathy levels. He suggests people avoid this fall by developing their face-to-face relationships without the use of technology.

Academic words

VOCABULARY

1 Complete the definitions with the words in bold.

1 Social networks **aid** the reunion of old school friends and distant family.
2 Most people are unable to **differentiate** between social media and social networking.
3 There is **empirical** evidence to show that social media has a negative impact on character.
4 The military first developed the system that would **evolve** into the Internet.
5 People should **modify** their use of technology when in the company of others.
6 The **perception** that only young people use social media is largely unfounded.
7 Many use social media to **pursue** friendships with like-minded individuals.
8 Crowdsourcing is a popular way of getting people together to **resolve** an issue.

a _____ (v) to see or show a difference between things
b _____ (n) the way you think about or understand something
c _____ (v) to gradually develop or change
d _____ (v) to find a satisfactory way of dealing with a problem
e _____ (v) to change something slightly in order to improve it
f _____ (v) to help
g _____ (v) to try to achieve something
h _____ (adj) based on real experience or scientific experiments

2 Complete the questions with words from Exercise 1. Change the form if necessary.

1 How sensible is it to _____ friendships with people you've never met face-to-face?
2 How do you think social networking both _____ and harms relationships with family?
3 Would you ever ask people online to help you _____ a serious issue?
4 How important is it to provide _____ evidence when making an academic argument?
5 How can a YouTube vlogger _____ their content from others?
6 How much do you _____ your use of technology when in class or with other people?
7 How important are people's _____ of you online?
8 How might social networks _____ in future?

3 Work with a partner. Discuss the questions from Exercise 2.

GATHERING UNIT 1 19

CRITICAL THINKING

Critical thinking

Identifying types of evidence

An academic argument needs to be supported by evidence. Evidence can be in the following form:

1 **Data, statistics, or research from credible and unbiased sources**

   You need to be realistic about how much money people will invest in your project. 69% have raised less than $10,000.

2 **An opinion from a credible and unbiased expert**

   All-or-nothing campaigns are perceived as less risky.
   (Economist, Thomas Kerr)

3 **Anecdotal evidence**

   I recently saw a campaign for a product called Flic—a small button in your house that allows you to wirelessly control apps on your phone … watch the video and within the first ten seconds you know exactly what it is and how it can benefit you.

1 Read *Are online "friends" a threat to development?* again. Find and underline arguments in the text that match sentences 1–8. Use the paragraph number in parentheses to help you.

   1 Technological developments have resulted in people being on the Internet for longer. (2)
   2 Claims that social networking causes people to lose friends are not supported by evidence. (3)
   3 Young people can talk to a wider range of people online. (3)
   4 Social networking can be advantageous for teenagers' emotional health. (4)
   5 Social networking is causing young people to think only of themselves. (5)
   6 Technology allows users to determine the nature of our friendships. (6)
   7 People do not want to be on their own anymore. (7)
   8 Parents ought to worry about the effect of using technology in the company of others. (7)

2 Skim the text again and decide whether the arguments in Exercise 1 are supported by statistics (S), research (R), an expert opinion (EO), or anecdotal evidence (AE).

3 Work with a partner. Assess the strengths and weaknesses of each type of evidence used to support the arguments in Exercise 1. Which do you think is the most effective type? Why?

Writing model

You are going to learn about concessive clauses, contrastive structures, and how to analyze essay questions. You are then going to use these to write an essay about the social and economic impacts of social media.

A Model

1 Match the essay introduction to the question it is answering.

> Since the inception of social media in the mid-2000s, its popularity has grown exponentially. Often defined as platforms such as Facebook and YouTube, the term *social media* most accurately describes the content which people share via those platforms (Taylor et al. 2015). Sharing content in this way has evolved to become an integral part of our social fabric, determining the way we communicate with each other, share and receive news, and work. Although some of these advancements will no doubt prove to be positive, understanding any detrimental effects will allow us to pursue solutions. This essay will therefore examine both the potential positive and negative impacts of social media use on our physical and mental well-being and assess their significance on society.

1 Evaluate the impact of social media on the health of its users today.
2 Justify the future use of social networking in education.
3 Outline the social and economic impacts of social media in the last decade.
4 Examine the impact of social media on society or on business and illustrate with examples.
5 Identify key social and economic impacts of teenagers owning smartphones.

2 Work with a partner. Discuss the questions.
   1 What are some positive effects of social media on our physical and mental well-being?
   2 What are some negative effects of social media on our physical and mental well-being?
   3 Do you think the positives outweigh the negatives or vice versa? Why?

B Analyze

1 Read the introduction more carefully. Which sentence(s):
   1 give any useful definitions?
   2 introduce the main topic of the essay?
   3 give an outline of what the essay will say?
   4 state why the topic is important?

2 Order the items in Exercise 1 to create a logical essay introduction. More than one answer may be possible.

GRAMMAR

Grammar

Concessive clauses and contrastive structures

Concessive clauses—those beginning with *although*, *though,* or *even though*—allow writers to acknowledge an alternative point of view, before presenting their own, often contrary position:

Even though *purchases can be made via social media, the feature is yet to catch on.*

Other structures which can be used to contrast information include:

It is true that *there are positives to social media.* ***Nevertheless****, there are also negatives.*
Much as *social media takes up a lot of our time, it does help to strengthen relationships.*

Note that *despite* and *in spite of* can be followed by either a noun or a gerund.

1 Match (1–6) to (a–f) to concede or contrast ideas.

1 Despite many adolescents using Facebook and YouTube,
2 Even though many parents monitor their children's online activity,
3 Although many of us take care to protect our privacy online,
4 Much as social media can be a useful tool,
5 It is true that social media can cause feelings of anxiety.
6 While traditional advertising can be expensive,

a its impact on our offline character is hugely disconcerting.
b promoting products on social media is not.
c it is impossible to protect them at all times.
d not all young people want to engage with social media.
e identity theft is still a prominent issue.
f Nevertheless, it has done a great deal to raise awareness of mental health.

2 Write sentences giving your opinions on the topics in bold, using the prompts provided and the words in parentheses.

1 **Children and smartphones:** necessary for safety / dangerous for health (Even though)
2 **Smartphones in schools:** can enhance education / can distract (although)
3 **Smartphones and sleep:** disrupt sleep / some apps aid sleep (in spite of)
4 **Social media in the workplace:** can increase productivity / can reduce productivity (It is true that / Nevertheless)
5 **Social media and privacy:** privacy issues / benefits—which are greater? (despite)

3 Compare sentences with a partner. How do your views differ?

Writing skill

> Before writing an essay, follow these steps to analyze the question:
> 1 Identify the key words in the question as this will help you to understand the main subject area and its particular focus.
> 2 Identify restricting words which limit what you should write (e.g., time periods, particular areas of a subject, number of things to write about).
> 3 Identify the meaning of the instruction word or phrase (e.g., *analyze, to what extent, discuss*).

WRITING

Analyzing essay questions

1 Underline the key words in the essay questions below.
   1 Evaluate the <u>impact of social media</u> on the <u>health of its users today</u>.
   2 Justify the <u>future use of social networking in education</u>.
   3 Outline the <u>social and economic impacts</u> of social media in the <u>last decade</u>.
   4 Examine the <u>impact of social media</u> on <u>society or on business</u> and illustrate with <u>examples</u>.

2 Identify the restricting words in the essay questions in Exercise 1.

3 Match the instruction words in the box with their meanings.

| analyze   describe   discuss   evaluate   examine   illustrate   justify   outline |

   1 _describe_ = give details about how and why something happens.
   2 _illustrate_ = give examples to support an idea or argument.
   3 _discuss_ = present an argument while exploring both sides of the issue.
   4 _analyze_ = look at the facts and issues in close detail and investigate what they mean.
   5 _evaluate_ = provide evidence for an argument, considering alternative views too.
   6 _justify_ = make a judgment about something.
   7 _outline_ = give the main points of something but not the small details.
   8 _examine_ = look at the component parts of something, discuss them, and show how they relate to each other.

4 Read the essay outline below. Which question in Exercise 1 is it answering?

Intro: Define social media, mention commercial impact, state essay purpose.
Main body: State how social media has impacted on advertising and revenue, client/colleague communication, and productivity. Suggest what each one means for companies.
Conclusion: Both benefits and issues. Benefits largely outweigh issues.

WRITING

Writing task

You are going to write an essay in response to the following question:
"Outline the social and economic impacts of social media."

Brainstorm

What are some key social and economic impacts of social media? Complete the spidergram.

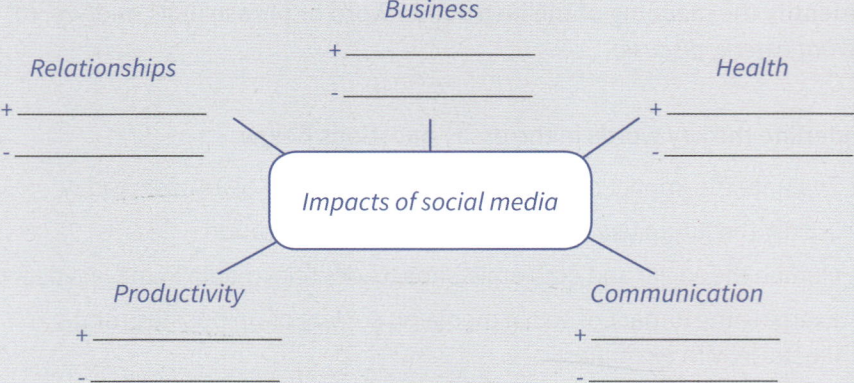

Plan

Read the essay question carefully. What exactly do you have to do? Decide which information you should include in your essay. Order the ideas so they are presented logically in your text. Check that your plan will help you to answer the essay question correctly.

Write

Use your plan to make sure you organize your ideas effectively and answer the question clearly. Remember to use concessive clauses and contrastive structures where appropriate and to select more formal academic words when choosing synonyms to bring a variety of vocabulary to your essay.

Share

Exchange your essay with a partner. Use the checklist on page 189 to help you provide feedback to your partner.

Rewrite and edit

Consider your partner's comments and write your final draft. Think about:

- whether you answered the question clearly
- whether you used concessive clauses and contrastive structures appropriately
- whether you analyzed the question sufficiently.

Review

Wordlist

MACMILLAN DICTIONARY

Vocabulary preview

acquaintance (n)	crowdfunding (n)	hyper-connected (adj)	start-up (n)
adolescent (n) *	empathy (n)	narcissist (n)	tangible (adj)
anti-social (adj)	entrepreneur (n)	nurture (n)	tie (n) **
backer (n)	equity (n)	philanthropic (adj)	venture capital (n)

Vocabulary development

advancement (n)	comprise (v) **	detriment (n)	repercussion (n)
assert (v) **	derive (v) **	disconcerting (adj)	
comprehend (v)	determine (v) **	eradicate (v)	

Academic words

aid (v) **	empirical (adj) *	modify (v) *	pursue (v) **
differentiate (v) *	evolve (v) **	perception (n) **	resolve (v) *

Academic words review

Complete the sentences using the correct form of the words in the box.

| aid | differentiate | empirical | perception | pursue |

1. When Ed graduated, he wanted to _pursue_ his dream of becoming a film director.
2. When reading a text, it is important to _differentiate_ between fact and opinion.
3. Some people think the government should spend less on overseas _aid_.
4. It is important to gather _empirical_ evidence to support your argument.
5. The public's _perception_ of crowdfunding has changed as people have become more familiar with it.

Unit review

Reading 1	☐ I can understand assumptions in questions.
Reading 2	☐ I can identify the writer's position.
Study skill	☐ I can edit my draft.
Vocabulary	☐ I can use synonyms and different registers.
Grammar	☐ I can use concessive clauses.
Writing	☐ I can analyze essay questions.

2 GAMES

Gaming by percentages

Discussion point

Discuss with a partner.

1 Do you think video games have a positive impact on children in your country? Why / why not?
2 Do you think video games are socially isolating? Why / why not?
3 What effects do video games have on academic performance and health?

Gamers by gender

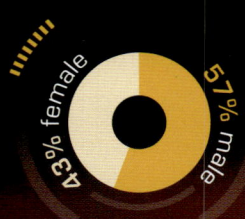
43% female / 57% male

66%

66% of parents say that gaming has a positive effect on their children's development

42%

42% of American households own a games console

75%

75% of teenagers prefer online gaming to playing alone

38%

Gaming can improve decision-making by 38%

VIDEO

MOBILE GAMING

Before you watch

Match the words in bold with the correct definitions.

1 **console** (n) — d
2 **gross** (v) — c
3 **platform** (n) — a
4 **value** (v) — b

a a technology for building software on
b judge how much money something could be sold for
c earn an amount of money before tax is paid and costs are deducted
d a device for playing games

26 UNIT 2 GAMES

UNIT AIMS

READING 1 Interpreting visual data
READING 2 Identifying stance and distancing
STUDY SKILL Questioning numbers and statistics
VOCABULARY Vocabulary for the description of data
GRAMMAR Inverted conditionals: real and unreal present
WRITING Using data to support opinions

Commentators at the DreamHack digital festival.

While you watch

Watch the video and choose *T* (True) or *F* (False).

1 The value of the mobile games industry is expected to double by next year. T / **F**
2 People like playing games on mobiles because it is convenient. **T** / F
3 Mobile games are starting to offer a gaming experience that is comparable to a console game. **T** / F
4 Mobile games now have the majority market share of the gaming industry. T / **F**

After you watch

Work with a partner. Discuss the questions.

1 Why have mobile devices broadened the popularity of video games?
2 The gaming industry generates a higher annual revenue than the movie and music industries combined. What possible explanations are there for this?
3 The concept of a "game", from ancient board games to modern mobile gaming, has been popular throughout the ages. Why do you think this is the case?

1 READING

Instant satisfaction

A Vocabulary preview

1 Complete the sentences with the words in the box.

| consumption | dominate | embrace | feasible |
| norm | sector | staggering | subscription |

1 _____-based streaming services have greatly improved the quality of television.
2 Massive online multiplayer games _____ the video game industry in my country.
3 Streaming is the _____ in my country—people rarely, if ever, purchase physical media these days.
4 A _____ proportion of young people in my country rarely watch traditionally broadcasted television anymore.
5 Young people are quicker to _____ new technology as they've grown up around it.
6 Pioneers of a new _____, such as Netflix, are usually the most successful.
7 It's _____ that streaming will destroy cinema within my lifetime.
8 _____ of physical media is likely to see a revival over the next decade.

2 Work with a partner. Discuss to what extent you agree with the sentences in Exercise 1.

B Before you read

Activating prior knowledge

Work with a partner. Discuss how technology has evolved over the past 50 years and the positive / negative impact these changes have had on society.

C Global reading

Identifying main ideas

Complete *Instant satisfaction* with the paragraph headings (a–f).

a Media and demographics
b The origins of media streaming
c Trends in the gaming industry
d The death of broadcasting?
e Transition in all sectors
f A trend toward digital consumption

Instant satisfaction

READING 1

1 _____

Streaming and on-demand services have demonstrated exponential growth in recent years, largely due to the widespread availability of high-speed Internet connections and improved wireless connectivity. Without the vast improvements in these fields, streaming as we know it simply would not be technologically feasible. While streaming has come to dominate several contemporary industries, its origins can actually be traced back to the early 80s when the hacking community used it for file sharing. Over the following two decades, the technology improved enough to facilitate the video sharing sites that have transformed how we consume media today. This report looks at media consumption trends in several industries and assesses their impact on society as a whole.

2 _____

Perhaps one of the biggest changes of the past 20 years is the shift away from physical media. No industry exemplifies this change more so than the music industry. Sales of physical singles and albums have dropped dramatically since the inception of digital media services such as iTunes and Spotify. Today the bulk of music is consumed digitally, although overall, the rate of digital downloads and streamed music has started to flatten out. As evidenced in Figure 1.1, income from digital sales, in all formats, now constitutes in excess of 50% of the market and has remained consistently higher than physical sales for the past three years. While an increasing number of people are choosing to buck this trend—sales of vinyl are at a 25-year high—the vast majority are embracing all forms of digital media. Should this trend continue, physical media may well become a thing of the past sooner than we think.

3 _____

There has also been a significant rise in online subscription video and on-demand TV services such as Amazon Prime and Netflix. Digital TV Research—a London-based media research company—forecasts that revenues from video streaming services will reach $32 billion in 2021, up from just under $2 billion in 2010. Countries such as China will see increases from just $37 million in 2010 to $3 billion in 2020. Without doubt, the leading video sharing site in the world is YouTube. A staggering 300 hours of video footage is uploaded to YouTube every minute and 5 billion videos are watched daily—1 billion of which are accessed via a mobile platform. Companies are also increasingly using it to advertise their products and to communicate directly with consumers. In terms of popularity, YouTube is second only to Google, and viewing figures far outstrip those of its direct competitors. Should growth rates continue in this way, on-demand and subscription viewing could surpass traditional broadcasting as the primary source of television.

4 _____

There are, however, distinct generational differences in media consumption. According to Ericsson (2015), 82% of 60–69-year-olds watch traditionally broadcasted television on a daily basis, while only 60% of 16–34 year olds consume media this way. Just over half of this younger generation watches all videos on a smartphone, laptop, or tablet. Broadly speaking, 90% of YouTube viewers are under 50—a statistic replicated across virtually all paid-for media platforms. People aged 14–25 are more likely to subscribe to a video streaming channel than to pay TV. In comparison, about a third more people over the age of 49 are likely to subscribe to pay TV. Newspapers, either in print or digital formats, appeal only to a minority of younger people, whereas approximately five times the number of pensioners consume news this way. Consequently, this is seen by many in the industry as an area of potential growth as it becomes the norm for the proportion of users in new formats to dominate traditional ones.

5 _____

Though it may seem counterintuitive, the trend towards digital media is far less pronounced in the video game sector. According to PwC (2016), physical sales still dominate the market, with digital media being outsold by 4 to 1. However, cross-platform games—those that can be available on desktops, consoles, and mobile devices—and massively multiplayer online games (MMOG), like *World of Warcraft*, look set to fuel an explosion in growth. Another key revenue stream for the industry is in-game purchases of supplementary content that, while not essential to the core gameplay, may enhance or personalize the overall experience.

6 _____

In many industries, sales of digital media are rapidly outstripping their physical counterparts. CD sales have been steadily declining for the past decade, and in the past three years, sales of digital media have dominated the market. Access to subscription TV services has also risen dramatically in recent years, with many predicting 1,000% growth over the next decade. This trend is likely to be exacerbated by the younger generation's preference for digital forms of media. However, sales of physical media in the gaming industry remain buoyant, arguably due to the huge file size of most digital games, which can be up to 16 times that of a standard movie. However, growth in in-game purchases and MMOG markets is likely to transform the industry in the years to come.

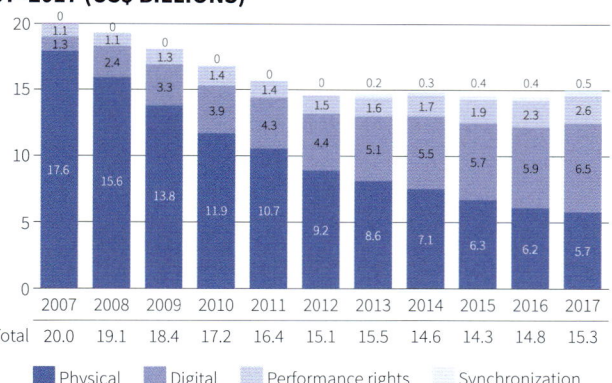

WORLDWIDE MUSIC INDUSTRY REVENUES 2007–2017 (US$ BILLIONS) — Figure 1.1

Legend: Physical, Digital, Performance rights, Synchronization

1 READING

Interpreting visual data

D Close reading

> Graphs and charts are an efficient way for an author to communicate large amounts of information using little space and few words. Interpreting graphs can give you a better understanding of the bigger picture behind the article.

1 Look at Figure 1.1 in *Instant satisfaction* again and complete the summary.

The graph shows changes in revenue streams in the music industry from 2007 to 2017. From 2007 to 2011 sales of physical media ¹*exceeded / were lower than* combined revenue from all other areas. Synchronization—revenue from the use of music in advertising, film, TV, etc.—provided ²*no / some* income until 2011. Between 2007 and 2017 the income from performance rights ³*doubled / halved*. There has been a ⁴*steady / slow* rise in digital sales and today it is the main income stream.

2 Look at Figure 1.1 again and complete the sentences.

1 In 2007, the total revenue generated from sales, performance rights, and synchronization was $___ billion.
2 In 2010, the industry generated $___ billion from physical sales.
3 In 2014, the combined revenue generated by physical and digital sales was $___ billion.
4 Between 2012 and 2017, revenue from digital sales increased by $___ billion.
5 In 2017, physical sales generated $___ billion less than they did a decade earlier.

3 Work with a partner. Discuss the questions.

1 In terms of total revenue, physical sales, and digital sales, what general trends are indicated in Figure 1.1?
2 What factors may have caused these changes?

E Critical thinking

Work in a group. Discuss the questions.

1 What do you think are the main reasons for the increased popularity of streaming and online gaming?
2 What are some of the disadvantages of streaming services? How can these affect performers?

Study skills: Questioning numbers and statistics

Numbers may appear to be convincing, but they may not be as reliable as they seem. When using any set of data, be objective and critical. Consider:

- Do these data measure what they purport to measure?
- How were they collected? Might this have led to mistakes and inaccuracies?
- Who wanted them collected? Why?
- Are they representative? Or do they refer only to particular sets of people or particular circumstances?

© Stella Cottrell (2013)

1 Read the descriptions of three data sets. What weaknesses might there be with each?

1. Data supporting the health benefits of the bacteria in yogurt. Research commissioned by a large dairy company.
2. Data on employee motivation focusing on accountants in one firm in America.
3. Survey data collected only on a smartphone app.

2 Read the descriptions of three more data sets and how students have interpreted them. What are the weaknesses of each interpretation?

1. A survey of Italian lawyers found that money was the greatest motivator at work.

    Money is clearly the greatest motivator and therefore all companies should pay higher salaries.

2. A survey showing the health benefits of cereals. Sponsored by a large cereal firm.

    The survey clearly shows the importance of eating a high-fiber diet for breakfast.

3. Research showing that farming methods of New Zealand lamb minimize the carbon footprint.

    Clearly it is better for the environment to import New Zealand lamb than to purchase local lamb.

3 Work with a partner. Discuss the questions.

1. Would you trust research commissioned by a company? Why / why not?
2. What would you want to know about the research methods before trusting the data?

2 READING

Gaming, society, and the individual

A Vocabulary preview

1 Complete the questions with the words in the box.

> aggression   analytical   awareness   deficit
> interaction   isolation   peers   prolonged

1 Do you think children who play video games are more likely to have better social skills than their non-gaming _____?
2 Do you agree that regular gaming increases levels of _____ in young people?
3 Does gaming have a positive or negative impact on social _____?
4 To what extent do you agree that _____ periods of online gaming could lead to health issues?
5 In what way might gaming improve cognitive and _____ ability?
6 How might playing video games improve your spatial _____?
7 What are the long-term health implications of a sleep _____ caused by gaming?
8 Is social _____ an inevitable consequence of gaming?

2 Work with a partner. Discuss the questions in Exercise 1.

B Before you read

Activating prior knowledge

Work in a group. Discuss whether gaming has a largely positive or negative impact on both individuals and society as a whole.

C Global reading

Identifying main ideas

Read *Gaming, society, and the individual*. Match the main ideas (a–f) with paragraphs (1–6).

a Online multiplayer games may actually enhance social skills ___
b Research indicates both positive and negative effects on academic performance ___
c The impact on physical and mental health is mixed ___
d Gaming has come to dominate our culture ___
e The link between gaming and violence is unfounded ___
f Despite many positives, continued research is necessary ___

32 UNIT 2 GAMES

GAMING, SOCIETY, AND THE INDIVIDUAL

READING 2

[1] Traditionally, gaming was solely the pursuit of a hardcore minority, but the rise of mobile gaming over the past five years has significantly expanded this user base. While there remains a dedicated core that plays anything up to 40 hours a week—the equivalent to a full-time job—hundreds of millions now play for a more leisurely half an hour to an hour a day. From the early arcade games of the 70s and console wars of the 90s, to the current boom in massively multiplayer online games (MMOG) and virtual reality, gaming has become ingrained in all aspects of modern society. While gaming is often reputed to have a negative impact on child development and behavior, an emerging body of research suggests we may have been a little quick to judge.

[2] Perhaps the most well publicized concern is that gaming is causally linked to increased levels of violent behavior, especially amongst children and adolescents. The general perception is that violent video games incite real-world violence, yet frankly there is considerable evidence to the contrary. Przybylski and Mishkin (2015) found that it is in fact the duration of game play, not the content of the game itself that is likely to have a detrimental influence on behavior. Furthermore, according to Ferguson (2010), many studies are purely observational and use measures to evaluate aggression that do not correspond to real-world violence, and that it is consequently impossible to demonstrate a cause-and-effect relationship. In this area at least, it seems there simply isn't enough robust data to support common wisdom.

[3] Another commonly held belief is that gaming leads to the social isolation of our youth. It is largely perceived as an insular activity that has a profoundly negative impact on the individual's ability to interact with their peers. While a superficially attractive theory, it fails to consider the role and prominence of massively multiplayer online gaming (MMOG). These games, by definition, require interaction; in fact it is often impossible to succeed in them without the cooperation of others. Rather than being socially isolating, they may actually improve real-world social skills—a notion that seems to be supported by the research. Kovess-Masfety et al. (2016) found that children who frequently play video games are actually more likely to have superior intellectual and social skills than those who play no games at all. Furthermore, in a review of recent research, Granic et al. (2014) concluded that gaming encourages both collaborative behavior and social interaction. While gamers undoubtedly spend less time socializing offline, the perception that gaming is socially isolating, simply isn't borne out by the research.

[4] However, one issue that is a little less clear-cut is the impact of gaming on academic performance.

2 READING

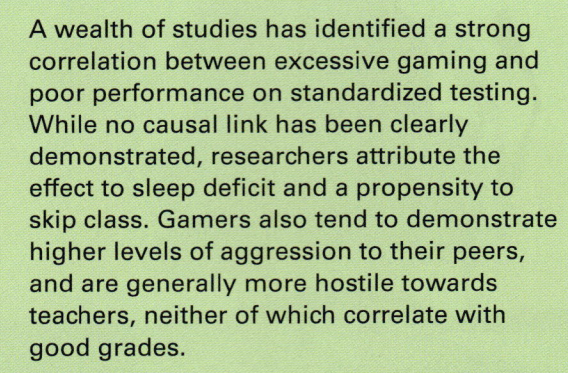

A wealth of studies has identified a strong correlation between excessive gaming and poor performance on standardized testing. While no causal link has been clearly demonstrated, researchers attribute the effect to sleep deficit and a propensity to skip class. Gamers also tend to demonstrate higher levels of aggression to their peers, and are generally more hostile towards teachers, neither of which correlate with good grades.

Yet perhaps somewhat counter-intuitively, gaming has been shown to be of benefit to children with attention deficit disorder (ADD). Furthermore, Bavelier et al. (2014) found that habitual action gamers are actually better analytical decision makers and can work faster and with a higher level of accuracy than their non-gaming counterparts—all of which are hugely beneficial in an academic environment.

[5]Another key area for discussion is the impact of gaming on physical and mental development. Gamers have repeatedly demonstrated greater hand-eye coordination, improved dexterity, and better spatial awareness than their non-gaming counterparts—largely due to the sheer speed at which they are expected to interpret and react to visual stimulus. Furthermore, gaming is arguably beneficial to mental health (Kovess-Masfety et al. 2016) and, according to a study by the Max-Planck Institute (2013), may even help prevent neurodegenerative diseases.

However, as the vast majority of games require little to no physical movement, one might reasonably claim them to be a contributory factor in childhood obesity. However, children also spend prolonged periods of time watching TV and using mobile devices, both of which contribute to a more sedentary lifestyle. It would therefore be unjust to infer that gaming alone is the direct cause of obesity.

[6]In conclusion, while there is research to suggest that gaming can have a negative impact on academic performance and our physical health, the commonly held beliefs that video games lead to violent behavior and are socially isolating simply aren't borne out by the evidence. In fact, collaboration and, by extension, social interaction, are intrinsic parts of massively multiplayer online gaming. Furthermore, gaming can enhance fine motor skills and may well prevent a range of mental health issues. However, as gaming continues to encroach on all aspects of society, one thing remains clear—we must continue to study its impact on all aspects of our lives.

REFERENCES:

Bavelier, D. et al. (2014) Action video game play facilitates the development of better perceptual templates. *Proceedings of the national academy of sciences*. 111(47)

Ferguson, C.J. (2010) Blazing Angels or Resident Evil? Can Violent Video Games Be a Force for Good? *Review of General Psychology*. 14(2), 68-81

Granic, I., Lobel, A. and Engels, R. C. M. E. (2013) The benefits of playing video games. *American Psychological Association*. 69(1), 66–78

Kovess-Masfety, V. et al. (2016) Is time spent playing video games associated with mental health, cognitive and social skills in young children? *Soc Psychiatry Psychiatr Epidemiol*. 51(3), 249–357

Kühn, S. et al. (2014) Playing Super Mario induces structural brain plasticity: gray matter changes resulting from training with a commercial video game. *Molecular Psychiatry*. 19(2), 265–271

Przybylski, A. K., & Mishkin, A. F. (2016) How the quantity and quality of electronic gaming relates to adolescents' academic engagement and psychosocial adjustment. *Psychology of Popular Media Culture*. 5(2), 145–156

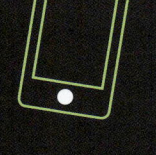

D Close reading

> In order to properly evaluate an argument or claim, it's important to distinguish the writer's opinion from others presented in the text. Although writers often explicitly state their attitude toward something, they also use a range of adverbs to indicate stance;
>
> *Admittedly*, it's unclear whether there is a direct causal link between the two.
>
> It is *obviously* too soon to assess the true impact of gaming on society.
>
> Writers may also use adverbs in the middle of a clause to distance themselves from what they're saying;
>
> The researchers were *apparently* unable to determine the exact cause of the phenomenon.

READING 2

Identifying stance and distancing

Read *Gaming, society, and the individual* again. Do the following statements agree with the views of the writer? Write *Y* (Yes) if they agree, *N* (No) if they disagree, and *NG* (Not Given) if it's impossible to say what the writer thinks of this.

1. Research supports the commonly held belief that gaming incites violence. ___
2. On the surface, the notion that gaming leads to social isolation is appealing. ___
3. Gamers almost certainly socialize less in the real-world than their peers. ___
4. Prohibiting mobile devices in the classroom would improve academic performance. ___
5. Gaming has an unexpectedly positive impact on behavioral disorders. ___
6. Non-gamers perform better in tests of agility and physical strength. ___
7. Arguing that gaming plays a role in childhood obesity is unjustified. ___
8. The general perception that games are too violent is unjustified. ___

E Critical thinking

Work with a partner. Discuss the questions.

1. Based on the text, do you think the effects of gaming are mainly positive or negative?
2. What else would you like to know about the studies mentioned in the reading? How might this change your stance on question 1?

VOCABULARY

Vocabulary development

Vocabulary for the description of data

1 Complete the definitions with the words and phrases in the box.

| account for   exceed   flatten out   negligibly   overwhelming majority |
| significant proportion   sizable   vastly |

1 _____ (v) to be greater than a given number or amount
2 _____ (n) a powerfully large proportion of
3 _____ (adv) of little importance or size
4 _____ (adj) fairly large
5 _____ (phr v) to explain the cause of something
6 _____ (phr v) to stop increasing and remain at the same level
7 _____ (adv) to a great degree
8 _____ (n) a noticeably large percentage of

2 Complete the description of the bar chart with words from Exercise 1. Change the form if necessary.

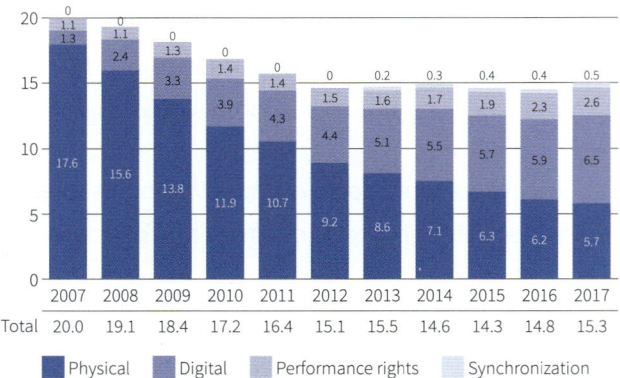

IFPI. (2016). Global Music Report. Available at: www.ifpi.org/downloads/GMR2016.pdf Accessed 15/05/2017

Physical sales [1]_____ [2]_____ digital sales in 2007, however, by 2014 they [3]_____ less than half of all income from music. Although income from synchronization has grown in recent years, as a proportion it has grown [4]_____ when compared to digital sales. Digital sales have been a [5]_____ of all sales since approximately 2010 and now the [6]_____ of income comes from digital sales. Performance rights are another area of growth and formed a [7]_____ section of all income, however, the growth appears to be [8]_____.

Academic words

VOCABULARY

1 Match the words in bold with the correct definitions.

1 **attribute** (v)
2 **bulk** (n)
3 **constitute** (v)
4 **format** (n)
5 **infer** (v)
6 **intrinsic** (adj)
7 **proportion** (n)
8 **solely** (adv)

a to be or form something
b the form that a film, program, or recording is produced in; the way something is designed or produced
c a part or share of a whole
d to say that something is the result of a particular situation, event, or person's actions
e involving nothing except the person or thing mentioned
f to form an opinion about something based on the information available
g the largest part or majority of something
h the essential qualities or features of something or someone

2 Complete the text with words from Exercise 1. Change the form if necessary.

Technology has become ¹ _____ to most aspects of society. The ² _____ of the changes that have occurred over the last 20 years can largely be ³ _____ to technological advancement. While many of the changes have been positive, there are areas of concern such as increased incidence of cybercrime which, in some countries ⁴ _____ approximately 40% of all crime committed—a disturbingly large ⁵ _____ of the total. From the available research, it seems reasonable to ⁶ _____ that this increase is, in part, due to the trend toward digital ⁷ _____ and the rise of streaming technology. In fact, many adolescents surveyed stated that they obtained music/media ⁸ _____ via illegal torrent sites.

3 Work with a partner. Discuss the questions.

1 To what extent do you agree that the bulk of technological advancements are positive?
2 In what ways has technology diminished our levels of privacy?
3 To what do you attribute increased levels of cybercrime?

CRITICAL THINKING

Critical thinking

> **Evaluating supporting data: 1**
>
> Data can be a simple way to support a claim or argument. However, it's important to assess whether the writer has deliberately misrepresented the data in order to strengthen the appearance of their argument. Some common ways to do this are;
>
> - Using percentages to make small sample sizes sound more impressive (e.g., 25% instead of 1 in 4)
> - Omitting results that contradict the main argument
> - Manipulating the presentation of a graph (e.g., presenting an axis ranging from 20–25, rather than 0–100).

1 Work in a group. Read the argument and supporting data. Then discuss the questions.

> Playing video games clearly leads to an increase in violence in children. In one study those that played violent games for more than two hours per day showed much higher levels of aggression toward peers and teachers. Therefore, it can be said that there is a clear cause-and-effect relationship between violent game time and violent behavior.

1 How large was the sample size? Why is it important to know this?
2 How was the level of aggression measured? Why is it important to know this?
3 What other information, such as the children's background, might influence our assessment of the data?
4 Do you agree with the writer that the data clearly indicates a cause-and-effect relationship?

2 Work in pairs. Read the arguments 1–3 and assess whether the data offered is sufficient.

1 In a case study of five boys, two showed much higher levels of aggression after playing video games. It is clear that over 40% of all children become more aggressive after playing video games.
2 As evidenced in Figure 1.1, there has been a huge spike in the number of violent crimes committed.
3 It was found that 30% of children failing at school play video games for in excess of two hours per week. Clearly, academic performance is hindered by video games.

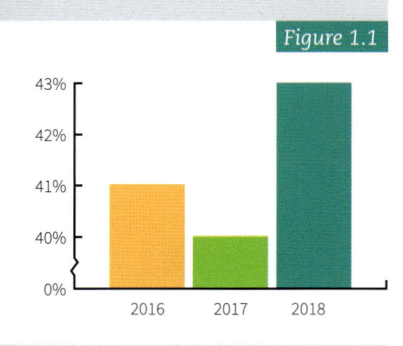

Figure 1.1

Writing model

You are going to learn about using inverted real and unreal conditionals, and using data to support opinions. You are then going to use these to write a short report about trends in the gaming industry.

A Analyze

Look at the graph and add an introductory sentence to the model below.

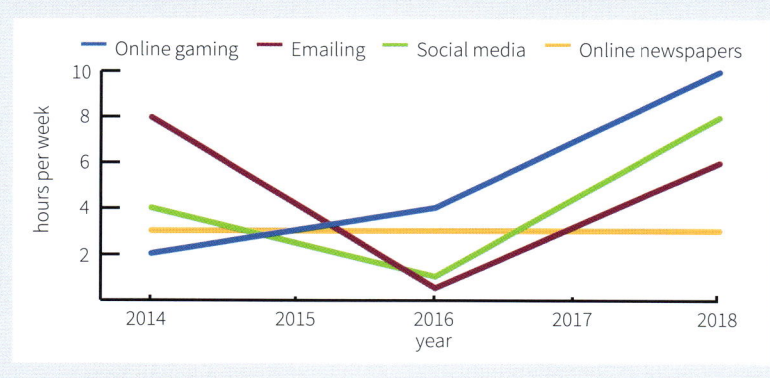

[Graph showing hours per week from 2014 to 2018 for Online gaming, Emailing, Social media, and Online newspapers]

B Model

Read the model and answer the questions.

In 2010 people spent vastly more time on email and it accounted for over 50% of the time spent online. It continued to take the overwhelming majority of people's time, as approximately twice as many hours were spent on email in comparison to all other activities until 2014. At this stage, a significant proportion of time was spent using social media. The rise in the number of hours spent on social media hours continued until 2016 when it flattened out at marginally more time than the hours spent on email. Were this trend to continue, technology would likely play an increasingly important social role.

Perhaps the most significant change is the vastly increased number of hours spent gaming online. Between 2016 and 2018 the number of hours spent gaming roughly doubled to exceed ten hours per week. Proportionally speaking, online gaming was also increasing, whereas reading online newspapers only negligibly changed. Although the graph does not state this, we could infer that this might be attributed to the increased bandwidth and better wireless technology that gaming requires. Should technology continue to accelerate in this way, physical games may become obsolete.

1. Which sentences describe single factors and which ones combine factors?
2. Which verbs are used to describe change?
3. Which adverbs are used to describe the verbs?
4. How does this graph compare to your own online use?

Grammar

> **Inverted conditionals: real and unreal present**
>
> Conditional sentences can be made to sound more formal using the following inverted constructions;
>
> **should + subject + base form**
>
> Should this trend continue, DVDs will become obsolete by the end of the decade.
> Should consumers not choose to adopt mobile gaming, the industry may collapse.
>
> **were + subject + to + base form**
>
> Were it easier to access high-speed Internet connections, more consumers would adopt Netflix.
> Were companies not to adapt, they would risk losing out to competitors.

1 Invert the following sentences using the verbs in bold.

1 Companies may stop investing in e-books if sales continue to stagnate.
   Should _____
2 Traditionally broadcasted TV may become a thing of the past if people continue to stream content on mobile devices.
   Should _____
3 Investors might well lose faith in the project if sales were to decline any further.
   Were _____
4 If companies choose not to invest in mobile gaming, they may well see a decline in revenue over the next decade.
   Should _____
5 E-readers would undoubtedly be more popular among consumers if they were easier to navigate.
   Were _____
6 If consumers don't adopt early, the product might fail in its first year.
   Were _____

2 Work with a partner. Make predictions about the following using inverted conditionals.

   a DVD sales
   b Online gaming
   c Music streaming

Writing skill

Data is often used to support an argument in academic writing. There are two main ways to do this;

1 State the opinion first then justify it with supporting data.
2 Present the data first as a basis for the opinion that follows.

Use of email for personal correspondence has declined steadily since 2010, while social media has seen a rise to prominence. This strongly indicates that social media has become the preferred method of communication.

Note that your choice of adverb shows the degree to which you believe in the data.

WRITING

Using data to support opinions

1 Work with a partner. Discuss what data sets might be used to support the following arguments;
   1 Social media has become the primary way to share photos.
   2 The gaming industry is still primarily rooted in physical media.
   3 Young people are no longer interested in physical media.
   4 Mobile gaming is the main reason for the growth in female gamers.

2 Write sentences to support the following arguments using data from the graph.

Age and media preference—% of Europeans ranking the three most important paid for media services

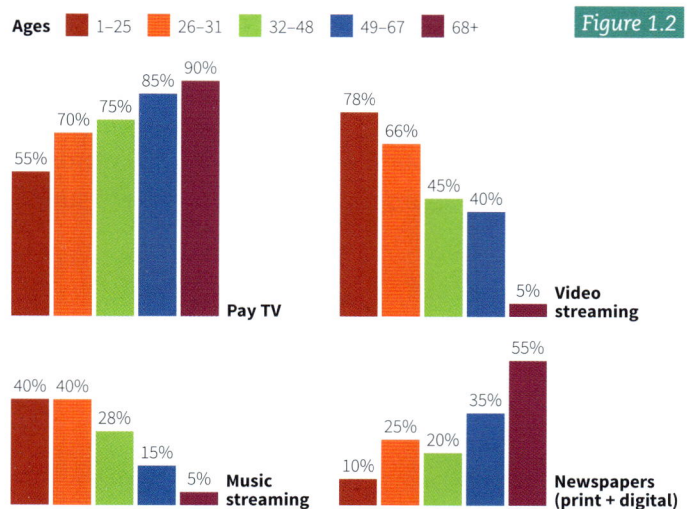

Figure 1.2

Ages: 1–25, 26–31, 32–48, 49–67, 68+

Pay TV: 55%, 70%, 75%, 85%, 90%
Video streaming: 78%, 66%, 45%, 40%, 5%
Music streaming: 40%, 40%, 28%, 15%, 5%
Newspapers (print + digital): 10%, 25%, 20%, 35%, 55%

1 Video streaming is far more popular among young people than pensioners.
2 Music marketing should be targeted squarely at adolescents.
3 Young people simply aren't interested in newspapers.
4 Pay TV will become obsolete within the next decade.

GAMES | UNIT 2 | 41

WRITING

Writing task

You are going to write a short report in response to the following:
"The graph shows current and predicted trends in the gaming industry. Summarize the information by selecting and reporting the main features, and make comparisons where necessary."

Brainstorm

Look at the graph and make notes about the main trends.

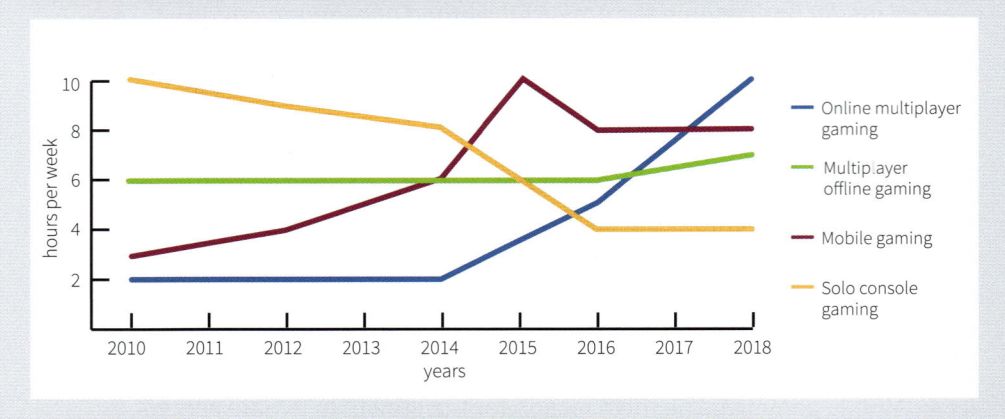

[Graph: hours per week (y-axis, 2–10) vs. years 2010–2018 (x-axis), showing four lines:
- *Online multiplayer gaming*
- *Multiplayer offline gaming*
- *Mobile gaming*
- *Solo console gaming]*

Plan

1. What are the main trends you will focus on?
2. What conclusions can be drawn about the data?
3. What might happen if these trends persist?

Write

Use your plan to help your write your report. Write 250–350 words. Remember to use inverted conditionals as appropriate and to use data to support your opinions.

Share

Exchange your report with a partner. Use the checklist on page 189 to help you provide feedback to your partner.

Rewrite and edit

Consider your partner's comments and write your final draft. Think about:

- whether you summarized the most relevant features
- whether you used inverted conditionals appropriately
- whether you used data to support your opinions.

Review

Wordlist

Vocabulary preview

aggression (n) **	deficit (n) **	interaction (n) **	prolonged (adj)
analytical (adj) *	dominate (v) **	isolation (n) **	sector (n) **
awareness (n) **	embrace (v) **	norm (n) **	staggering (adj)
consumption (n) **	feasible (adj) *	peer (n) **	subscription (n) *

Vocabulary development

account for (phr v) ***	negligibly (adv)	significant proportion (phr)	vastly (adv)
exceed (v) **	overwhelming majority (phr)		
flatten out (phr v)		sizable (adj)	

Academic words

attribute (v) **	constitute (v) **	infer (v) *	proportion (n) ***
bulk (n) **	format (n) **	intrinsic (adj)	solely (adv) **

Academic words review

Complete the sentences using the correct form of the words in the box.

| bulk | constitute | modify | proportion | resolve |

1. Adnan was extremely disappointed with his exam results, so he _____ to work harder in future.
2. The captain maneuvered the ship's vast _____ skillfully into the port.
3. Sales of e-books declined by 18.7% in the U.S. last year, and this _____ a downward trend as consumers switch to tablets and cell phones to download digital books.
4. Crowdfunding has become increasingly common as a means to _____ funding issues for business ventures.
5. A significant _____ of the students at the college were dissatisfied with their study programs.

Unit review

Reading 1	I can interpret visual data.
Reading 2	I can identify perspective.
Study skill	I can question numbers and statistics.
Vocabulary	I can use phrases for change.
Grammar	I can use inverted conditionals in the real and unreal present.
Writing	I can use data to support opinions.

3 ENERGY

Discussion point

Discuss with a partner.

1. What are the main sources of energy in your country?
2. What energy does your country produce?
3. Do you think we should continue to use fossil fuels? Why / why not?

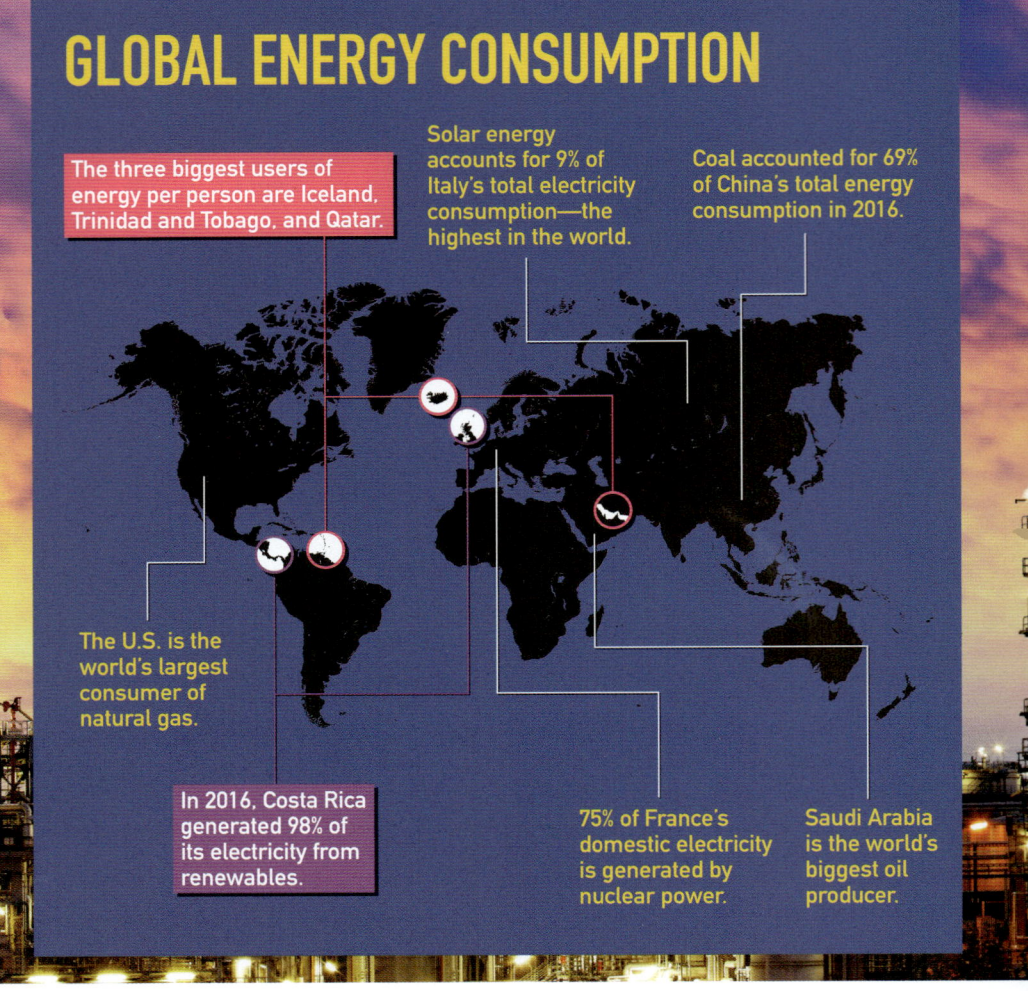

GLOBAL ENERGY CONSUMPTION

The three biggest users of energy per person are Iceland, Trinidad and Tobago, and Qatar.

Solar energy accounts for 9% of Italy's total electricity consumption—the highest in the world.

Coal accounted for 69% of China's total energy consumption in 2016.

The U.S. is the world's largest consumer of natural gas.

In 2016, Costa Rica generated 98% of its electricity from renewables.

75% of France's domestic electricity is generated by nuclear power.

Saudi Arabia is the world's biggest oil producer.

VIDEO

THE NUCLEAR DEBATE

Before you watch

Match the words in bold with the correct definitions.

1. **go to the polls** (phrase)
2. **outdated** (adj)
3. **referendum** (n)
4. **subject** (sth) **to** (phr v)
5. **vessel** (n)

a. a container
b. a democratic vote of a specific topic
c. vote
d. make something experience something unpleasant or unfair
e. no longer suitable for modern purposes

UNIT AIMS

READING 1 Completing flow charts
READING 2 Inferring meaning of technical vocabulary
STUDY SKILL Stages of the memory process
VOCABULARY Words to describe energy production
GRAMMAR Transitive and intransitive verbs
WRITING Writing definitions

An oil refinery at dusk.

While you watch

Watch the video and underline the correct ending for each sentence.

1 The purpose of the referendum is to decide **whether to use nuclear power or renewable energy sources / how quickly to close down nuclear plants**.
2 Anti-nuclear campaigners believe **renewable energy sources will be cheaper / nuclear power poses a significant safety risk**.
3 Pro-nuclear campaigners believe **energy prices will rise if nuclear plants are closed / safety concerns can be allayed through the modernization of nuclear plants**.

After you watch

Work in a group. Discuss the questions.

1 How would you vote if the referendum was in your country? Why?
2 Do you believe such decisions should be put in the hands of the people, rather than the government? Why / why not?
3 Why do you think it is taking so long for countries to move towards using cleaner, renewable energy sources?

1 READING

The oldest energy source

A Vocabulary preview

1 Complete the sentences with the words in the box.

> adverse carbon-neutral cultivate excessive
> inedible minimize proponents renewable

1 Biomass is arguably an efficient way to utilize __inedible__ agricultural waste.
2 Reykjavík—the capital of Iceland—recently announced its aim to become __carbon-neutral__ by 2040.
3 __Proponents__ of biomass fail to recognize how long it takes for a forest to regrow.
4 Denmark aims to supply 100% of its total energy from __renewable__ sources by 2050.
5 Car ownership has reached __excessive__ levels—it's time we looked to greener methods of transportation.
6 Pine is a highly valued form of biomass as it's relatively inexpensive and easy to __cultivate__.
7 Taking fewer flights each year is a simple way to __minimize__ your carbon footprint.
8 The __adverse__ effects of the biomass industry far outweigh the potential benefit.

2 Work with a partner. Discuss the questions.

1 How could you minimize the adverse environmental effects of your lifestyle?
2 Do you think the world will ever become carbon-neutral? Why / why not?
3 Which sources of energy are predominantly used in your country?

B Before you read

Activating prior knowledge

Work in a group. Discuss the advantages and disadvantages of burning biomass—organic matter such as plants or animal waste—in order to create electricity.

C Global reading

Identifying main ideas

Read *The oldest energy source*. Complete the article with the headings (a–f).

a The negative impact of energy crops
b The carbon-neutrality debate
c Biomass is not the solution
d An ancient solution to a modern crisis?
e How is bioenergy produced?
f What is biomass?

The oldest energy source

1 d

When tasked with listing renewable forms of energy, people tend to mention solar, wind, or hydro. Few bring up geothermal, and fewer still raise the oldest renewable of all—biomass. Since our ancestors discovered the controlled use of fire, biomass has played a prominent role in global energy production and has recently been heralded as the answer to our ever diminishing fossil fuel supply. Yet critics argue it has a hugely detrimental impact on the environment. So what is biomass energy and what does the research say about it?

2 f

Biomass is any organic, decomposable matter that can be used either as a fuel in the production of heat or electricity, or converted into liquid fuel substitutes for gasoline and diesel. Broadly speaking, biomass can be divided into four distinct categories—wood and agricultural products such as logs, sawdust, and agricultural waste; solid waste (i.e., garbage); landfill gas (i.e., methane); and liquid fuels such as biodiesel and ethanol, which are produced by extracting the sugars from crops such as wheat, corn, sugar beets, and sugar cane. As biomass is derived from living, or recently living, plants and animals that can be replaced in a relatively short period of time, it is generally considered to be a renewable source of energy.

3 e

Although the production process varies slightly depending on the type of biomass used, it is in essence not dissimilar to that of a traditional coal-fired power station. Biomass—typically wood chips or pellets—is burned in a combustion chamber in place of coal to boil water. This produces high-pressure steam that is passed through a turbine, causing it to rotate. This in turn powers a generator which creates electricity. A transformer then increases the voltage of the electricity before distributing it to homes and businesses. Methane gas captured from the anaerobic digestion of animal waste or collected from landfills can also be used as a fuel during the initial stages of the process. Since this is a relatively simplistic process that is modeled on existing technology, there has been a significant growth in the number of biomass power plants around the world. However, the adverse environmental impact should not be underestimated.

4 b

During the process of photosynthesis, plants harness radiant energy from the sun in order to convert water and carbon dioxide (CO_2) into oxygen and carbohydrates. As the amount of CO_2 released into the atmosphere when biomass is burned is equal to the amount captured during photosynthesis, proponents of bioenergy claim that it is a carbon-neutral source of energy. However, this is debatable for several reasons. Firstly, biomass can help to minimize carbon emissions if fast-growing crops such as willow are cultivated on unproductive land. However, cutting down forests for energy releases CO_2 that otherwise would have been captured, and it can take centuries to re-establish these forests and pay off this carbon debt. Secondly, proponents fail to take into the account that harvesting and transporting biomass over great distances generates hazardous air pollutants which are not offset during the process. While the effects of burning biomass can be mitigated to a certain extent by choosing to burn biomass that is less polluting, it is highly doubtful that it can ever be classed as truly carbon-neutral.

5 a

The other primary use of biomass is the production of liquid fuels such as biodiesel and ethanol from crops high in cellulose, such as wheat, corn, and sugar cane. These "energy crops" are predominantly inedible and, as they are cultivated on an industrial scale, are associated with the same environmental concerns as any other mass agricultural practice—namely, the pollution of water and soil from pest control, the excessive use of water, and the erosion of soil. In addition, since the production of energy crops has required large-scale deforestation in many areas, it has also directly contributed to increased levels of greenhouse gases. Furthermore, since energy crops are hugely profitable, farmers are now dedicating more land to their production than food crops. With close to a billion people suffering from food shortages, we can scarcely afford to allocate more land to the energy sector. In fact, the IEEP (2012) forecasts that the increased demand for energy crops could raise the prices of vital foodstuffs such as oilseeds, vegetable oils, and maize by as much as 20 to 30%—a change that would disproportionately affect the poorest members of society. Furthermore, many small farmers have been forced off their land as large biofuel companies attempt to satisfy the growing demand for energy crop production.

6 & c

In conclusion, if fast-growing biomass is cultivated on unproductive land or harnesses otherwise waste products, it is arguably a renewable alternative to fossil fuels. However, proponents of the carbon-neutral theory fail to take into account the length of time it takes to pay off the carbon debt of mass deforestation, and the hazardous pollutants emitted during harvest and transportation. In addition, a greater emphasis on energy crop production has diverted vital foodstuffs from a rapidly expanding global population and taken away the livelihood of many small farmers. While it is vital that we find a sustainable alternative to fossil fuels, a process that has such a potentially devastating impact on both the environment and the poor is not the answer.

References:

Kretschmer, B., Bowyer, C., Buckwell, A. (2012) EU Biofuel use and agricultural commodity prices: a review of the evidence base. London: Institute for European Environmental Policy (IEEP), p6. Available at: https://ieep.eu/uploads/articles/attachments/9d109cf4-8b49-4ed0-9ac7-4c5678d83b53/IEEP_Biofuels_and_food_prices_June_2012.pdf?v=63664509780 [Accessed: 19th October 2017]

1 READING

Completing flow charts

D Close reading

> When reading about a process it can help you to understand the different stages by noting them down in the form of a flow chart. This visual representation clearly shows the stages and the order in which they happen.

1 Read the third paragraph of *The oldest energy source* again. Complete each blank in the flow chart with no more than two words from the article.

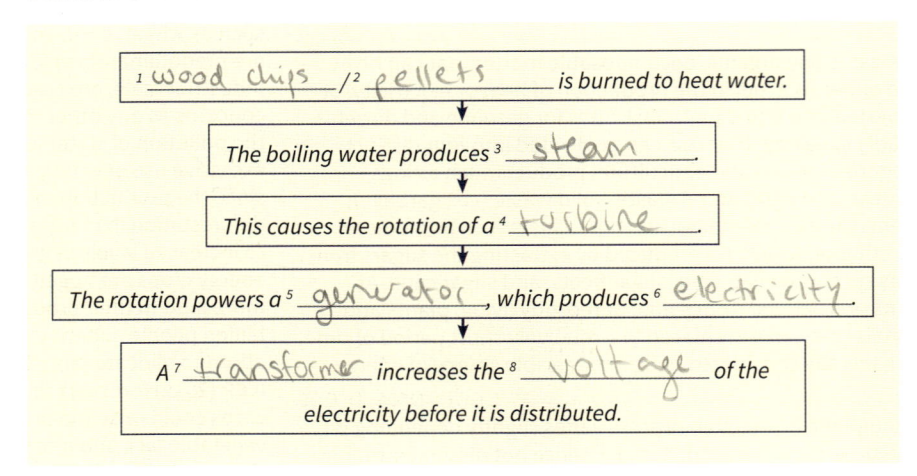

¹ __wood chips__ /² __pellets__ is burned to heat water.
↓
The boiling water produces ³ __steam__.
↓
This causes the rotation of a ⁴ __turbine__.
↓
The rotation powers a ⁵ __generator__, which produces ⁶ __electricity__.
↓
A ⁷ __transformer__ increases the ⁸ __voltage__ of the electricity before it is distributed.

2 Read *The oldest energy source* again. Are these sentences *T* (True), *F* (False), or *NG* (Not Given)?

1 Ethanol can be used as a substitute for gasoline or diesel. __T__
2 Methane increases the efficiency of bioenergy production. __NG__
3 Critics argue it can take centuries to offset the effects of deforestation. __T__
4 Energy crops have had detrimental effect on food prices. __T__
5 Biofuel companies are working in conjunction with local farmers. __F__

E Critical thinking

Work with a partner. Discuss the questions.

1 Based on the arguments in the text, do you think it is a good or bad idea that more and more biomass energy plants are being built?
2 What should a company proposing a new biomass power plant have to prove before they are allowed to build it?

48 UNIT 3 ENERGY

Study skills: Stages of the memory process

A way of using the brain to improve memory is to work with the four stages of the memory process:
1 *Taking in information* – noticing or attending to information, and absorbing it.
2 *Retaining it* – short-term memory
3 *Encoding it* – interacting with the information in working memory so that the brain can store it in long-term memory.
4 *Recalling it* – retrieving or remembering information.

© Stella Cottrell (2013)

1 Work with a partner. Discuss the questions.
　1 What skills and techniques do you use when trying to take information in (e.g., taking notes, highlighting, writing research questions, etc.)?
　2 What skills and techniques do you use for memorizing information (e.g., organizing information into groups, testing yourself on definitions, etc.)?
　3 How many times do you think you need to review something to store it in your long-term memory? What are the most effective techniques you use?
　4 How do you recall information under pressure (e.g., in exams or during a presentation)?

2 How do you remember new vocabulary? Complete the flowchart describing the best techniques for you to use at each stage of the memory process.

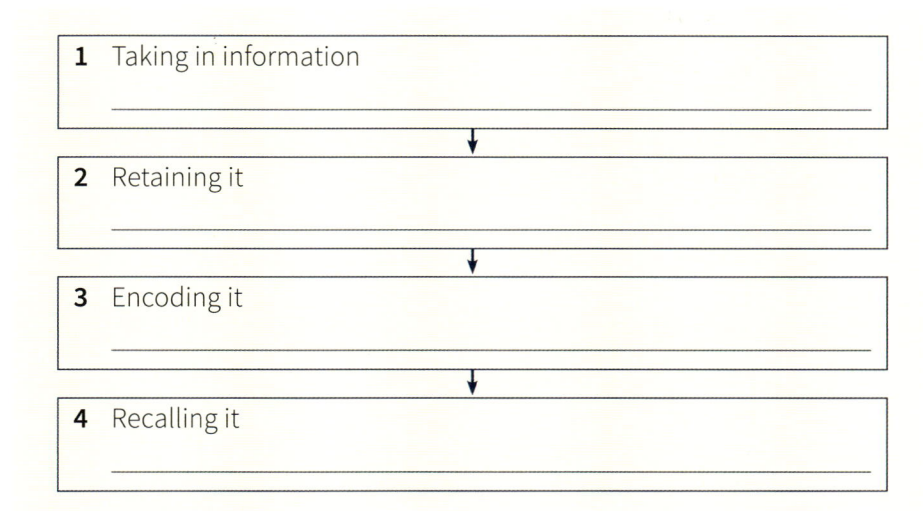

   1 Taking in information
   _____
           ↓
   2 Retaining it
   _____
           ↓
   3 Encoding it
   _____
           ↓
   4 Recalling it
   _____

3 Explain your chart to a partner.

2 READING

Fracking—the future?

A Vocabulary preview

Complete the sentences with the words in the box.

> additives   contaminate   drill   formations
> horizontal   mining   pump   vertical

1. Protests continue over the company's plans to _____ for oil off the north coast of Alaska.
2. Next, developers _____ cold water into the rock where it absorbs heat.
3. The chemical _____ in fracking solution include hydrochloric acid and sodium chloride.
4. Small holes are made in the _____ section of the pipe that runs parallel to the shale formations.
5. Researchers claim the results of the decade-long study prove fracking can _____ drinking water.
6. Critics argue that _____ significantly damages the environment and should be banned.
7. Fracking enables the extraction of natural gas from rock _____ deep below the Earth's surface.
8. The _____ wells can extend to a depth of 2,000 meters below ground level.

B Before you read

Activating prior knowledge

In a group, discuss where fossil fuels such as oil and natural gas are found and how they are extracted.

C Global reading

Identifying main ideas

Read *Fracking—the future?* Match the research questions (a–h) to paragraphs (1–8).

a How is shale gas extracted? 3
b What claims do proponents make? 4
c How does fracking impact drinking water? 6
d Which countries currently lead the drive toward renewables? 1
e How are waste products dealt with? 5
f What other detrimental effects is fracking linked to? 7
g How is oil and natural gas traditionally extracted? 2
h Is fracking a viable alternative to renewables? 8

50   UNIT 3   ENERGY

Fracking— the future?

[1] In 2014, 99% of Costa Rica's electrical energy was derived from renewable energy sources. In 2015, Denmark produced 42% of its electricity from wind turbines. The Scottish government recently announced plans to generate 100% of its electricity from renewables by 2020. Yet despite a global trend away from fossil fuels, larger industrialized nations, such as the U.S. and Russia, are still heavily reliant on oil and natural gas. So how are these natural resources obtained, and what is the environmental impact?

[2] Oil and natural gas is most commonly found in porous rock formations called reservoirs. Tiny holes, or pores, in the rock allow it to absorb large quantities of oil, water, and natural gas, which is trapped in place by thicker rock above and below. To extract the resources, mining companies drill a deep vertical well through the thick rock, directly into the reservoir. The oil and natural gas is then pumped back to the surface. Although this is a relatively simple process, most known reservoirs are nearing exhaustion and companies are being forced to rely on increasingly complex mining techniques such as fracking.

[3] Hydraulic fracturing, or fracking, is a technique used to extract oil and natural gas from sedimentary rock formations called shale. Unlike reservoirs, the resources trapped in shale do not gather in large pools that can be easily drained. Instead, they are spread across tiny cracks in the rock. To release the trapped resources, the rock must be split, or fractured, open. To achieve this, deep vertical wells are drilled down to the level of the shale. The depth of these wells varies, but can extend as far as 2,000 meters into the ground. Once the desired depth has been reached, the drill takes a 90-degree turn and continues horizontally, parallel to the layer of shale rock. Small holes are then made along the horizontal section of the well, exposing it to the rock. Millions of gallons of high-pressure fracking solution, a mixture of water, sand, and chemical additives, is then pumped through the well into the surrounding rock for an average of 72 hours. The extreme pressure causes the fissures, or cracks, in the rock to widen, allowing the oil and natural gas to flow into the well and be pumped back to the surface.

2 READING

[4]This process may be very simple, but it is proving to be as profitable as it is controversial and therein lies the dilemma. Currently, shale gas is produced at a commercial rate in very few countries. The U.S. and Canada lead the way in the mining of shale gas, but there are around 40 countries with the potential to exploit such assets. As many of these countries are currently net importers of fossil fuels, tapping into a domestic supply of shale gas would significantly reduce their dependence on foreign energy sources and could potentially lead to a new source of income. It would also provide thousands of new jobs and help lower household gas and electricity bills. Fracking proponents further argue that it actually has a positive effect on the environment as it produces up to three times less carbon emissions than coal. Given these factors, it is no surprise that there is much enthusiasm for the practice.

[5]One of the major concerns is associated not with the shale gas itself, but with the sheer volume of chemical additives being pumped into the ground. Over 750 additives, including formaldehyde, hydrochloric acid, and sodium hydroxide, are used or have been used in fracturing operations, many of which are known carcinogens. These additives constitute anything up to 2% of the fracking mixture which, when extrapolated to an industrial scale, equates to around 300 tons of additive per 15 million liters (Earthworks, n.d.). The fear is that chemicals in the fracking solution could leach into the soil or groundwater, potentially affecting food production and contaminating the supply of safe drinking water in the area. Furthermore, as the cracks created during the fracturing process can extend as far as 1.6 km from the original well, it's possible that additives may also contaminate drinking water far from the site.

[6]Management of the billions of liters of waste water generated during the fracking process also presents a huge issue, as it often contains high levels of methane and radioactive waste. While much of the waste water is pumped back to the surface, it's estimated that as much as 50% of it is left in the wells, again raising concerns that pollutants will leach into the groundwater. If true, this could result in a range of health issues including asthma and several forms of cancer. Such are the concerns with the levels of radioactive material entering waste water that some feel employees of fracking corporations should be monitored in the same way as those working in nuclear power plants. Any water that does return to the surface either needs to be treated for re-use or disposed of safely. The high concentrations of heavy metals and radionuclides in recovered hydrofrac water can make treatment a difficult and expensive process (Soeder and Kappel, 2009), which few facilities currently have the capacity to deal with. Disposal is equally difficult. Most waste-water is simply injected back into porous rock formations via disposal wells or released into river systems, jeopardizing aquatic ecosystems.

[7]Another concern often cited by critics is the risk that the fracking process and its after-effects can lead to earthquakes. Indeed, despite claims that fracking-related earthquakes are not common, microearthquakes—those of a magnitude of under 2.0 on the Richter scale—are frequently experienced in and around fracking sites. Furthermore, many scientists believe that waste-water injection can be directly linked to several huge earthquakes in the U.S. midcontinent, including one that reached a magnitude of 5.6. While Ellsworth (2013) argues that certain techniques can be employed to lessen the risk of earthquakes, until regulation is in place to enforce these practices, homes will continue to be destroyed and lives will be lost.

[8]Fracking will almost inevitably grow in the coming years as governments chase reliable fuel sources and industry seeks larger profits—this despite the ever-increasing list of devastating issues associated with the process. And yet it is perhaps the unknown we should fear most. Industrial fracking on this scale is still in its relative infancy, and its use should, at the very least, be restricted until enough studies have been conducted for us to fully quantify its impact. While there are huge volumes of untapped shale gas sequestered beneath the Earth's surface, its extraction may have profound effects on the environment, and with such progress being made in the renewables industry, it seems crazy to take such huge risks with the future of our planet for the sake of profits. Rather than wasting time and money extracting what is, after all, another finite resource, it would make sense to invest in reliable, environmentally friendly renewable energy production.

References:

Ellsworth, W. L. (2013). Injection induced earthquakes. *Science*. 341(6142, 1225942) Available: http://www.normalesup.org/~dublanch/sismiciteinduite/EllsworthScience2013.pdf [Accessed: 19th October 2017]

Hydraulic Fracturing 101 (n.d.) *Earthworks*. Available: https://www.earthworksaction.org/issues/detail/hydraulic_fracturing_101#.Wei5aVtSxhE [Accessed: 19th October 2017]

Soeder, D. J., and Kappel, W. M. (2009). Water resources and natural gas production from the Marcellus shale: U.S. Geological Survey Fact Sheet 2009–3032. Available: https://pubs.usgs.gov/fs/2009/3032/pdf/FS2009-3032.pdf [Accessed: 19th October 2017]

D Close reading

> Often a text will contain technical terms that you may not be familiar with. However, it's sometimes possible to infer their meaning from context. For example;
>
> Millions of **gallons** of high-pressure fracking solution, a mixture of water, sand, and chemical additives, is then pumped through the well.
>
> We can infer from the context that "gallons" is a unit for measuring liquid.

1 Read *Fracking—the future?* again. Use context to help you complete the definitions with the words in the box. Then explain to a partner how you inferred each meaning.

   fissures   leach   magnitude   porous   well

   a _porous_ (adj) containing many small holes that allow water or air to pass through
   b _well_ (n) a deep hole made into the ground to obtain water, gas, or oil
   c _fissures_ (n) deep, narrow cracks in rocks or earth
   d _magni_ (v) to remove a chemical from soil as a result of water passing through it
   e _leach_ (n) the strength of an earthquake

2 Read *Fracking—the future?* again. Are these sentences T (True), F (False), or NG (Not Given)?

   1 The shale gas extraction process can take several days. T
   2 Hydraulic fracturing is a technique commonly employed in coastal regions. NG
   3 All countries have access to large bodies of untapped shale gas. F
   4 Waste water is known to contain dangerous levels of pollutants. T
   5 The disposal of waste water is not causally linked to earthquakes. F
   6 There is insufficient data to reliably assess the impact of fracking. ___

E Critical thinking

Work in a group. Discuss the questions.

1 Based on the arguments in the text, do you think fracking is a good way to meet global energy needs?
2 Profits often drive environmental decisions. What can be done to better control this?

READING 2

Inferring meaning of technical vocabulary

VOCABULARY

Vocabulary development

Words to describe energy production

1 Match the words in bold with the correct definitions.

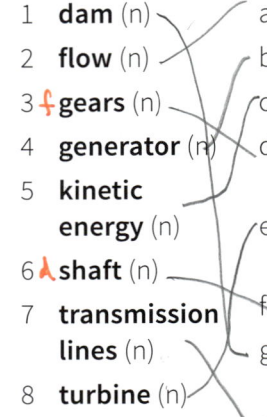

1 **dam** (n)
2 **flow** (n)
3 **gears** (n)
4 **generator** (n)
5 **kinetic energy** (n)
6 **shaft** (n)
7 **transmission lines** (n)
8 **turbine** (n)

a the continuous movement of a liquid in one direction
b a machine that produces electricity
c the energy an object has as a result of movement
d a long, narrow passage that people or liquids, gases, etc. can move through
e a machine or engine which uses air, gas, water, or steam to turn a wheel and produce power
f part(s) of an engine that convert power into movement
g a barrier built across a river to stop the water from flowing, usually to create a lake or to produce electricity
h the cables used to carry electricity over long distances

2 Complete the sentences with words from Exercise 1. Change the form if necessary.

1 Grand Coulee is the largest hydroelectric _____ in North America.
2 The penstock is a long _____ that carries water from the reservoir to a water wheel.
3 High-pressure steam causes the _shaft_ to rotate at speeds of up to 3,600 rpm.
4 This is then converted into _kinetic energy_ as the water _flows_ down the penstock.
5 Higher _gears_ are used to increase the speed of movement.
6 The hydroelectric _generator_ then converts this mechanical energy into electricity.
7 Finally, _transmission lines_ conduct the electricity to homes and businesses across the country.

Academic words

1 Match the words in bold with the correct definitions.

1. **cite** (v)
2. **diminish** (v)
3. **dispose** (v)
4. **erosion** (n)
5. **parallel** (adj)
6. **predominantly** (adv)
7. **restrict** (v)
8. **sustainable** (adj)

a the process by which the surface of land or rock is gradually destroyed by the action of water, wind, rain, etc.
b mainly, or mostly
c to get rid of something that you no longer need or want
d used to describe two or more lines that are the same distance apart at every point
e using methods that do not harm the environment, and can therefore continue for a long time
f to become or cause something to become smaller or weaker
g to keep something within strict limits
h to mention something as an example, explanation, or proof of something

2 Complete the sentences with words from Exercise 1. Change the form if necessary.

1. Current levels of energy consumption are no longer _sustainable_ – it's time to embrace renewables.
2. Use of private vehicles must be _restricted_ in order to limit individual carbon footprints.
3. A commonly _cited_ argument in favor of biomass is that it is a carbon-neutral process.
4. Despite advances in renewable technology, the world still relies _predominantly_ on fossil fuels.
5. Horizontal wells run _parallel_ to the shale rock formations for hundreds of meters.
6. A viable alternative to our _diminishing_ supply of fossil fuels has yet to be identified.
7. Arguably, the biggest challenge of nuclear power is how to safely _dispose_ of the waste.
8. Extreme weather over the past few weeks has caused large-scale _erosions_ along the coast.

3 Work with a partner. Discuss the questions.

1. Should fracking be restricted until sufficient data has been collected to assess its impact? Why / why not?
2. How could your country make its energy consumption more sustainable?
3. Is erosion a common issue in your country? How is it usually dealt with?

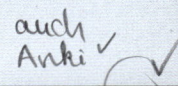

Critical thinking

Identifying bias

Bias is an attitude that someone has that makes them treat someone in a way that is unfair or different. It is also when someone prefers a thing or idea in a way that is unfair. People can show their bias in a number of ways, such as selecting arguments from only one side, showing preference for one side despite strong evidence on the other, or allowing other influences on their life to affect their judgement. This will often be shown via language that makes an argument sound more or less important than it is.

1 Read the text and answer the questions.

> Despite concerns, fracking has proven to be a relatively safe way of extracting shale gas. Most of the criticisms come from environmental lobbyists with limited scientific data to support their weak claims. According to experts at the Kilnbrook it is a much safer and environmentally friendly method of extracting fossil fuels than most other techniques.

   1 Does the writer give a balanced view?
   2 What experts does the writer refer to?
   3 What words indicate bias in their argument?

2 Look at the responses to the reading texts in this unit. How is each writer showing bias?

   1 Earthquakes, water contamination, global warming, and damaging ecosystems show that the damage caused by fracking clearly outweighs any possible benefits.
   2 Our research shows that there are very few dangers associated with fracking. (Frank Smith, CEO of Fracking UK)
   3 Clearly, fracking is only being pushed aggressively forward due to the vast profits dubious corporate associations can gain from exploiting the fragile environment.

3 Work with a partner. Discuss the questions.

   1 In which situation might someone present a biased argument?
   2 Why is it important to keep bias out of academic writing?
   3 How can you combat biased arguments?

Writing model

You are going to learn about transitive and intransitive verbs, and writing definitions. You will then use these to write a description of how hydroelectricity is produced.

A Analyze

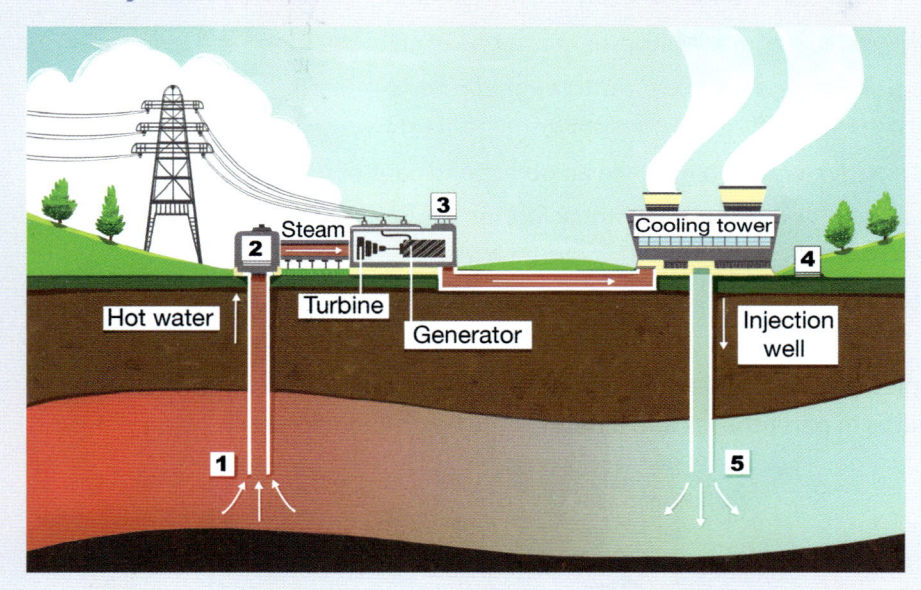

Look at the diagram of a geothermal energy power plant. How do you think the process is similar or different than the production of hydroelectricity?

B Model

Geothermal energy is a clean form of renewable energy that uses heat stored within the Earth's crust to generate electricity. There are three different types of geothermal power plant: dry steam, flash steam, and binary cycle. The diagram above shows a flash steam power plant—the most predominant form of geothermal power plant in operation. Flash steam power plants pump hot water from underground reservoirs back to the surface under intense pressure. The water is fed into large low-pressure tanks, generating steam which is used to rotate a turbine. A turbine is an engine or machine that uses the pressure of liquid or gas on a wheel to move.

The movement of this turbine is then converted into a source of electricity via a generator. The electricity is then directed via transmission lines to homes and businesses around the country. Any remaining water is pumped to a cooling station and then injected back into the reservoir to be heated again. This reuse of water makes geothermal energy a sustainable form of energy.

Work with a partner. Discuss the questions.

1. What terms in this process do you think need defining?
2. How can you further explain a definition to the reader?
3. What renewable sources of energy are produced in your country?

Grammar

> ### Transitive and intransitive verbs
>
> **Transitive verbs** require an object and can usually be used in the active and passive;
>
> The movement **increases** the temperature. (TRANSITIVE ACTIVE)
> The temperature **is increased** by the movement. (TRANSITIVE PASSIVE)
>
> However, some transitive verbs cannot be used in the passive;
>
> The sluice gates **let** water flow through the dam.
> ~~The water **is let** through the dam by the sluice gates.~~
>
> **Intransitive verbs** do not take an object and cannot be used in the passive;
>
> Fossil fuels **exist** in particular rock formations.
> ~~Renewable energy **is existed** in many forms.~~
>
> Note that some verbs are always intransitive (e.g., *occur, look, appear, exist*).

Complete the description of how a wind turbine works. Use the correct form of the verbs in parentheses and a noun in the box when necessary.

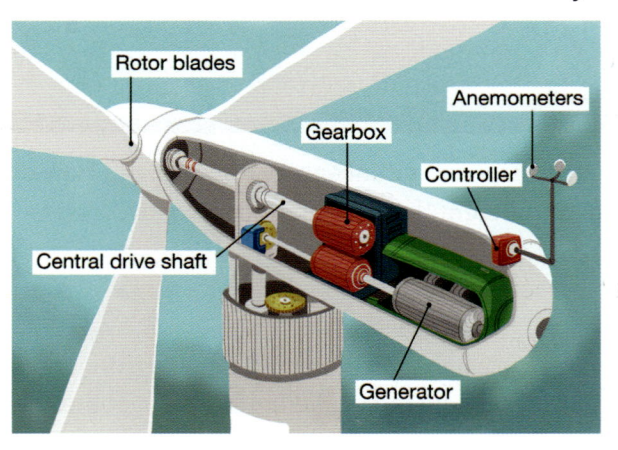

electrical energy   the kinetic energy   the low-speed rotation   the speed   the turbine

Wind ¹**blows** (blow) toward the turbine's rotor blades. The blades spin around, slowly rotating a central drive shaft. A gearbox ² **converts the low-speed rotation** (convert) of the drive shaft into the high speeds required by the generator. Next, the generator ³ _uses the speed_ (use) of the spinning drive shaft to ⁴ _generate the ke_ (generate). Finally, this energy is converted to a high enough voltage to ⁵ _be transmitted_ (transmit) to the power grid. The anemometers at the back of the main body are used ⁶ _to measure the speed_ (measure) of the wind and this data ⁷ _is transmitted_ (transmit) to a controller. Using these measurements, the controller is able ⁸ _rotate_ (rotate) so it always points directly into the wind. If it becomes too windy, brakes ⁹ _are applied_ (apply) to prevent the rotor blades from turning.

Writing skill

WRITING

Writing definitions

Descriptions of scientific processes are likely to contain technical vocabulary that your reader may not understand. Often these words can be guessed from context, but if it is key to understanding the process, it may help to provide a definition. Here are four ways to write definitions:

1 **Noun + relative clause**
   A turbine is a machine that uses a wheel rotated by liquid or gas to generate electricity.

2 **Physical description + relative clause**
   A wind turbine is a large metal structure with blades that rotates in the wind to generate electricity.

3 **Explanation between em dashes (—)**
   Fracking fluid—a mixture of water, sand, and additives—is pumped into the well.

4 **Similar word / object + *or* + noun**
   Tiny holes, or pores, in the rock allow it to absorb large quantities of oil, water, and natural gas.

1 Complete the definitions.
   1 A generator is a machine which _transforms (movement)_ into energy. [kinetic energy] ✓
   2 A solar panel is a _sustainable way_ to generate electricity.
   3 Hybrid cars— _cars that drive with fuel and electricity_ —have grown in popularity.
   4 _speed / energy_ [kinetic], or force, from the waves turns the turbines to generate electricity.

2 Write definitions for the following terms using each of the techniques in the *Writing definitions* box. ✓
   1 Mining
   Mining is a process where ressources are built from the underground ← extracting substances from deep underground
   2 Recycling
   Recycling is a process of reusing something.
   3 Carbon footprint
   The Carbon footprint — the emission [amount of] — is rising [growing] every year.
   4 A dam
   a dam, or a big well

✓

WRITING

Writing task

You are going to write a process description in response to the following:
"The diagram illustrates how hydroelectric energy is produced. Summarize the information by selecting and reporting the main features, and make comparisons where necessary."

Brainstorm

Look at the diagram and describe the process to a partner.

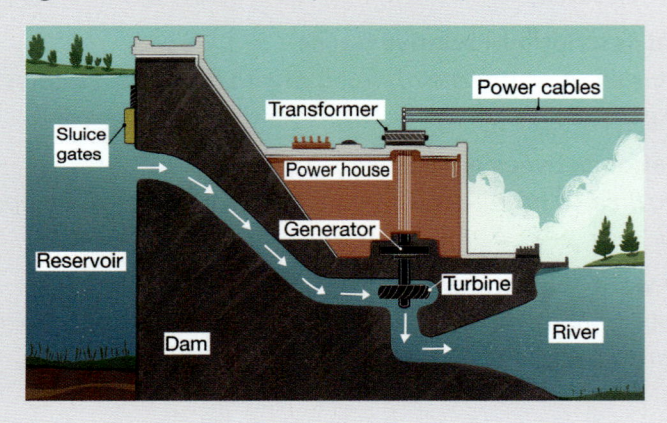

Plan

Draw a flow chart to help you explain the stages of hydroelectric energy production.

Write

Use your plan to help you write a description of how hydroelectricity is produced. Remember to check your use of transitive and intransitive verbs and define key terms as appropriate. Your text should be at least 150 words long.

Share

Exchange your description with a partner. Use the checklist on page 189 to help you provide feedback to your partner.

Rewrite and edit

Consider your partner's comments and write your final draft. Think about:

- whether you described the most relevant features
- whether you used transitive and intransitive verbs appropriately
- whether you defined key terms appropriately.

Review

Wordlist

Vocabulary preview

additive (n)	cultivate (v) *	horizontal (adj) **	proponent (n)
adverse (adj) *	drill (v) *	inedible (adj)	pump (v) *
carbon-neutral (adj)	excessive (adj) **	minimize (v) *	renewable (adj)
contaminate (v)	formation (n) ***	mining pump (n)	vertical (adj) **

Vocabulary development

dam (n)	gear (n) **	kinetic energy (n)	transmission line (n)
flow (n) ***	generator (n) *	shaft (n) **	turbine (n)

Academic words

cite (v) *	dispose (v) **	parallel (adj) **	restrict (v) **
diminish (v) **	erosion (n) **	predominantly (adv) *	sustainable (adj)

Academic words review

Complete the sentences using the correct form of the words in the box.

| cite | infer | parallel | restrict | solely |

1. Opponents of nuclear power often _____ the Fukushima disaster of 2011 to argue that nuclear power is fundamentally unsafe.
2. In Costa Rica, hydro, wind, and geothermal resources are used in _____ to supply the country with 98% of its energy.
3. For safety reasons, access to the power plant is _____ to authorized personnel only.
4. From the data collected, researchers were able to _____ the reasons for the sudden increase in demand for electricity.
5. You mustn't rely _____ on one source of information; you need to refer to other sources to ensure that you form a balanced view.

Unit review

Reading 1	☐ I can complete flow charts.
Reading 2	☐ I can infer the meaning of technical vocabulary.
Study skill	☐ I can talk about the stages of the memory process.
Vocabulary	☐ I can describe processes.
Grammar	☐ I can use transitive and intransitive verbs.
Writing	☐ I can write definitions.

4 RISK

Discussion point

Discuss with a partner.

1 Which person in the infographic do you think took the biggest risk? Why?
2 How important do you think risk is in business? Why? How can business people mitigate risks?
3 What risks do people take in their family life, social life, work life, and leisure time?

Six business risks that paid off

1 **Elon Musk, CEO of Tesla and SpaceX**
Invested his last $35m to keep Tesla afloat in 2008. Company now worth $2.5bn.

2 **Sylvester Stallone, actor/screenwriter**
Refused to sell screenplay for *Rocky* unless he had the lead role. Accepted a much smaller price as a result. Film earned him millions and launched his career.

3 **Renee Lawson Hardy of Whole Foods Market**
Started a whole food company in the 1970s when local, organic food wasn't on consumers' radar. Now one of the biggest supermarkets in the U.S.

4 **David Choe, graffiti artist**
Agreed to decorate the first Facebook office in exchange for company stocks not cash. That stock's now worth $200m.

5 **Zhou Qunfrei, founder of Lens Technology**
Gave her customers the names of her key competitors in a bid to expand the size of the market. Now worth $9bn.

6 **Mark Pincus, CEO of Zynga**
Rejected final chance at funding of first company to maintain control. Managed to receive funding later and sold the company at a good profit.

VIDEO

GREEK AUSTERITY

Before you watch

Match the words in bold with the correct definitions.

1 **austerity** (n)
2 **bid** (n)
3 **flagging** (adj)
4 **make ends meet** (phrase)
5 **thrift** (n)

a a system of reducing public spending
b have just enough money to pay for the things you need
c the practice of spending money carefully and avoiding waste
d an attempt to achieve something
e becoming weaker

UNIT AIMS	READING 1 Identifying the sequence of past events	VOCABULARY Attributive language
	READING 2 Summarizing an argument	GRAMMAR Infinitive phrases
	STUDY SKILL The Harvard system	WRITING Integrating sources into your writing

Trading floor of the Chicago Mercantile Exchange.

While you watch

Watch the video and choose *T* (True) or *F* (False).

1 Austerity in Greece has pushed some people deeper into poverty. T / F
2 In 2015 around 7.6% of Greeks were at risk of poverty. T / F
3 Although difficult, austerity has been successful for the majority of Greeks. T / F
4 The people who use the "Ithaca" laundry service are homeless. T / F
5 There are signs that austerity will start to have a positive impact soon. T / F

After you watch

Work in a group. Discuss the questions.

1 Do you think austerity is a useful way to tackle a struggling economy? What other approaches could be successful?
2 Who do you think has ultimate responsibility for the economic performance of a country? Why?
3 Do you think a difficult economic situation fosters a stronger or weaker sense of community in the affected country?

1 READING

The credit crunch: Whose fault was it anyway?

A Vocabulary preview

Complete the definitions with the words or phrases in the box.

> bail them out   credit crunch   default on your mortgage   file for bankruptcy
> housing bubble   recession   regulator   stimulate the economy

1 A period of time when banks are not willing to lend much money is called a _____.
2 When you fail to pay back money you borrowed to buy a house or apartment, you _____.
3 A _____ occurs when demand to buy accommodation and related prices are high.
4 A _____'s job is to make sure that companies or organizations follow systems and rules.
5 If you have to officially state that you do not have enough money to pay your debts, you _____.
6 When a company is in a bad financial situation, another company might _____.
7 An economic decline over a period of several months or more is a _____.
8 When it is in decline, governments usually try to _____ so it improves.

B Before you read

Activating prior knowledge

Work with a partner. Discuss the questions.

1 How does an increase or decrease in interest rates affect homeowners, savers, companies, and banks?
2 What do you know about the financial crisis in 2007/8 (e.g., causes, effects, etc.)?

C Global reading

Identifying main ideas

Read *The credit crunch: Whose fault was it anyway?* Match the ideas (a–f) to the paragraphs (1–6) that the information can be found in.

a A surprising bankruptcy despite government intervention ___
b The effects of interest rates on banks and property owners ___
c Examples of proposed changes to the banking system ___
d Institutions that the author believes helped to create the financial crisis ___
e The impact of the financial crisis on a manufacturing industry ___
f The first signs that banks were in trouble ___

The credit crunch: Whose fault was it anyway?

READING 1

[1]The causes of the global economic downturn in 2008 have been much debated. While experts and academics agree the downturn was the result of a credit crunch, the causes of this credit crunch are more contentious. Blame is often apportioned to commercial banks due to the large number of risky investments they had undertaken. However, this paper will argue that central banks, regulators, and governments were also to blame. It will begin by outlining the key events before and during the global economic downturn and will then move on to an analysis of these key events to determine the major causes of the credit crunch and subsequent financial crisis.

The global economic downturn: key events

[2]By the mid-2000s, interest rates in the U.S. had risen to over 5% from just 1%. This had a particular impact on the subprime market where millions of people with few or no savings had been persuaded to take out a mortgage. They struggled to afford the interest rate increase and began to default on their mortgage repayments. This impacted not only on subprime mortgage lenders but also on the big banks, as they had previously bought up these debts from subprime banks. Such debts were considered to be low risk by large banks as they were bundled together from different parts of the country. The banks anticipated property markets rising and falling differently across regions, so that falls and losses in one area would be offset by rises and gains in another. Ratings agencies, funded by the banks, also found these investments to be low risk. However, once customers started defaulting on their mortgages and banks began to withdraw mortgage products from the market, the credit crunch started to take hold. Customers previously able to obtain mortgages no longer could. The housing bubble, which had gone unchecked by government and regulators for years, eventually burst in 2006. The bundled subprime loans were now very much high-risk debts.

[3]In April, 2007, the first subprime bank went bankrupt. Three months later, the U.S. bank Bear Stearns, subsequently bought by JP Morgan, told investors that they would receive little or no return on their investment. These were the initial indicators that there was a potential credit crunch. By September, the rate at which banks lend money to each other was at its highest for almost 20 years. Commercial banks were clearly nervous about their own credit and the credit of others. For the rest of the year, banks and related organizations warned of and/or declared subprime related losses. On December 13th, in an unprecedented action, the U.S. government persuaded five banks to lend to other banks in a bid to increase credit levels. In the week preceding this, President Bush had already promised financial support to a million homeowners struggling to keep their homes.

[4]In 2008, the financial crisis became a reality and the U.S. government tried to limit its effects: it reduced interest rates to 3.5% in January, set aside an allocation of $50bn for credit-squeezed banks in April, and bailed out the U.S.'s largest lenders Freddie Mac and Fannie Mae, owners of $5 trillion worth of mortgage debts, in July. Yet, despite these interventions, the fourth largest investment bank in the U.S. and a significant international bank, Lehman Brothers, filed for bankruptcy eight months later. This collapse of a major bank caused shockwaves throughout the industry and large losses in financial markets. The U.S. government only now created a $700bn rescue plan that included purchasing bad debts from banks to prevent a collapse of the world's financial system. By the end of the year, interest rates had been lowered to just 0.25% and another $600bn had been injected into the economy to try to prevent a recession. Other governments around the world in Europe and Asia were taking similar steps to stimulate their economies.

[5]The crisis continued into 2009. On June 1st, General Motors filed for administration. Chrysler had already done this four weeks prior, despite both organizations having had financial support the previous year. Over the next few weeks, General Motors reorganized, received financial support from the governments, and was able to come out of bankruptcy, while many of Chrysler's assets were bought by Fiat. On June 24th, the Organization for Economic Co-operation and Development (OECD) announced that the world economy was in its worst recession since World War II. The U.S. government, as well as those in Japan and Europe, declared that their economies had shrunk over the last 12 months. Financial markets continued to suffer losses and the effects reached other industries.

[6]In July 2009, 10% of the biggest banks in the U.S. failed a stress test showing they had still not put aside sufficient funds to absorb bad debts. In the previous month, President Obama had announced proposals for legislation to reform U.S. banks in an attempt to prevent the same situation happening again. These reforms—which had not been in place previously—included requiring banks to put aside more money to absorb losses, a greater regulation of mortgages and credit cards, and authority given to the Federal Reserve to inspect and monitor the major banks.

GLOSSARY

Federal Reserve (n) the central bank of the U.S.

interest rate (n) the percentage that an institution such as a bank charges when lending money, or pays out when borrowing money

subprime (adj) used to describe the practice of lending money to people who are less likely to be able to pay it back

1 READING

Identifying the sequence of past events

D Close reading

Identify the following language to help you understand a sequence of past events in a complex academic text:

Tenses
Writers often mix tenses when describing a sequence. Recognizing which tense has been used and why will help you establish the order in which events occurred (e.g., the simple past presents completed actions in chronological order; the past perfect describes one action that happened before another past event, etc.).

Time expressions
Writers also use time expressions to signify exactly when an action happened (e.g., *In March, On April 6th*) or when one action happened in relation to another (e.g., *Six months later, three weeks prior to that, previously, subsequently, the following month*, etc.).

Read *The credit crunch: Whose fault was it anyway?* again. Put the events (a–j) in the order they occurred.

___ a Homeowners were unable to repay their mortgage debts.
___ b A major global bank went bankrupt.
___ c Chrysler filed for bankruptcy.
___ d General Motors entered bankruptcy.
___ e The U.S. government attempted to prevent a crisis by reducing interest rates and bailing out banks.
___ f Banks lent money to people with little credit and then sold those debts to large banks.
___ g The government reduced interest rates again and tried to boost the economy with hundreds of billions of dollars.
___ h Banks failed a stress test.
___ i The government announced bank reforms.
___ j The OECD announced that there was a global recession.

E Critical thinking

Work with a partner. Discuss the questions.

1 What reasons do you think the writer will give to support his claim that central banks, regulators, and governments were also to blame for the financial crisis? Use information in the paper to help you.
2 What risks do ordinary people take with money every day? How can these risks be avoided?

Study skills — The Harvard system

When you have used, quoted or paraphrased a source, acknowledge it. Either within the sentence or at the end of the sentence, write in brackets the author's name, the date of publication and, if required, page numbers.

The film was deliberately inaccurate about José Martí, who spent much of his life in poverty (Colon 1982, pp.81–82)

References

In the 'References:' at the end of the essay, the reference to Colon would appear in this form (and in alphabetical order):

Colon, K. (1982). *A Puerto Rican in New York and Other Sketches*, 2nd edn. New York: International Publishers.

© Stella Cottrell (2013)

1 Look at the reference list below and answer the questions.

   1 What is the order of information when referencing a book?
   2 What extra information do you need to include when you reference a journal?
   3 How are online articles referenced differently to books?

   References:

   Carter, P. and Thwaite, D. (2015) *Risk-taking: biology and psychology*, 2nd edn. Sydney: Black & White Publishing
   Morton, V. (2012) Financial risks in the 21st century, *The Financial Review* vol. 3, March, pp. 112–117.
   Young, A. (2014) Risky behavior: the banking system, *Financial Times* [Online], Available: http://www.finance.free.com/thebankingsystem.htm [Accessed 4 March 2017].

2 Identify the missing information for each source in the reference list below.

   References:

   Arita, R, The dangers of risk-taking, *riskmgment.com*, Available: www.riskmgment.com/articles/423502.htm [Accessed 7 April 2018]
   Graham, (2017), *Why we take risks*, 2nd ed, London: Macmillan
   Hamilton, D, (2016), Risk: a risky business, Available: www.riskresearch.com/article0421.html
   Leigh, W, (2016), *Risk Management in the 21st century*, New Jersey
   Smith, T, (2014), Developing risk literacy, *Journal of Risk Literacy*, pps 29–30
   Yang, Y, (2017), How to teach risk, *Journal of Risk Literacy*, Vol 10, Available: www.JRL.com/articles/2017/Vol10/39276.htm [Accessed 4 April 2018]

2 READING

Risk-takers: Who are they?

A Vocabulary preview

Complete the paragraph with the words in the box.

> addictive   disregard   gene   peer pressure
> personality trait   sound judgment   susceptible   triggered

Why do some people actively seek risky activities and participate in them with complete [1] _____ for the consequences? Do they have a [2] _____, like disinhibition, that makes them [3] _____ to decision-making without [4] _____? Is the pull of [5] _____ too strong for them because they want to fit in? Is it the fact that chemicals [6] _____ in the brain during risky activities are [7] _____? Or is it simply physical, i.e., their biological makeup? In other words, a [8] _____ that they inherited from their parents?

B Before you read

Activating prior knowledge

Imagine a typical risk-taker. Write notes about the person's age, character, gender, job, and social life. Then compare with a partner.

C Global reading

Note-taking for summaries

> Summarizing the key points in a text enables you to gain a good understanding of the content. Follow these steps for effective notes:
> 1. Read the text to understand the main idea.
> 2. Write a thesis statement—a sentence which summarizes the main argument in the whole text. Include the writer's name and the article date.
> 3. Reread the text more carefully. Divide it into sections and take notes of the main point and supporting evidence in each, ignoring what isn't important.

1. Read *Risk takers: Who are they?* and check the causes discussed.

   ☐ Social background   ☐ Brain chemicals   ☐ Work experience
   ☐ Genetic factors   ☐ Age   ☐ Gender

2. Which of the following is the most appropriate thesis statement? Why?

   1. Wittman (2012) believes that risk-taking is inherited through our parents' genes.
   2. Wittman (2012) suggests that age, gender, brain, and biology cause risk-taking.
   3. Wittman (2012) states that risk-taking is determined by psychology rather than biology.

3. Read the text again and take notes following step three in the *Note-taking for summaries* box.

Risk-takers: Who are they?

READING 2

By Dr. Charlie Wittman, December 3, 2012

[1] Jamie is a risk-taker; a 24-year-old banker who spends his earnings on motorbikes and kite-surfing. Risk is something we face daily, whether it is deciding how a company should invest to ensure its future or whether it is making the decision to take an umbrella to work or not. However, some people, like Jamie, have a greater orientation towards risk-taking than others. Biological and psychological evidence indicates that this is likely to be because of the way Jamie's brain processes dopamine; because he is a novelty-seeker; and because he is young and male. This paper explores that evidence.

Biological reasons for risk-taking

[2] Biologists appear to have discovered a physical reason for risk-taking that explains the behavior of people like Jamie. Dopamine is a neurotransmitter—a chemical that transmits signals between nerve cells (neurons). It is associated with the brain's reward system and is the chemical that makes us feel good, and scientists believe it to be linked to risk-taking. Our nerve cells have dopamine receptors which control the amount of dopamine that each cell receives, but not all receptors may be active. When a person has few active receptors to control the amount of dopamine that is received, a cell can become flooded, triggering a feeling of euphoria.

[3] Researchers at Vanderbilt University in Nashville and Albert Einstein College of Medicine in New York asked 34 men and women to complete a questionnaire about their risk-taking to assess whether they seek new opportunities or are cautious in life. This was then followed by a brain scan using a technique called *positron emission tomography* (PET) to analyze the number of dopamine receptors that the participants had. In their article in the *Journal of Neuroscience* (2008), the researchers observed that people who are risk-takers have fewer dopamine receptors than people who are not; mirroring the outcome found in studies carried out with rats. This suggests that the rush of pleasure a risk-taker receives when a cell becomes flooded with dopamine can become addictive for some people. They therefore pursue fresh, exhilarating activities in order to try to repeat this feeling, and as a result their concern for risk is invariably reduced.

Psychological reasons for risk-taking

[4] Dopamine gives us a biological reason for risk-taking, but scientists believe there may be psychological reasons too. Sensation-seeking is a personality trait that describes the desire to find activities that bring us pleasure. In 1964, psychologist Marvin Zuckerman created the sensation-seeking scale—a personality test which was designed to show how much of the trait a person has. His 40-item questionnaire, still in use today, was given to people who actively sought out novel experiences, as well as those content to lead a tranquil life. From the results, Zuckerman's deduction was that there are four components of sensation-seeking. The first is *thrill and adventure seeking*; for example doing extreme sports. The second is *experience seeking*; looking for new experiences. The third is *disinhibition*; the desire to take risks in social activities. The fourth is *boredom susceptibility*; a low tolerance of monotony. Zuckerman further asserted that, while risk-taking is not a trait in itself, it is very much connected to sensation-seeking, as a high sensation-seeker does not appraise risk in the same way that a low sensation-seeker does. An overwhelming desire to achieve pleasure means that there is a greater willingness to participate in activities which pose more risks.

[5] Studies of identical twins have been carried out to ascertain whether sensation-seeking is a result of nature or nurture. Pairs of twins who had grown up together and pairs of twins who had grown up apart were studied (Zuckerman, 2007). The study determined that a fairly high proportion—60%—of the sensation-seeking trait can be attributed to genes, showing just how influential genes are in risk-taking. This is higher than many other traits which usually range from 30–50%, suggesting that the sensation-seeking trait, and a tendency towards risk-taking, can in fact be inherited.

Age and risk-taking

[6] Age is also relevant to the area of risk-taking. Adolescents seem to conduct themselves with a clear disregard for safety, and while this can be as a result of peer pressure, it now appears there may also be neurological reasons behind it. Dr. Jay Giedd from the National Institute of Mental Health in the U.S. (2008) conducted a study in which 145 children underwent a brain scan every two years for ten years using an MRI (magnetic resonance image) scanner. According to Giedd, the area of the brain that sits just behind the forehead—the prefrontal cortex—does not fully develop until as late as 25. This part of the brain is known to control the way we organize, plan, make sound judgments, and reason, so it is essential for calculating risk. If teenagers and young adults are dependent on a part of their brain which is not fully formed until their mid-20s, it is logical that they will sometimes miscalculate risk and therefore fail to minimize it.

Gender and risk-taking

[7] Some people may believe that Jamie, the risk-taker introduced at the beginning of this paper, takes risks simply because he is male, assuming that fewer women are risk-takers. However, researchers at the Columbia Business School in the U.S. (2011) contend that gender affects the type of risk-taking that takes place, not whether it actually occurs. They claim that financial risks are more typical of men, whereas social risks, such as giving a controversial opinion in public or making a significant career change, are more representative of women. These differences may be related to a person's perception of how risky an action is. The researchers further suggest that when you are less familiar with a situation, you are more likely to perceive it as risky. As a person's gender can cause them to have different life experiences, the researchers argue that there is a correlation between gender and perceptions of situations. So, while Jamie may not be involved in risky behavior as a direct result of being male, his gender and life experiences to date could have impacted on his choice of career, encouraging him to work in an industry that entails significant risk without him necessarily perceiving that risk.

Conclusion

[8] There has been considerable research that examines risk-taking and why different people behave differently. The research presented in this paper indicates that there are both biological and psychological explanations as to why people like Jamie may choose to take more risks than others. However, none of these explanations are conclusive. It is possible that the brain's reward system, a person's sensation-seeking character, age, and gender all impact on risk-taking behavior.

Sources

Figner, B. and Weber, E.U. (2011). Who takes risks and why? Determinants of risk-taking. *Current Directions in Psychological Science*. 20(4), 211–216

Giedd, J.N. (2008). The Teen Brain: Insights from Neuroimaging. *The Journal of Adolescent Health*. 42(4), 335–343

Zald, D.H. et al. (2008). Midbrain dopamine receptor availability is inversely associated with novelty-seeking. *The Journal of Neuroscience*. 28(53)

Zuckerman, M. (1964). Development of a sensation-seeking scale. *The Journal of Consulting Psychology*. 28(6), 477–482

Zuckerman, M. (2007). *Sensation Seeking and Risky Behavior*. 1st ed. Washington DC: American Psychological Association

D Close reading

1 Read *Risk-takers: Who are they?* again. Complete the statements with no more than one word from the article.

1. Dopamine is only able to fill a cell when the receptor is not _____.
2. In a study in New York, participants had to say if they were _____ about or keen on doing new activities.
3. The New York research produced similar results to studies conducted on _____.
4. Dopamine creates a feeling of pleasure which some people find _____.
5. Sensation-seeking is a characteristic which causes people to seek _____ in new activities.
6. Zuckerman's research suggests the sensation-seeking trait has _____ key aspects to it.

2 Read the text again. Are these sentences *T* (True), *F* (False), or *NG* (Not Given)?

1. Risk-taking is a characteristic like sensation-seeking. ___
2. Whether a person has the sensation-seeking trait is partially decided by a person's biological makeup. ___
3. A person's prefrontal cortex is fully formed before they reach adulthood. ___
4. It is possible to work out when a prefrontal cortex will develop in some children. ___
5. Women are more likely to take risks in situations they have less experience of. ___
6. The writer concludes that the causes of risk-taking discussed in the article are definitive. ___

E Critical thinking

Work in a group. Discuss the questions.

1. Do you agree that young people take more risks than older people? Why / why not?
2. How do parents, schools, the government, etc., try to minimize the risk that young people take in your country? Is it their responsibility to do so? Why / why not?
3. Whose responsibility is it to teach children how to calculate risk so they make safer decisions in their lives? Why? How can they do it?
4. How do you assess risk in your own life? Do you think you do this successfully, or are there things you should do differently? If so, what are they?

READING 2

Reading for specific information

VOCABULARY

Vocabulary development

Attributive language

To attribute information in a text to other authors, we use:

- Reporting verbs (e.g., *advocate, determine, refute*, etc.), often in conjunction with adverbs (e.g., *Schmidt **further** asserts…, Collins **consistently** argued…, Verma **directly** states that…*, etc.)
- Verb and noun collocations (e.g., *propose a theory, offer a definition, describe a process*, etc.)
- Set phrases (e.g., *As Mattel points out… / Writing in* The Lancet, *Xu argues that…, To quote Farhad, …,* etc.).

1 Scan *Risk-takers: Who are they?* and underline the language used to attribute information to researchers.

2 Circle the incorrect word in each group. Explain your answers to a partner.

1 Vance (2017) **acknowledges/admits/concedes/endorses** that risks are not gender-specific.
2 As the researchers **emphasized/examined/noted/stated**, young people take larger risks than adults.
3 According to Harley, he **disagrees/disputes/refutes/rejects** the results of Hunter's research.
4 Stephens **briefly/consequently/initially/predominantly** denied that the findings were correct.
5 Cummins was unable to **establish/identify/make/prove** a relationship between risk-taking and wealth.
6 Columbia researchers (2011) **argue/assert/believe/compare** that gender impacts on perceptions of risks.

3 Complete the paragraph with the words in the box.

| according to   advised   concluded   evidence   further |
| observation   recommended   writing |

¹ _____ researchers at the University of Iowa, children under 14 should not cross the road without an adult. During an experiment in a virtual environment, they made the ² _____ that only people over 14 were able to cross without accident, and ³ _____ that this was caused by underdeveloped visual judgment and motor skills. The researchers found ⁴ _____ of two key issues: not waiting for a gap in traffic and not crossing quickly. ⁵ _____ in the *Journal of Experimental Psychology*, Professor Jodie Plumert ⁶ _____ that parents help children develop patience and speed. She ⁷ _____ ⁸ _____ city planners to increase traffic crossings.

Academic words

VOCABULARY

1 Complete the definitions with the words in bold.

1 Most people take out a mortgage to **fund** a property investment.
2 There was no **allocation** of funds at some banks to deal with the financial crisis.
3 The raising of interest rates **preceded** the credit crunch.
4 Parents tend to **transmit** their beliefs about money to their children.
5 Higher house prices can be **offset** by lower interest rates.
6 The government may **inspect** the activities of banks more closely in the future.
7 **Deduction** suggests there are multiple causes of risk-taking behavior.
8 Some people have an **orientation** toward risk-taking.

a _____ (n) something that you know from the evidence you have
b _____ (n) someone's basic attitudes or beliefs
c _____ (v) to come before something else in a series
d _____ (v) to provide the money for something that costs a lot
e _____ (v) to look at something carefully in order to check it's correct or good enough
f _____ (n) an amount of something used for a particular purpose
g _____ (v) balance the effect of something so there is no advantage or disadvantage
h _____ (v) to pass information or attitudes to other people

2 Complete the statements with words from Exercise 1. Change the form if necessary.

1 Governments must _____ money to reducing health risks.
2 Teachers should avoid _____ their personal values to students.
3 _____ health education is as important as paying for healthcare.
4 Young people today can _____ risk better than young people could a generation ago.
5 Students must play sports to _____ the harmful effects of sitting for long periods in class.
6 As young people have an _____ toward risk, they should study how to calculate it.
7 Road safety lessons should _____ all school trips.
8 School _____ should include risk assessments of local roads.

3 With a partner, discuss whether you agree or disagree with the statements in Exercise 2.

CRITICAL THINKING

Critical thinking

> **Assessing whether research supports an argument**
>
> When assessing cited research, ask yourself these questions:
>
> **Currency**—Is the research up-to-date?
>
> **Reliability**—Were the results obtained once, or have the results been replicated? Was the research carried out by a reliable, independent organization?
>
> **Validity**—Was the sample large enough for the results to be significant? Could the results have been caused by something else?
>
> **Relevance**—Is the research relevant to the argument being made? Do the results of the survey directly support the conclusions being drawn?

1. Read the text below. Why is the research mentioned not current, reliable, valid, or relevant?

   > Teenagers are just as likely as adults to avoid risk by wearing a helmet when cycling. 1996 research by the helmet manufacturer Safemet involved 20 teenagers and 20 adults who had recently bought helmets. They answered 30 questions anonymously online about their cycling habits. A total of 80% of both groups said that they liked their helmets. This suggests that the view of teenagers taking risks by rejecting helmets on the grounds of fashion is untrue.

2. Scan *Risk-takers: Who are they?* again and find the source of each piece of information:
   1. Risk-takers have fewer dopamine receptors in their nerve cells. _____
   2. Sensation-seeking is a personality trait which causes you to look for excitement. _____
   3. The sensation-seeking trait can be passed on to children. _____
   4. Our prefrontal cortex may not fully develop until as late as 25. _____
   5. Men and women take different types of risks. _____
   6. Perceptions of risk are different depending on a person's past experience and familiarity with the situation he or she is in. _____

3. Look at the research you identified in Exercise 2 and answer the questions.
   1. How is the dopamine receptor research valid?
   2. How is the sensation-seeking personality trait research relevant?
   3. How is the research showing that sensation-seeking can be passed on to children valid?
   4. How is the prefrontal cortex research reliable?
   5. Does the research into male/female differences and perceptions of risk have currency? Is it relevant?

Writing model

You are going to learn about using infinitive phrases and integrating sources in your writing. You are then going to use these to write a summary of an academic paper.

A Analyze

Complete the students' notes with no more than one word from the model in each blank.

> Patricia Hughes (2017)–risk literacy (RL) is [1] _____ every day so [2] _____ for school RL lessons are needed. Two studies support this: 1. 2016 study with 16-year-olds at University of Derbyshire. RL lessons on offsetting [3] _____ risk = more successful decision-making re. saving/investing money. 2. Barker (2015), risk literacy in London [4] _____ schools = similar conclusion.
> Conclusion: "both primary and secondary schools ought to be doing more to teach risk literacy in math lessons." Specialized teacher training + [5] _____ for upper primary–upper secondary needed.

B Model

Read the summary of an academic paper written using the notes above. Answer the questions.

> In her article "The need to learn risk" (2017), in the *Journal of Risk Literacy* (Vol. 2, Issue 4), Patricia Hughes argues strongly that risk literacy is essential in our daily lives and funds should be allocated to allow young people to learn to calculate risk better in schools. To support her argument, Hughes provides evidence that risk literacy education has been successful among 16-year-olds in a 2016 study undertaken at the University of Derbyshire. The teenage participants were more successful in making decisions on how to save or invest money by offsetting calculated risk after risk literacy lessons. Hughes also quotes Barker (2015) who examined the role of risk literacy in a study in London primary schools and came to similar conclusions. Hughes ultimately concludes that "both primary and secondary schools ought to be doing more to teach risk literacy in math lessons" and goes on to suggest the need for specialized teacher training and a syllabus that goes from upper primary to upper secondary schools.

1. Identify the sentence where the university student presents the main idea of the paper.
2. Identify the purpose of the rest of the summary.
3. Underline language that the student uses to attribute ideas to other authors. How varied is it?

Grammar

> **Infinitive phrases**
>
> **Perfect infinitive** is used to suggest that the action took place before the time we're talking about.
>
> *(to) have + past participle*
>
> *Biologists appear **to have discovered** a physical reason for risk-taking.*
>
> **Continuous infinitive** is used to suggest that the action is in progress around the time we are talking about.
>
> *(to) be + ing verb*
>
> *We **should be trying** to reduce risk-taking among young people.*
>
> **Passive infinitive** is used to focus on the object, not the subject.
>
> *(to) be + past participle*
>
> *His research suggests that the sensation-seeking trait **can** in fact **be inherited**.*

1 What is the difference in meaning between each pair of sentences?

1. a Some adults appear to take regular risks.
   b Some adults appear to have taken regular risks.
2. a Risky behavior is likely to be causing unnecessary accidents.
   b Risky behavior is likely to have caused unnecessary accidents.
3. a Some people would like to take more risks in life.
   b Many people would like to have taken more risks in life.
4. a Without risk-taking, humans would not have achieved so much.
   b Without risk-taking, so much would not have been achieved.
5. a Schools should be taking greater care to teach risk literacy.
   b Schools should take greater care to teach risk literacy.

2 Complete the text with the correct infinitive form of the verbs in parentheses.

> Parents these days seem ¹ _____ (protect) their children more than ever. Yet the truth is children must ² _____ (give) the opportunity to take risks in order to develop. By the time a child becomes an adult, he/she needs ³ _____ (learn) how to deal with the successes and failures associated with risk-taking, as these skills will ⁴ _____ (need) in the adult world. It's a shame that children today appear ⁵ _____ (miss out) on typical childhood activities because of their parents' fear of injury, especially as many of those parents are likely ⁶ _____ (enjoy) such activities when they were young. Children today should ⁷ _____ (nurture), but they should also ⁸ _____ (provide) with the independence they need to take risks in as safe an environment as possible.

Writing skill

WRITING

Intergrating sources in your writing

When integrating information from other sources into your writing, you can:

Use a short quotation (i.e., one or two sentences only)

Gluckman (2014): "Peer pressure affects how teenagers act."

Paraphrase / summarize information in your own words

Gluckman (2014) suggests that peers influence teenage behavior.

Note, you can mention the author at the beginning or end of a sentence.

Helen Atkins (2016) claims that peer pressure can influence risk-taking.

Peer pressure can influence risk-taking (Atkins, 2016).

1 Read the following excerpt of a 2017 paper by professor of sociology Dr. Philip Bauman. What is the topic?

> Peer pressure may be having an effect on today's teenage drivers. In a study at Temple University, teenagers and adults playing a video game had to decide whether to stop at yellow lights or not. When they believed two same-sex friends were watching them, the teenagers drove through 40% more yellow lights, causing 60% more crashes. Such results help to explain the higher number of car accidents among this age group.

2 Look at the summary below. Why is it ineffective? Think about both content and referencing.

> Peer pressure might be having an impact on teenage drivers today. In a study, young drivers playing a video game had to decide whether to stop at traffic lights. Dr. Bauman says the results can explain why teenagers have a higher number of accidents.

3 Continue the paper below with reference to Dr. Baumann's paper above. Write it in three different ways:

   1 With the first line of Dr. Bauman's paper as a quotation.
   2 With a paraphrase of the first line of the paper.
   3 With a summary of the whole paragraph.

> Peer pressure can have a significant impact on risk-taking among teenagers and young adults. Professor of sociology …

RISK UNIT 4

WRITING

Writing task

You are going to write a summary in response to the following:
"Write a summary of 'Risk-takers: Who are they?' on pages 69 & 70."

Brainstorm

Read through the notes you took on *Risk-takers: Who are they?* (page 68, Exercise 3). Make sure you've omitted anything unnecessary, before putting the notes into your own words.

Plan

Use the thesis statement on page 68 and your notes to help you plan a summary of *Risk-takers: Who are they?* Think about the most important information to include and the order in which it should be presented.

Write

Use your brainstorm and plan to help you write your summary. Remember to use infinitive phrases where appropriate and to integrate sources into your writing.

Share

Exchange your summary with a partner. Use the checklist on page 189 to help you provide feedback to your partner.

Rewrite and edit

Consider your partner's comments and write your final draft. Think about:

- whether you summarized the most relevant information
- whether you used infinitive phrases where appropriate
- whether you integrated sources into your writing.

Review

Wordlist

Vocabulary preview

addictive (adj)	file for bankruptcy (phr)	recession (n) **	susceptible (adj)
bail (sb) out (phr v)	gene (n) **	regulator (n)	trigger (v)
credit crunch (n)	housing bubble (n)	sound judgment (n phr)	
default on sth (v)	peer pressure (n)	stimulate (the economy) (v) **	
disregard (v)	personality trait (n)		

Vocabulary development

acknowledge (v) **	conclude (v) ***	endorse (v) **	repeatedly (adv) **
concede (v) **	dispute (v) ***	predominantly (adv) *	

Academic words

allocation (n) *	fund (v) ***	offset (v) *	precede (v) **
deduction (n)	inspect (v) **	orientation (n)	transmit (v) **

Academic words review

Complete the sentences using the correct form of the words in the box.

| allocation | orientation | predominantly | sustainable | transmit |

1 Governments should aim to achieve _____ economic growth and economic development.
2 Students were invited to attend an _____ week prior to the commencement of their courses.
3 The company carries out a careful risk assessment before an _____ of funds can be made to any one project.
4 The university's student intake is from _____ middle-class backgrounds and it is looking for ways to address this imbalance.
5 Economic uncertainty usually _____ itself to the financial markets causing share prices and currency values to drop.

Unit review

Reading 1	☐	I can identify the sequence of past events.
Reading 2	☐	I can summarize and argument.
Study skill	☐	I can use the Harvard System to reference texts.
Vocabulary	☐	I can use attributive language.
Grammar	☐	I can use infinitive phrases.
Writing	☐	I can integrate sources into my writing.

5 SPRAWL

Discussion point

Discuss with a partner.

1 Why do you think the cities have expanded at a faster rate than the suburbs?
2 Why might poverty be a greater issue in the suburbs?
3 Why might the number of jobs within a typical commute distance be decreasing in both suburbs and cities?

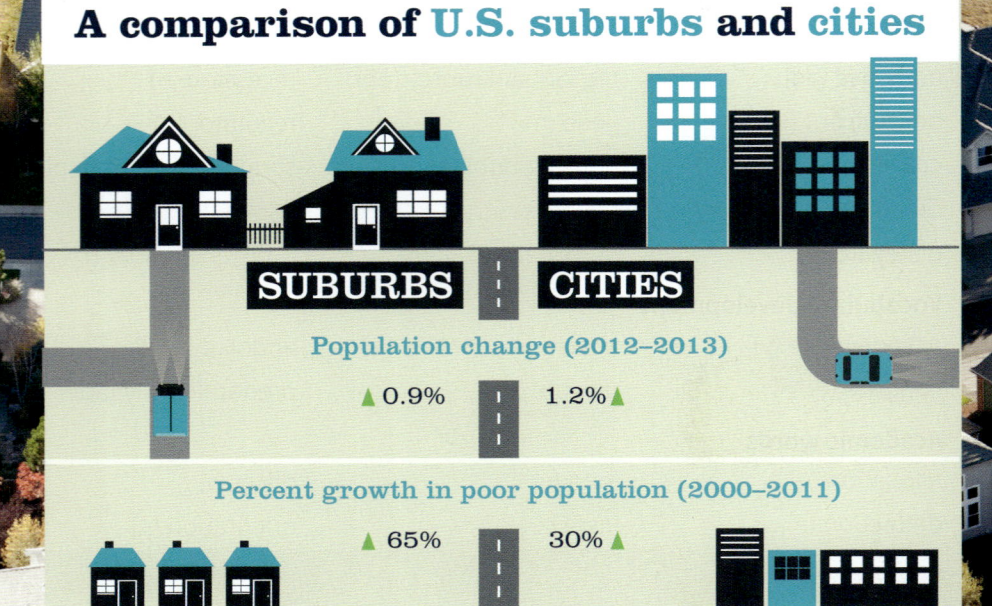

A comparison of U.S. suburbs and cities

SUBURBS | CITIES

Population change (2012–2013)
▲ 0.9% | 1.2% ▲

Percent growth in poor population (2000–2011)
▲ 65% | 30% ▲

Number of jobs within a typical commute distance (2000–2012)
▼ 8% | 4% ▼

Average cost of living per year (2015)
$35,000 | $45,000

VIDEO

SLUM RENEWAL

Before you watch

Match the words in bold with the correct definitions.

1 **hold sway** (v)
2 **initiative** (n)
3 **lurk** (v)
4 **regeneration** (n)
5 **slum** (n)

a have control
b a new plan or process started in order to solve a problem
c part of a city with improvised housing and poor sanitation
d the process of rebuilding in order to improve
e remain hidden

UNIT AIMS

READING 1 Questioning while reading
READING 2 Finding similarities and differences
STUDY SKILL Reflective learning
VOCABULARY Phrasal verb academic alternatives
GRAMMAR Parallel structures
WRITING Direct quotations

Suburban housing in Superior, Colorado.

While you watch

Watch the video and choose *T* (True) or *F* (False).

1 Both local residents and city authorities are helping to transform the slums. T / F
2 Medellin has a history of violent crime. T / F
3 The project has only improved conditions for the wealthy people of the city. T / F
4 The regeneration project has changed how the area looks, but has not improved community relations. T / F
5 The problem of organized crime still exists in the slum areas. T / F

After you watch

Work in a group. Discuss the questions.

1 What aspects of the regeneration of Medellin do you think are the most important? Why?
2 How can governments and local authorities decide which areas would benefit most from regeneration projects?
3 "It is the people who live in our community, not the facilities or whether it looks nice, that influence how we feel about where we live." To what extent do you agree with this statement?

1 READING

Rust Belt dystopia

A Vocabulary preview

1 Complete the paragraph with the words in the box.

> automation   booming   coal   desired
> domestically   fallout   impacted   restructure

Globalization and increasing ¹ _____ have led to a decline in manufacturing levels in some corners of the world. Industries that were once ² _____ have been forced to ³ _____ in order to survive and others, like ⁴ _____ mining, have all but disappeared. In addition, cheaper workforces abroad have made it difficult for companies to justify manufacturing ⁵ _____. The ⁶ _____ of such changes are far-reaching, but in particular they have ⁷ _____ employees who were made redundant. These people can no longer find their ⁸ _____ employment and have been forced to move or retrain.

2 Work with a partner. Discuss how areas in your country have been affected by the issues described in Exercise 1.

B Before you read

Activating prior knowledge

Look at *Rust Belt dystopia*. Read the title, sub-headings, and introduction and answer the questions.

1 What information do you think you will find in the research paper? Why?
2 What do you already know about this topic?

C Global reading

Identifying research questions

1 Use the table to write down three questions you have about the Rust Belt. Then read the research paper and try to answer your questions.

	Questions	Answers
1		
2		
3		

2 Work with a partner. What were your questions and did you find answers in the text?

Rust Belt dystopia

[1]The Rust Belt is a region of the U.S. that stretches from the Great Lakes to the upper Midwest States. Although once known for its booming industry, over the past three decades the area has come to be characterized by economic decline, population loss, and urban decay. Regeneration of this region has become a staple policy of presidential candidates; often dictating the implementation of country, state, and city-wide initiatives. This paper will evaluate the benefits and challenges of three such initiatives: increased tourism, economic restructuring, and smart decline.

The factory belt decline

[2]In the first half of the 20th century, the Rust Belt was the industrial heartland of the country, and business was booming. Transportation links to the eastern states made this area attractive to automobile companies, steel and coal mining companies, and manufacturers of materials for heavy industry. These in turn attracted employees, including many migrant workers from Eastern Europe. By the middle of the 20th century the industrial landscape was changing. Companies began to move manufacturing bases southwest, drawn by the promise of cheaper labor and less unionization. Automation forced thousands out of work and free trade agreements curtailed demand as the subsequent globalization and foreign monetary policies meant that coal and steel were cheaper to import than to produce domestically. Lee Ohanian (2014) also believes that, as domestic companies had faced little to no competition, they had had no incentive to expand productivity and were simply unable to compete with their international counterparts. The fallout of these changes reached far and wide in Rust Belt communities as manufacturing was such an integral part of their economies. The area now had a much smaller share of manufacturing jobs in the country. This resulted in a decline in both population and the economy which, in turn, produced a heavy reliance on social security and a deficit in government spending.

Regeneration initiatives

Tourism

[3]"Tourism constitutes a major portion of most urban economies today, and the industry is a top priority of elected officials" (Cowan, 2016), however, tourist attractions must be managed carefully to ensure they are of benefit. Rogerson (2002, as cited in Eyles, 2008) believes that if tourist attractions are not managed in the long-term, they will not be sustainable or contribute to a positive image; an attraction in decline could actually be detrimental to an area. He suggests that, in order to create a successful tourist industry, planners must, in consultation with local citizens, develop "a total tourism portfolio" highlighting natural features such as waterfronts and urban parks, buildings of interest, and promotion of local culture. The portfolio must enhance the lives of inhabitants as well as visitors, and create a positive image of the area to both build a brand and instil a sense of pride in local people.

[4]Another consideration when using tourism as a means to local economic growth is wages. While a well-designed tourist portfolio can attract wealth to the area, employment in the tourism industry tends to be low, especially compared to traditional manufacturing jobs and especially in urban areas (Lacher & Oh, 2011). This impacts on both the economy and on people's standard of living.

Economic restructuring

[5]Some experts suggest that greater stability can be achieved through the production of "new knowledge, innovations, and cutting edge technologies or [being] a light, flexible manufacturer" (Siddiqui, 2013), implying that diversification is vital for the continued importance of industry in the region.

[6]However, diversification requires investment, and while tax reductions, incentive payments, and no-interest loans may tempt businesses back to the area, they can also be costly to local tax payers. One company moved its operations to Cleveland after being promised $93.5 million in state incentives over 15 years. This worked out as $53,429 for each of its 1,750 jobs (Beyerlein, 2012). Such jobs are often in the service industry, meaning they are low-paid with few benefits and may not enhance the local economy significantly.

Smart decline

[7]Most Rust Belt cities, such as Detroit and St. Louis, continue to pursue growth policies, yet there is a school of thought that reducing the size of the city would be more effective. Known as "smart decline," this approach "focuses on strategies that improve the lives of existing residents rather than exhaust city resources through hopeless efforts to increase population" (Heins, 2012). Indeed, Lee and Newman (2017) cited a U.S. government survey that found cities with declining populations allocated the majority of their property funding to the care of vacant buildings.

[8]By disposing of unwanted buildings and unused facilities, the funding could be used elsewhere. However, smart decline has not been implemented in sufficient breadth to conclusively prove its efficacy in regenerating a region. Hackworth (2016) examined 269 neighborhoods in 49 cities where buildings had been demolished. He found that, in fact, the demolition resulted in increased housing loss without "market rebound or a decrease in social marginality."

Conclusion

[9]None of the three approaches examined in this paper have been fully able to revitalize the Rust Belt. Both tourism and diversified manufacturing have resulted in lower-paid work and a heavy burden on city finances, although some towns and cities have survived as a result. Smart decline is untested in practice, but it should not be disregarded due to its potential benefits in theory. Towns and cities in the Rust Belt may well benefit from a two-pronged approach, using tourism and commerce to improve the local economy in order to increase the standard of living for the existing population without trying to return to population sizes of the past.

1 READING

Questioning while reading

D Close reading

Asking questions while reading a text can help you better process the information and reflect on the content. Answering these questions as you go will help you to adjust your understanding as you read. Questions might relate to:
- the meaning of certain terms or concepts
- reasons or principles behind a concept mentioned
- what is missing from the text
- validity of claims or arguments that the writer is making.

1 Read *Rust Belt dystopia* again. Stop after each section and note down any questions you have.

2 Work with a partner. Try to answers the questions you listed in Exercise 1, using information from the text or your own knowledge. Look up anything you cannot find.

3 Complete the sentences with no more than two words from the paper.
 1 Companies chose to settle in the factory belt region because of its _____.
 2 In the mid-1900s, _____ deals with other countries made it less cost-effective to manufacture goods at home.
 3 Plans for attracting visitors to a city should also inspire a feeling of _____ among residents.
 4 The cost of economic incentives is footed by _____.
 5 State governments in areas with dwindling populations are required to finance the maintenance of _____.
 6 There is no proof that _____ an area can be positively affected by demolishing buildings.

E Critical thinking

Work with a partner. Discuss the questions.
1 Are there any areas in your country that have been affected by the issues described in *Rust Belt dystopia*? What initiatives have been introduced to address them?
2 Smart decline has yet to be fully implemented and proven. How effective do you think it could be as a strategy to deal with deindustrialization? What might the disadvantages be?

Study skills — Reflective learning

Your performance as a student is likely to improve if you develop the habit of putting time aside to reflect on how you learn. You will find that you study more effectively if you consider, for example:
- changes in your motivation levels
- changes in your attitudes and ideas
- the appropriateness of your current study strategies to the tasks you are undertaking
- which skills you need for different kinds of assignment
- what is blocking your learning
- gaps in your knowledge or your skills

© Stella Cottrell (2013)

1 Complete the questionnaire below about your reading and writing skills.

GETTING TO KNOW YOUR SKILLS

A Your reading skills
Think about an academic text you have recently read in English.
1 What motivated you to read it? / What reduced your motivation? Why?
2 What reading skills did you need in order to read and understand the text?
3 How effectively did you understand the text?
4 What helped your understanding of the text? What prevented it?

B Your writing skills
Think about a piece of writing you are currently working on.
1 What is the best way to approach this piece of writing?
2 What skills do you need to be able to complete this piece of writing?
3 Of those skills, which are your strengths and which are weaknesses?
4 How easy do you find it to focus when writing? What distracts you?

2 Discuss these questions with a partner.
1 What conclusions can you draw from your answers to the questionnaire?
2 How can you address any issues your conclusions have raised?

2 READING

Suburbs of the future

A Vocabulary preview

Complete the sentences with the words in the box.

| bungalows | downsize | ethnicities | inaccessible |
| insufficient | millennials | reside | unsustainable |

1 People are drawn to urban cores—they are a melting pot of cultures and _____.
2 Nearly 8.5m people _____ in New York City—twice the population of Los Angeles.
3 Over 40% of _____ in New York still live with their parents.
4 The property ladder in London is simply _____ to people of my generation.
5 Experts suggest that current rents are _____ and are predicting a crash.
6 _____ affordable housing pushes many young families out to the suburbs.
7 Three-bedroom _____ in the suburbs of London sell for around £2.5m.
8 Most people _____ to a smaller property when they retire.

B Before you read

Activating prior knowledge

Work with a partner. Discuss the questions.

1 What do you think are the main benefits and issues associated with living in modern suburbia?
2 What do you think suburbs of the future will look like? Explain your reasons.

C Global reading

Identifying main ideas

Read *Suburbs of the future*. Check (✓) the topics the writers talk about.

- [ ] types of housing
- [ ] education
- [ ] transportation
- [ ] environmental issues
- [ ] technological innovation in the home
- [ ] communication networks
- [ ] community diversity
- [ ] business investment

SUBURBS OF THE FUTURE

READING 2

Despite the lure of bright city lights, it is the suburbs which account for the highest percentage of population growth. We asked four leading futurists to give their opinions on the changing face of suburbia.

Sarah Kalensky, regular contributor to *The Forecaster*

[1] As suburban populations grow, so too does suburban sprawl, leading to more and more people commuting into the city for work, shopping, and entertainment. However, the future looks different. Sprawl is making way for density as an approach to suburbanization. Developments aim to provide housing, offices, shops, and other facilities in one area so that residents are no longer required to use their own vehicles to get around and commuting hours are reduced. As a result, the cost of maintaining infrastructure, including roads, could fall by up to 50% per capita according to some.

[2] New developments are likely to provide apartments and houses of varying sizes in the same area, which will allow single people, couples, and families all to reside there. However, properties will need to be affordable, a task which developers have struggled to accomplish in recent years. People on lower incomes have regularly been priced out of the market, making predictions in this area difficult. Even if housing is affordable at first, the longer-term impact may not be quite as desired. Once first-time buyers sell their property on, the price—determined by market forces—may be considerably higher than the original purchase price. The types of people who were originally able to live there are priced out of the market and the area becomes middle-class, with people from similar backgrounds and with similar income levels. Those on lower incomes or from different backgrounds are excluded. As well as price, construction companies must also consider the local geography before they commence with the construction of buildings, to ensure they are as ecologically sustainable as possible. Homes no longer need to rely on unsustainable energy to run—they can even be carbon-neutral, although this of course depends on sun and wind levels in the area. Companies must be aware that what works in one area may not necessarily be successful in another.

2 READING

Yoichi Katayama, author of *The Eco Futurist*

[3] One often quoted benefit of urban density over urban sprawl is the lowering of emissions, as facilities can be more easily reached on foot or by bicycle. However, mixed-use developments are often required to provide substantial parking facilities outside shops and restaurants in the area, which will logically encourage people to use cars or motorbikes rather than greener alternatives. As well as that, increased density means increased numbers of people and therefore vehicles, meaning the reduction in emissions will be somewhat limited and emissions could arguably increase in that particular area. Having said that, suburbs of the future can still help to reduce the harm we inflict on our environment. Heating bills do not need to cost the Earth, literally. By integrating energy-saving features into new buildings in new developments, it is possible for the area to have a much less significant impact on the world around us.

[4] Energy-saving features will cost less financially too. This is significant as new developments must be within budget for not only older generations, but also younger generations. It is very challenging for most millennials to get onto the property ladder in today's risk-averse property market. Denser suburbs promise affordable homes which will allow millennials to overcome this obstacle and purchase their own homes just as their parents did. Those millennials are likely to come from a range of backgrounds. While suburbs are often considered to be places where similar people live together in rows of houses which all look the same, the truth is that suburbs are already full of people from very different backgrounds, be that ethnicity, class, or income-level. According to a survey commissioned by the Urban Land Institute (2016), "seventy-six percent of the minority population in the top 50 metro areas lives in the suburbs" and there is nothing to suggest that this will not remain the case or increase in the future.

Matt Crawford, founder of the *Forward Thinking Housing Association*

[5] One possible prediction for modern suburbs is the depression of the housing market. When existing home owners reach an age where their home is too large or no longer suitable for their needs, they will look to sell that home and downsize to, for example, a smaller bungalow. As young adults today are struggling to afford to buy their own homes, sellers may not find buyers, and as a result, prices will fall. Similarly, eco-friendly features such as solar panels may reduce reliance on fossil fuels, but they may also significantly increase the price of homes which could also contribute to the depression of the housing market. One way to prevent such a depression is to continue to encourage multi-cultural suburbs through planning and pricing. Mixed housing, i.e., flats, houses, and bungalows in one area, allows people of all backgrounds to live together and share community life. Multi-generational families —many of whom are immigrants—will look to buy the larger homes vacated by retirees. Of course, should there be a depression, it may well help young adults and those on a lower income to get onto the property ladder as prices fall to a more acceptable level. Mortgages may still prove difficult to obtain, however.

[6] One attraction of living in new mixed-use developments in the suburbs is that most people will benefit from more free time to spend on alternative activities. The suburbs of the future will be more walkable. No longer will residents have to drive to the city to work, go shopping, or see a film at the cinema—they will be able to do this in the area where they live, meaning less time spent in the car. This is likely to lead to a reduction in both congestion and emissions.

Marisa Tomes, CEO of the *Neo Construction Group*

[7] Construction companies are becoming better at producing properties that are comfortable and warm without endangering the planet. Providing companies adapt to features in the local surroundings, mixed-use developments have the opportunity to be friendlier to the environment than we ever have before. However, it is not only buildings which will contribute to this; transportation will too. The suburbs tend to be inaccessible to those who are unable to drive as public transportation is insufficient as a means of traveling to the workplace. Modern suburbs have a chance to attract those people as they will not need to rely on cars or indeed public transportation to get around, providing them with more opportunities without a loss of independence. In fact, fewer people in the suburbs will need to learn to drive which will keep cars off the road and help to improve poor air quality.

[8] Mixed housing has proven to be very popular in areas like Washington, D.C.'s Georgetown. The fact that there will be a range of housing types in future suburbs will make it easier for people to move from a small apartment to a larger apartment, or an apartment to a house, without having to move to a different area completely. Unfortunately, construction companies have focused on properties in the higher-end of the market in recent years as they have struggled to build truly affordable properties to aid first-time buyers. The potential to supply a number of cheaper options for the younger generation and other lower-income families is certainly there, but it is unclear if the potential can be realized or not. Building companies do need to plan with a variety of people in mind before they proceed with their projects.

D Close reading

> Identifying similarities and differences between multiple viewpoints can help you form a broader understanding of the topic being discussed. To do this you can:
> 1 Identify the parts of texts where writers talk about the same topic.
> 2 Take brief notes on what each writer says about that topic.
> 3 Use the notes to identify key similarities and differences.

READING 2

Looking for similarities and differences

1 Read *Suburbs of the future* again. For each question, underline the parts of the text that deal with that topic. Then take notes on what each writer says to help you answer the question.
   1 Who has a similar view to Sarah Kalensky on the use of private transportation in future suburbs?
   2 Which writer has a different opinion to the others on diversity in suburban areas?
   3 Who shares the same opinion as Marisa Tomes on the future of housing opportunities for people in their 20s?
   4 Who expresses the same view as Yoichi Katayama on the potential of achieving greener homes?
   5 Which writer expresses a different view to the others about the future of pollution?

2 Scan Sarah Kalensky's part of the text again. Complete the summary with no more than two words from the article in each blank.

Urban sprawl is being replaced by a policy of ¹_____ as a means of creating better suburbs for the future. These suburbs will provide a one-stop place for people to live and work, reducing the need to use ²_____ and cutting costs in ³_____ maintenance. These suburbs have the potential to supply different types of homes for people from various ⁴_____, providing that they are sufficiently ⁵_____ for everyone. They can also be ⁶_____ in terms of the environment. However, for this to be the case, the homes must be constructed with the ⁷_____ in mind.

E Critical thinking

Work in a group. Discuss the questions.
1 Which of the predictions made in the text do you think are least likely to happen? Why?
2 What are some of the key development issues in your area and how might they be addressed?

Vocabulary development

Phrasal verb academic alternatives

1 Replace the phrasal verbs in bold with their more formal equivalents in the box.

| accomplish cite curtail dispose of |
| disregard exhaust proceeding relocate |

1 Urban sprawl occurs when people **move away** from its downtown area to the suburbs.
2 A city with urban sprawl will **use up** more resources on infrastructure.
3 The need to **cut down** pollution is apparent in some suburban neighborhoods.
4 To **pull off** a reduction in pollution, road use must be lowered.
5 It's impossible to **write off** the lack of employment opportunity in the suburbs.
6 Proponents of sprawl may **refer to** a greater sense of community as an advantage.
7 In cities with decreased populations, planners should **get rid of** abandoned facilities.
8 City planners should plan urban expansion carefully before **going ahead** with it.

2 Complete the text with the formal verbs in Exercise 1. Change the form if necessary.

People who live in a city have wonderful facilities on their doorstep, but stress associated with the cost of living, crowds, and noise can be problematic. This kind of stress can be [1]_____ if the decision is taken to [2]_____ from the city to the suburbs. Larger homes, fewer people, nature, tranquility, and a sense of community are all [3]_____ as the advantages of suburban life. However, before [4]_____ with the move, it is important not to [5]_____ potential issues. There will be longer commutes which may [6]_____ funds more quickly, as well as reduce the number of tasks you can [7]_____ each day. In addition, environmentally conscious people may be concerned about their increased effect on the environment, as more resources are required to provide them with electricity, gas, and water, as well as [8]_____ their trash.

3 Think about the comparison between city living and suburban living in Exercises 1 and 2. Discuss these questions with a partner.

1 What do you think are the benefits of and issues with both city life and suburban living in your country?
2 Would you argue that it is better for people to live in cities or suburbs? Consider issues related to homes, lifestyle, facilities, transportation, and the environment.

Academic words

VOCABULARY

1 Match the words in bold with the correct definitions.

1 **commence** (v)
2 **commission** (v)
3 **diversify** (v)
4 **implementation** (n)
5 **integral** (adj)
6 **labor** (n)
7 **panel** (n)
8 **somewhat** (adv)

a to develop new products or services in addition to the ones you already provide
b a flat piece of wood, glass, or other material that forms part of something
c to start
d the workers in a particular industry or company considered as a group
e the process of making a plan, idea, etc., start to work and be used
f to officially ask for a piece of work to be done for you
g to some degree, but not a large degree
h forming an essential part of something

2 Complete the text with words from Exercise 1. Change the form if necessary.

Making homes green

Many people think only of solar ¹_____ when they imagine an eco-friendly home, but there are other options too, for example, wood from sustainable forests for kitchens, flooring, or under floor heating. The source of materials is ²_____ to eco-friendly homes and materials should be natural and locally sourced where possible. Access to these materials has ³_____ improved in recent years, with some construction supply companies choosing to ⁴_____ and offer greener alternatives.
Some land owners are choosing to build their own eco-friendly homes, but before ⁵_____ a project, they should devise a clear plan in consultation with construction professionals so that its ⁶_____ is as smooth as possible. They should ensure sufficient funds are allocated to the project and decide whether to supply the ⁷_____ themselves or ⁸_____ a third party.

3 Work with a partner. Discuss the questions.

1 How eco-friendly do you think the homes are in your area? Why?
2 What would make them more eco-friendly?
3 Would you ever consider building your own home? Why / why not?

CRITICAL THINKING

Critical thinking

Evaluating conclusions

Once you've identified the conclusion of a formal argument, it's important to evaluate its logic. One way to do this is to look for flaws in the way it is presented. Common logical fallacies associated with conclusions are;

- **Irrelevant conclusions**—where the conclusion given is thematically related to the topic, but does not logically follow the evidence.
- **Begging the question**—using the conclusion as evidence without proving it (e.g., *One expert suggested X so let us look at ways to implement this*).
- **Hasty generalizations**—Jumping to conclusions through poor inductive reasoning (e.g., *Two people said X so it must be true*).
- **False cause**—identifying a non-existent cause/effect relationship; mistaking correlation for causation; or assuming that only one factor led to an effect.

1. Underline the conclusions in each argument.

    1. Incomes steadily increased for many years. These increases allowed people to afford longer commutes, either on public transportation or in private vehicles. Relocations to suburban areas increased as a result.
    2. Many experts believe that urban density is preferable to urban sprawl. Thus, there is a need to address the implementation of such an approach. From here on in, this paper will examine how density as an approach can be exploited to its best effect.
    3. Urban sprawl has been shown to be harmful to the environment. Research shows that it increases traffic, creates more air and water pollution, and results in a loss of wildlife. For these reasons, agricultural capacity must be protected from the building of new developments.
    4. Urban sprawl is a never-ending cycle, hence the need to break it by considering alternative options. People move out of densely populated areas due to a loss of green spaces, traffic congestion, and overpopulation. As those people move into the suburbs, research shows those areas too become more densely populated and people leave to move into quieter, newer suburbs.
    5. Taxes are generally higher in urban areas than in the suburbs. A study of 30 people who moved to a suburban area showed that one benefit of moving was the reduction in taxes. This demonstrates a significant need to address the high taxes in cities in order to persuade residents to stay.

2. Work with a partner. Discuss whether the conclusions in Exercise 1 are logically supported by the evidence or if a logical fallacy if has been committed.

Writing model

You are going to learn about using parallel structures and integrating direct quotations in your writing. You are then going to use these to write an argumentative essay.

A Analyze

1 You are going to read part of an essay that argues for the expansion of existing suburbs. Thinking about what you have read about this so far, add ideas to the brainstorm below.

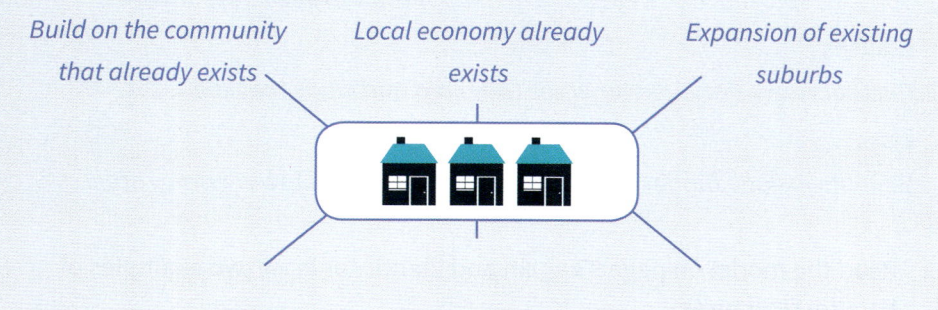

Build on the community that already exists   *Local economy already exists*   *Expansion of existing suburbs*

2 Read the model. Which ideas are included from the brainstorm?

B Model

Abandoning existing suburban areas for new ones will be expensive both financially and ecologically. Money and resources have been spent on the creation and the maintenance of road systems, utility supplies, and communication networks in those suburbs. In a 2015 study commissioned by the Century Foundation, Paul A. Jargowsky, noted that when people moved out of cities into suburbs, "existing infrastructure was abandoned and underutilized in the urban core." By relocating to new suburbs, the same situation could happen again in existing suburbs, with the money and resources allocated to that infrastructure going to waste. By expanding and improving existing suburbs, cities can not only create more modern areas that suit today's needs, but they can also make more use of existing infrastructure without exhausting funds or further damaging the environment.

1 Read the model again and answer the questions.
   1 What is the writer's main point?
   2 What evidence does the writer use to support this point?
   3 What is the writer's conclusion? Is this conclusion effective?
   4 What impact does the direct quotation have on the paragraph?

2 Work with a partner. How persuasive is the writer's point of view? Explain your reasoning.

GRAMMAR

Grammar

Using parallel structures

Parallel sentences use repeated grammar structures—parts of speech, verb patterns, clauses, etc.—to add emphasis and to make a text easier to read. Common parallel structures are formed with:

Conjunctions—*and, but, yet, so, not only… but also, either… or, neither… nor*
*Sprawl is neither **cheap** nor **eco-friendly**.*

Comparisons with *than* or *as*
*Some people much prefer **to live** in the city than **to live** in the suburbs.*

Clauses
*Planners were criticized for **what they said** and **what they did**.*

Lists
*Benefits include **bigger houses, better schools, and lower crime rates**.*

1 Read the model on page 93 again and identify at least two examples of parallel structures.

2 Rewrite the sentences using parallel structures. More than one answer is possible.
   1 There are many people who like to live in an urban area rather than living in a suburban one.
   2 Some people would rather be close to city facilities than to be far from them.
   3 Urban areas can be stressful due to constant noise and places that are crowded.
   4 The plan for a modern suburb was ambitious, an innovation but not cheap.
   5 The development was praised for its public transportation system, having a network of cycle lanes and local parking.
   6 Planners tried not only to convince residents to use public transportation but also that they should walk around the area.

3 Complete each sentence with an idea of your own and a parallel structure.
   1 Empty urban areas should be demolished or…
   2 The city was congratulated for its ability to provide eco-friendly transportation and…
   3 A new suburb's cost to the environment is just as important as…
   4 Creating a suburb of the future means…
   5 Homes in mixed use developments will be neither the same size nor…
   6 The development plan set out to change where people lived as well as…

Writing skill

WRITING

Direct quotations

Follow these guidelines to use direct quotations effectively in your writing:
1 Make sure the quotation integrates well with the content around it.
2 If you want to omit words from a quotation, use an ellipsis (…) to show this but, make sure the meaning does not change from the original.
3 If you want to use a word of your own to make a quotation clearer, put it in square brackets [ ].
4 Do not forget to attribute the quotation to the author, include a date and include a page number if appropriate.

1 Read the three excerpts (1–3) from essays below. Then select the most appropriate quotation (A–C) to be used in each one.

A Thomas Berberich—"Developments appear at the end of newly built highways which encourages them to relocate out of the city and into those developments" (2014)

B Alana Lei—"these induce demand which would otherwise not have existed" (2016)

C Matthew Turner and Gilles Duranton—"If a city increased its road capacity by 10% between 1980 and 1990, then the amount of driving in that city went up by 10%. If the amount of roads in the same city then went up by 11% between 1990 and 2000, the total number of miles driven also went up by 11%. It's like the two figures were moving in perfect lockstep, changing at the same exact rate" (2009)

1 When a new highway is built, the result is a rise in travel miles as people commence using that road. The question is therefore whether such a highway brings any benefits at all and whether construction of new roads should be more carefully considered before they proceed. ___

2 It is generally assumed that the building of a new highway will increase traffic rather than lower it. In a study of road expansion and traffic between 1980 and 1990, this was proven. It is certainly clear that there is a correlation between new roads and increased traffic. ___

3 Although large-scale highway construction may seem to produce more congestion, congestion surely stays the same. There are no more cars on the highway than there were prior to the road being built. It is therefore simply the number of travel miles that increases as people travel further afield. ___

2 Decide where and how to integrate each quotation into each text. Link the quotation to the previous and/or subsequent sentence as appropriate; select an appropriate reporting verb and edit the quotation if necessary.

WRITING

Writing task

You're going to write an argumentative essay in response to the following: *"Suburbanization is increasing as people move out of cities into suburban areas. Is it better to build more homes in existing suburbs or create new modern suburbs in rural areas?"*

Brainstorm

Read *Suburbs of the future* again. Think about the advantages and disadvantages of both expanding existing suburbs and building new ones.

	Advantages	Disadvantages
Building more homes in existing suburbs		
Creating new modern suburbs in rural areas		

Plan

Plan your essay. Prepare to write five paragraphs that include an introduction, the advantages of the option you choose, the potential drawbacks, and a conclusion.

Write

Use your plan to help you write your essay. Remember to use parallel structures where appropriate and to integrate direct quotations into your writing. Your essay should be at least 300 words long.

Share

Exchange your essay with a partner. Use the checklist on page 189 to help you provide feedback to your partner.

Rewrite and edit

Consider your partner's comments and write your final draft. Think about:

- whether you give a balanced viewpoint, including both benefits and drawbacks
- whether you used parallel structures appropriately
- whether you included direct quotations where appropriate.

Review

Wordlist

Vocabulary preview

automation (n)	desired (adj)	fallout (n)	millennial (n)
booming (adj) *	domestically (adv)	impact (v)	reside (v)
bungalow (n)	downsize (v)	inaccessible (adj)	restructure (v) *
coal (n) ***	ethnicity (n)	insufficient (adj) **	unsustainable (adj)

Vocabulary development

accomplish (v) **	curtail (v)	disregard (v)	proceed (v) ***
cite (v) *	dispose of (phr v) **	exhaust (v) *	relocate (v)

Academic words

commence (v) **	diversify (v)	integral (adj) *	panel (n) ***
commission (v) ***	implementation (n) **	labor (n) ***	somewhat (adv) ***

Academic words review

Complete the sentences using the correct form of the words in the box.

commence   deduction   diversify   labor   somewhat

1 Companies are using cheap foreign _____ to fill vacancies and this is causing friction within the local workforce.
2 Traffic congestion has improved _____ in the city, but not enough to satisfy local residents.
3 Oil-rich nations like Saudi Arabia and the UAE are _____ their economies so that they are less dependent on oil revenues.
4 The opening ceremony is scheduled to _____ at 5:30 p.m. Latecomers will not be admitted.
5 Your net income is your earnings after all _____, such as income tax and social security, have been made.

Unit review

Reading 1	☐	I can use questions to look for information from a text.
Reading 2	☐	I can find similarities and differences.
Study skill	☐	I can use reflective learning techniques.
Vocabulary	☐	I can use academic alternatives to phrasal verbs.
Grammar	☐	I can use parallel structures.
Writing	☐	I can use direct quotations.

6 BEHAVIOR

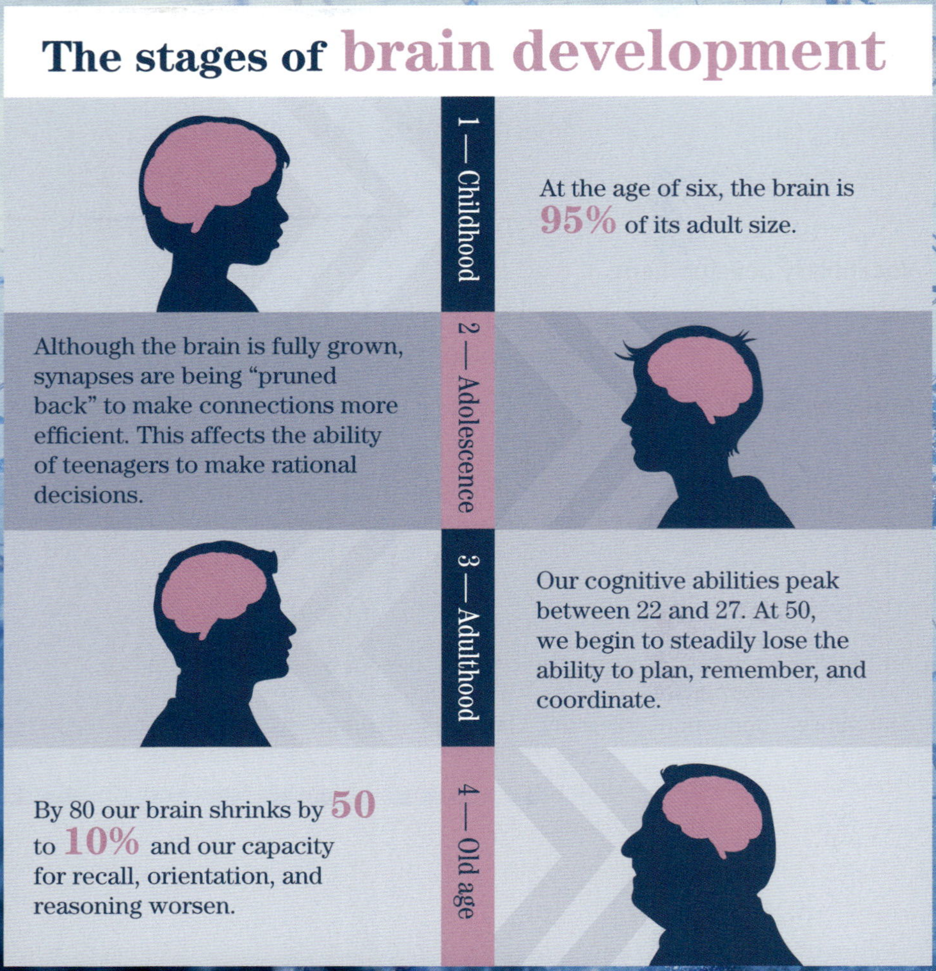

The stages of brain development

1 — Childhood
At the age of six, the brain is **95%** of its adult size.

2 — Adolescence
Although the brain is fully grown, synapses are being "pruned back" to make connections more efficient. This affects the ability of teenagers to make rational decisions.

3 — Adulthood
Our cognitive abilities peak between 22 and 27. At 50, we begin to steadily lose the ability to plan, remember, and coordinate.

4 — Old age
By 80 our brain shrinks by **50** to **10%** and our capacity for recall, orientation, and reasoning worsen.

Discussion point

Discuss with a partner.

1 Are you surprised by any of the statistics in the infographic? Why / why not?
2 Should we excuse teenagers for irrational behavior as their brains are not fully developed? Why / why not?
3 What can we do to slow the decline of our cognitive functions?

VIDEO

KITCHEN REHAB

Before you watch

Match the words in bold with the correct definitions.

1 **at risk** (phrase)
2 **culinary** (adj)
3 **screen** (v)
4 **nurture** (v)
5 **turn** (sth) **around** (v)

a related to cooking
b in a dangerous situation, vulnerable
c to help something grow
d check someone or something to see if it is suitable
e change a situation in a positive way

UNIT AIMS

READING 1 Identifying in-text referencing
READING 2 Identifying cause and effect
STUDY SKILL Aiming for clarity
VOCABULARY Consequence phrases
GRAMMAR Inverted conditionals: unreal past
WRITING Anaphoric and cataphoric referencing

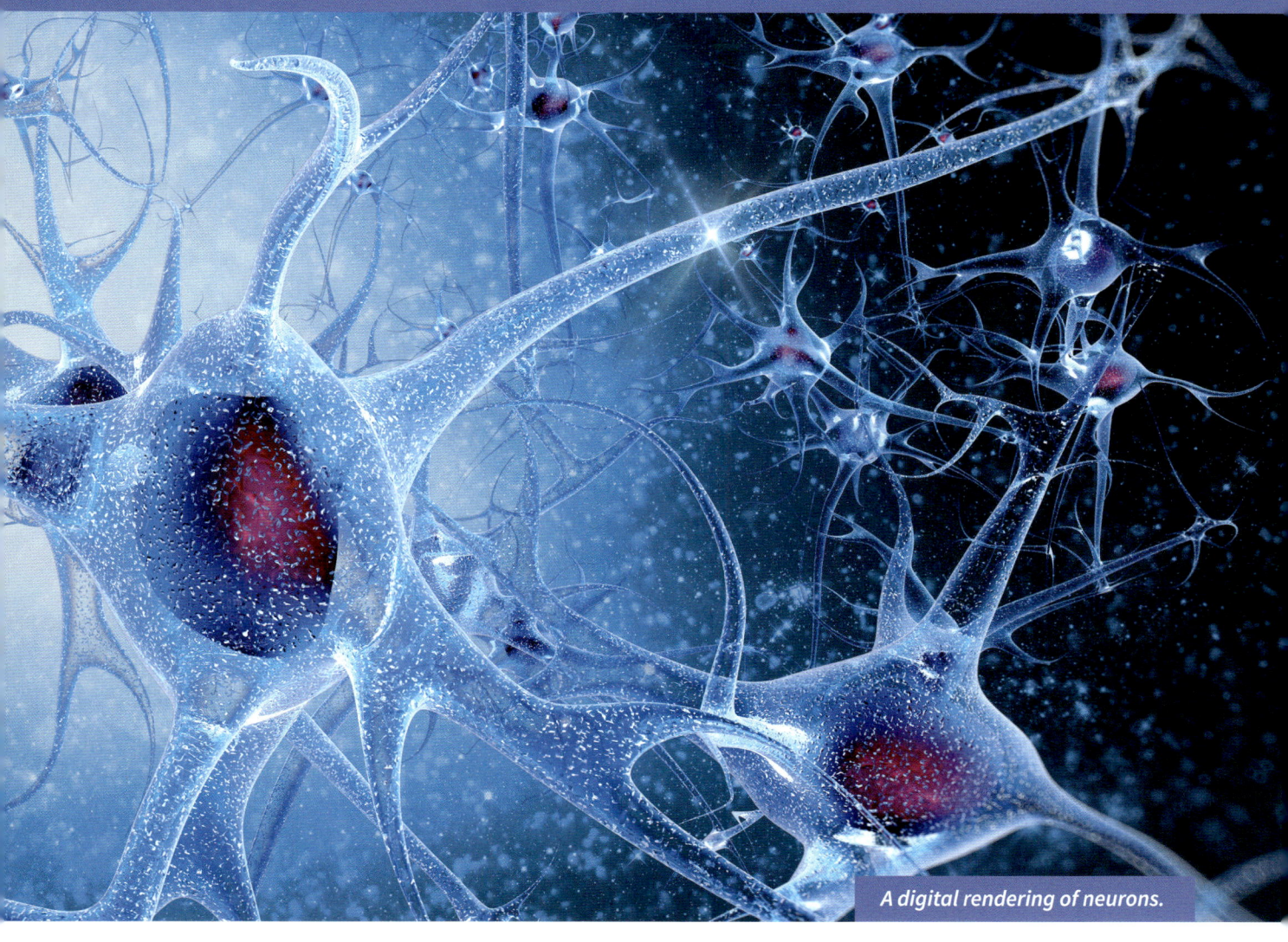

A digital rendering of neurons.

While you watch

Read the sentences. Watch the video and choose the correct ending for each sentence.

1 The aim of the culinary school is to **provide free food for students** / **teach young people how to cook**.
2 The courses are available to **all young people** / **only those who show a genuine interest in learning how to cook**.
3 Many of the school's graduates go on to **work in kitchens around the world** / **work in kitchens around the country**.

After you watch

Work in a group. Discuss the questions.

1 What do you think the motivation for running these courses could be for chef Zanele Mdokwana?
2 Other than the cooking skills they develop, what do you think a course like this teaches young people?
3 In general, do you think schools all over the world should focus more on providing young people with transferable skills than on academic subjects?

BEHAVIOR UNIT 6

1 READING

Born criminal?

A Vocabulary preview

Complete the sentences with the words in the box.

> delinquent   deviant   genetic   inherit
> notion   prominent   propensity   tendencies

1 Cystic fibrosis is a _____ condition that affects the lungs, liver, kidneys, and intestines.
2 The _____ that our personality is purely dictated by upbringing is clearly flawed.
3 Upbringing undoubtedly plays a role in the development of criminal _____.
4 The study using brain scans of _____ teens indicates that they're wired differently.
5 Economics and urban planning have played _____ roles in the development of criminal theory.
6 Subjects with abusive parents tend to show a greater _____ for violence.
7 Aggressive and _____ behaviors positively correlate with sleep deprivation.
8 If both parents carry the faulty gene, there is a one in four chance that their offspring will _____ the condition.

B Before you read

Activating prior knowledge

Work in a group. Discuss the questions.

1 Do you think criminal tendencies are inherited? Why / why not?
2 What other factors play a prominent role in determining the propensity toward criminality?
3 To what extent is our behavior dictated by the way we are publicly perceived?

C Global reading

Identifying main ideas

Read *Born criminal?* Match the headings (a–g) to paragraphs (1–7).

a Paternal influence on criminal tendency ___
b Nature or nurture? ___
c The correlation between intellect and crime ___
d A biological predisposition toward criminality? ___
e Society's influence on self-identity and behavior ___
f Siblings, genetics, and upbringing ___
g What is criminology? ___

Born criminal?

[1] In his 1885 publication, *Criminologia: Studio sul Delitto, Sulle sue Cause e sui Mezzi di Repressione*, Italian lawyer Raffaele Garofalo argued that scientific study was the only way to understand the criminal mind. He named this new field "criminology" and in the 250 years since its inception, theorists have struggled to answer one fundamental question—are we born criminal?

[2] Cesare Lombroso—often referred to as the father of criminology—rejected the classical belief that crime was a personality trait of human nature. Instead, he developed a theory of anthropological criminology stating not only that criminality was inherited, but that criminals could be identified by a series of prominent physical defects which confirmed their atavistic and savage nature. In his most influential work, *L'uomo delinquente*, Lombroso argued that thieves could be identified by their expressive faces, manual dexterity, and small wandering eyes, while murderers had cold glass-like stares, bloodshot eyes, and big hawk-like noses. Female criminals tended to be shorter, more wrinkled, and had darker hair and smaller skulls than "normal" women. The notion that physical appearance was innately bound to a propensity toward criminality was furthered by William Sheldon in *The Atlas of Men* (1954), in which he proposed a taxonomy for categorizing the human physique. Sheldon argued that humans could be categorized into three broad types—ectomorph, mesomorph, and endomorph—then scored within these categories to determine mental characteristics. Those with a muscular physique and athletic appearance showed greater criminal tendencies than tall, thinner people who he believed to be more intellectual. While superficially compelling, no evidence has been found to substantiate these theories, and they have since been widely discredited.

[3] Other early theorists laid the foundations for the most prominent school of thought in the 50s and 60s—"labeling theory," which hypothesizes that negative labels given to individuals by society actually promote deviant behavior. The origins of this theory can be traced back to Edwin M. Lemert, a sociology professor at the University of California. In *Social pathology: a systematic approach to the theory of sociopathic behavior* (1951), Lemert introduced the concept of "primary" and "secondary deviance." "Primary deviance" refers to an initial act that deviates from social norms—say getting caught for a minor traffic offense or taking stationery from work. Those that commit these acts are usually reprimanded and feel guilty enough not to replicate them. However, some go on to commit further, repeated or more serious acts—secondary deviance—and are labeled as criminals. Howard Becker further developed this notion in his 1963 publication, *Outsiders*, claiming that while society labels people as criminals to justify its condemnation, the deviants themselves use it to justify their criminal behavior. Essentially, they commit further criminal offenses because it's simply "who they are." Critics of labeling theory argue that while the label may encourage later criminal behavior, it fails to consider the influence of genetic or environmental factors that must have led to the initial crime.

[4] Perhaps the most influential study is *The Cambridge Study in Delinquent Development* (2013), which has been following the development of 411 males since 1961. Over the 50-year period that has elapsed since the start of the study, psychologists have interviewed the test subjects nine times, moving from a focus on their school attendance, to employment and fatherhood. It was found that a significant number of delinquent youths had criminal fathers. Under 10% of children from non-offending fathers went onto become chronic offenders, whereas just under 40% of the offspring of criminal fathers went on to regularly offend. While this data, and other studies like it, strongly imply that criminal parents are likely to produce criminal offspring, it remains unclear whether this intergenerational deviance is genetically determined or largely due to the environment in which we are raised.

[5] Various studies have also found a correlation between intelligence and crime. Moffitt et al. found that men with a lower IQ went on to commit two or more crimes by the age of twenty. Denno (1994) also tested the intelligence of nearly 1,000 children at different points in their life and found a consistent negative correlation between IQ and criminal behavior. However, others, such as Menard and Morse have claimed that the association is too weak to be considered statistically significant. Yet regardless of the extent to which intelligence affects propensity toward criminal behavior, it does appear to be a factor, which raises another question—are we born intelligent, and by extension, law-abiding? Researchers at the University of Queensland found that only up to a maximum of 40% of intelligence is inherited and the rest is determined by environmental factors. If this is true, both nature and nurture have a role to play in the development of criminal tendencies.

[6] One area of research that tests this hypothesis compares the behavior of identical monozygotic twins—those sharing an identical genetic makeup—to that of fraternal dizygotic twins, who share, on average, 50% of the same genes. A literature review on studies into identical twins and criminal behavior found that 60% exhibited criminal behavior concurrently, whereas only one third of non-identical twins had similarly related behavior. In the Minnesota Twin Family Study, researchers are currently comparing monozygotic and dizygotic twins who were both raised together with those separated at birth. The study has found remarkable similarities in those raised apart—strongly suggesting that genetics, not upbringing, determines behavior and personality. However, critics of the genetic connection argue that poor research methodology and design have distorted the findings leaving us with little conclusive proof that crime is genetically determined.

[7] So are we born criminal? While research strongly indicates a certain level of genetic predisposition toward criminality, it's clear that upbringing plays an integral role in the development of criminal tendencies. To blame our genes for criminal behavior wilfully ignores a broader societal responsibility to ensure that the environment in which we're raised doesn't promote criminal behavior.

1 READING

Identifying in-text referencing

D Close reading

> One of the most common ways to support or counter an argument is to cite information from other sources, either by quoting them directly;
>
> *"Peer pressure affects how teenagers act." Gluckman (2014)*
>
> Or paraphrasing the information;
>
> *Gluckman (2014) suggests that friends influence the behavior of a teenager.*
>
> References usually include the author's name, date of publication, and occasionally the page number.

1 Read *Born criminal?* again. Match the arguments (1–6) to the source(s) used to support them in the text.

1 Criminal tendencies are directly associated with physical attributes. ___
2 Branding someone a criminal often inspires further deviant behavior. ___
3 Criminal fathers are more likely to spawn criminal offspring. ___
4 There is a clear association between criminal behavior and intelligence. ___
5 The correlation between criminal tendency and IQ is insignificant. ___
6 Twins raised in different environments have similar personalities. ___

2 Scan the text again. Are these sentences *T* (True), *F* (False), or *NG* (Not Given)?

1 Cesare Lombroso believed that it is in our nature to behave like criminals. ___
2 Critics argue that labeling theory doesn't justify the primary act of deviance. ___
3 Few subjects in the Cambridge Study in Delinquent Development had criminal mothers. ___
4 According to Denno, people with high IQs show less propensity toward criminality. ___
5 Intelligence is largely dictated by genetics. ___
6 Statistically, monozygotic twins commit more crime than dizygotic twins. ___

E Critical thinking

Work in a group. Discuss the questions.

1 Do you agree that criminals live up to the label given to them by society? Why / why not?
2 Some argue that siblings who live together are not always brought up in the same environment. What might be different?

Study skills — Aiming for clarity

Write so your reader can easily follow what you are trying to say. Do not use long words and technical jargon simply in order to sound impressive. Avoid antiquated language, convoluted sentences or mannerisms—as well as using up your word limit, these could be off-putting to your readers.

Be concise: edit out unnecessary words.

Be precise: As you write, keep checking for precision. Ask yourself questions such as 'when exactly?', 'why exactly' or 'who?'. Check that you have given your readers enough detail for them to know exactly what you are talking about.

© Stella Cottrell (2013)

1 Work with a partner. Look at a modified version of the opening paragraph to an essay on bad behavior in teenagers. Cross out any words that are unnecessary.

The impact and importance of educational performance is extremely key during teenage years, yet this drastically coincides with one of the most ultimately challenging developmental stages. The development of the adolescent brain at this exact, precise point exerts a direct, clear influence on the physical and emotional behavior of teenagers, with radically diminished levels of fear and a massively heightened pursuit of risk commonplace. However, this can have an extraordinarily detrimental effect on educational performance and environment as a whole.

2 Compare your answers to Exercise 1 with a partner. Whose paragraph reads more concisely?

3 Work with a partner. Rewrite the following sentences so that they are more precise. Facts can be taken from the reading texts on page 101 and pages 105–106. Do not write more than one sentence for each answer.

1 Research suggests that many delinquent youths have criminal fathers.
2 Around 40% of intelligence is inherited.
3 Teenagers are hard-wired to be more impulsive, according to one study.
4 One study conducted in 2009 showed that brain speed and problem solving declined noticeably before the subjects were 30 and average memory started to fall at around 37.

STUDY SKILLS

2 READING

Is your brain ready yet?

A Vocabulary preview

Complete the sentences with the words in the box.

| counterparts | facial | impulses | neurological |
| oversimplification | rational | regulate | systematically |

1 Alzheimer's is a _____ disorder that affects an estimated 5.5 million people in the U.S.
2 During puberty, teenagers develop the ability to _____ test solutions.
3 It is a(n) _____ to claim that teenagers are incapable of self-control.
4 Adults are better equipped to reach a(n) _____ conclusion than teenagers.
5 Adults are more likely to be able to control their _____ than teenagers.
6 Adolescents use their prefrontal cortex less than their adult _____ during decision-making.
7 Children become consistently better at recognizing _____ expressions as they get older.
8 The prefrontal cortex is the part of the brain used to _____ behavior.

B Before you read

Activating prior knowledge

Write down three stereotypes about teenagers and how they behave. Compare your ideas in small groups.

C Global reading

Identifying main ideas

Read *Is your brain ready yet?* Complete the article with the headings (a–f).

a Impulse control under pressure
b Peak performance and rapid decline
c Questioning the stereotype
d Synaptic pruning in the adolescent brain
e A call for delayed decision-making
f Hormones, risk, and reward

Is your brain ready yet?

READING 2

1

Adolescence is a challenging period in our lives. Teenagers on the cusp of adulthood seem self-possessed one minute and foolhardy the next, or, as Bell and McBride (2010) put it, "all gasoline, no brakes, and no steering wheel." They are expected to make decisions that will profoundly affect the rest of their lives at a time when they seem particularly incapable of rationality—often throwing themselves headlong into dangerous or risky situations. So, what is the neurological explanation for this seemingly erratic behavior and does it present any advantages?

2

Perhaps the most often cited cause of stereotypical teenage behavior is the underdevelopment of the prefrontal cortex—the section of our brains that governs impulses and emotions, and makes rational decisions. The prefrontal cortex communicates with other sections of the brain via neuronal junctions called synapses. During childhood, we accumulate an overabundance of synapses, and as we move into adolescence over half are systematically removed, while others are strengthened in order to make communication more efficient; a process known in neuroscience as "synaptic pruning." During synaptic pruning, the brain operates a "use it or lose it" policy, keeping and strengthening connections that are regularly engaged and shedding those that aren't. If, for example you regularly engage the part of your brain associated with learning a foreign language, the synapses in this area will develop strong connections and will not be trimmed back. However, if this is an underutilized section, the synapses may well be eliminated. In fact, many researchers suggest that if we don't develop a skill at this point in our lives, we're unlikely to develop it at all. Brain imaging indicates that the process of synaptic pruning in adolescents begins at the back of the brain and systematically moves forward towards the frontal lobe, leaving pruning of the prefrontal cortex until last. As a result, teenagers are forced to do the majority of brain processing at the back of their brain, rather than in the prefrontal cortex which goes someway to explaining their seeming inability to evaluate risk and make logical decisions.

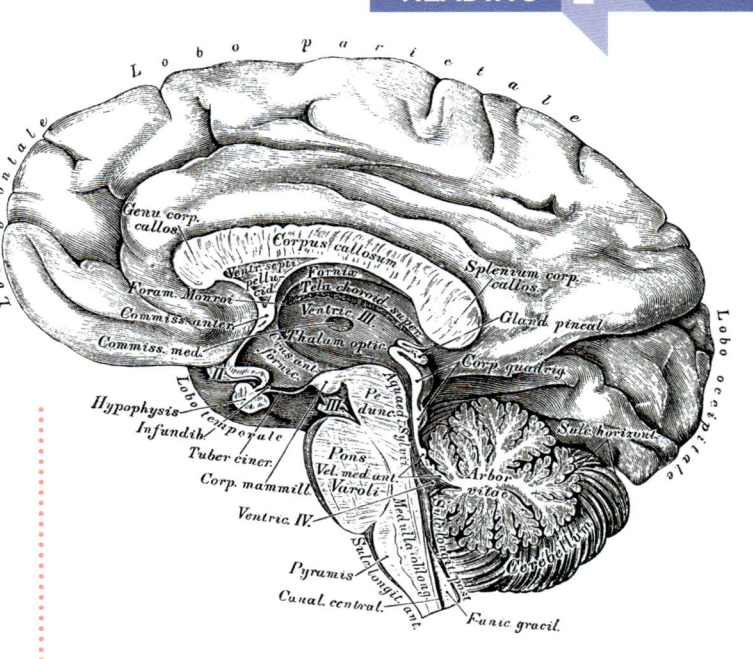

3

According to Luna et al., synaptic pruning is not the only factor that distinguishes adolescent brains from their adult counterparts. Luna's group used functional MRI (fMRI) scans to track blood flow through different regions of adolescent brains and the results showed that despite being underdeveloped, the prefrontal cortex is actually active during this period. However, the ability of teenagers to make rational decisions is overridden by the rush of dopamine—the hormone which triggers feelings of happiness—that occurs when they take risks. Essentially, the chemical reward is so great that teenagers actively seek out risk. Furthermore, the nucleus accumbens—the part of the brain that seeks pleasure and reward—is reasonably well established in the teenage brain, and actually seems to directly compete with the prefrontal cortex in the decision-making process. Research conducted at Cornell University in New York, measured brain activity in subjects

2 READING

that were rewarded for performing small tasks. In adolescents, the reward center reacted far more strongly when given a medium or large reward than in both adults and young children. When given a small reward, teenagers reacted as if they had been given no reward at all. Again, this seems to coincide with the notion that teenage brains are hard-wired to be impulsive. Neurologically, they are capable of both effective decision-making and self-control, yet at times the temptation to seek out risk or reward intervenes, outweighing their rationality.

4 _____

Many would argue that Bell and McBride's "all gasoline, no brakes, and no steering wheel" analogy is a gross oversimplification of teenage brain development. In fact, according to research conducted by Casey and Caudle (2013), adolescents are actually better able to regulate impulses than adults under certain circumstances. During a series of laboratory experiments, Somerville, Hare, and Casey (2011) showed test subjects images of positive, negative, and neutral facial expressions and measured their ability to regulate their responses. When no emotional information was present (i.e., the facial expression was neutral), teenagers performed as well as adults, if not better. However, when emotional cues were present, either positive or negative, adolescents were far less able to suppress their response. This diminished ability was not observed in adults or children, who find it equally difficult to regulate control whether emotional cues are present or not. This seems to contradict the oversimplification that teenagers are generally unable to act rationally or make good decisions. While this may be true in heated or stressful situations, perhaps because they tend to rely on the amygdala—the part of the brain that guides instinct—rather than the prefrontal cortex, in neutral situations adolescents are actually better equipped to control impulses and make rational decisions than adults.

5 _____

It's also worth considering that while adolescent brains may still be in development, our ability to plan and recall events, as well as task coordination actually begins to decline fairly rapidly in our mid to late twenties. In one study conducted by Timothy Salthouse, at the University of Virginia, 2,000 participants between the ages of 18 and 60 were asked to solve puzzles, recall words and stories, and identify patterns, repeatedly, over a seven-year period. The results suggested a sharp decline in skills such as the ability to make quick comparisons, to recall unconnected information, and to notice patterns and relationships. In particular brain speed and problem-solving declined noticeably at 27 and average memory started to fall at around 37 (Salthouse, 2009). While most people compensate for this loss by accumulating knowledge and experience, there is a definite decline in some mental skills in comparison to the burgeoning adolescent brain.

6 _____

Overall, the teenage brain is, in many ways, not different to its adult counterpart. However, synaptic pruning, regular influxes of dopamine, and the competition between the prefrontal cortex and the brain's reward center all affect the ability of teenagers to make clear, rational decisions. Yet, perhaps this increased propensity for risk-taking should be seen as beneficial as it is undoubtedly one of the factors that drives adolescents to leave home, search for a partner, or seek out the kind of new experiences that might shape their careers. Having said that, it could also be argued that as the brain is still in development during this period, key decisions should be delayed until later life—when we are better able to balance risk and logical decision-making more effectively. Given that the desire to seek out risk and short-term rewards is so strong, this is perhaps not the best time to make decisions that will profoundly affect the rest of our lives.

References:

Bell, C.C., McBride, D.F. (2010). Affect regulation and prevention of risky behaviors. *The Journal of the American Medical Association*. 304(5), 565–566

Casey, B.J., Caudle, K. (2013). The Teenage Brain: Self Control. *Current Directions in Psychological Science*. 22(2), 82–87

Galvan, A. (2006). Earlier Development of the Accumbens Relative to Orbitofrontal Cortex Might Underlie Risk-Taking Behavior in Adolescents. *Journal of Neuroscience*. 26(25), 6885–6892

Luna, B. et al. (2001). What has fMRI told us about the development of cognitive control through adolescence? *Brain and Cognition*. 72(1), 101–113

Salthouse, A. (2009). When does age-related cognitive decline begin? *Neurobiology of Aging*. 30(4), 507–514

D Close reading

> Academic writers who use scientific research to support their arguments often need to clearly explain cause-and-effect relationships to the reader.
>
> Sometimes this relationship is explicitly stated using signaling words (e.g., *affect, lead to, trigger, as a result,* etc.). However, sometimes the relationship is defined over multiple lines.

READING 2

Identifying cause and effect

1 Read *Is your brain ready yet?* again. Match the causes (1–6) to their effects (a–f).

1 Underutilized connections in the brain are ___
2 The prefrontal cortex is last to be pruned, ___
3 Risk-taking floods the brain with ___
4 Small and medium rewards cause ___
5 Stress and high emotion renders adolescents ___
6 Aging leads to a ___

a less able to regulate self-control than adults.
b a strong reaction in the reward center of the adolescent brain.
c a pleasurable rush of dopamine.
d eliminated during adolescent development.
e steady decline in pattern recognition skills.
f leading teenagers to rely on the back of their brains for decision-making.

2 Complete the sentences with no more than two words from the article.

1 Over half of the _____ produced during childhood are eliminated during adolescence.
2 Synapses that are _____ will be strengthened, while underutilized connections are removed.
3 Despite its immaturity, the prefrontal cortex is _____ during adolescence.
4 Teenagers were better able to regulate control when _____ cues were absent.
5 Cognitive speed and _____ abilities decline rapidly in our late twenties.

E Critical thinking

With a partner, discuss whether institutions should adapt to suit the different stages of brain development. Explain your reasoning.

VOCABULARY

Vocabulary development

Consequence phrases

1 Match the causes (1–8) with their effects (a–h).

1 **As a consequence of** their upbringing children with ___
2 Teenager behavior **may be influenced by** ___
3 Poor academic performance **may result in** ___
4 The desire to gain the approval of their peers **may prompt** ___
5 Risk-taking can **trigger** ___
6 The onset of adolescence **may bring about** ___
7 Criminal tendencies **stem from** ___
8 Sleep deprivation can **exert a direct influence on** ___

a low self-esteem and a propensity toward criminality.
b teenagers to behave in a delinquent manner.
c criminal parents are more likely to display criminal tendencies.
d a combination of genetics and social environment.
e a hard-wired desire to seek out risk.
f teenage emotions and behavior.
g an increase in delinquent behavior.
h a rush of dopamine in the adolescent brain.

2 Choose the correct word or phrase to complete the sentences.

1 Labeling someone a criminal **can trigger** / **may result from** increased propensity for crime.
2 Criminal behavior may **be influenced by** / **exert a direct influence on** levels of intelligence.
3 Teenage delinquency may **prompt** / **result from** a desire to seek out reward.
4 Many claim that criminal tendencies **trigger** / **stem from** a disruptive upbringing.
5 Better understanding of teenage brain development **may prompt** / **result from** changes in the judicial system.
6 The onset of adolescence **stems from** / **brings about** dramatic changes in the teenage brain.

3 Work with a partner. Discuss the questions.

1 What factors may prompt teenage delinquency?
2 What events can trigger dramatic changes in someone's personality?
3 What exerts a greater influence on teenage behavior; genetics or upbringing?

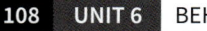

Academic words

1 Complete the definitions with the words in the box.

| accumulate | analogy | coincide | distort | evaluate | imply | integral | intervene |

1. _____ (v) to change something so that it is no longer true or accurate
2. _____ (v) to suggest you think something without saying it directly
3. _____ (v) to gradually get more of something over a period of time
4. _____ (v) to become involved in a situation in order to try to stop or change it
5. _____ (adj) forming an essential part of something
6. _____ (n) a comparison between one thing and another, usually to clarify an explanation
7. _____ (v) to happen at the same time as something else
8. _____ (v) to think carefully about something before making a judgment about its value, importance, or quality

2 Complete the sentences with words from Exercise 1. Change the form if necessary.

1. The findings _____ that social background has a strong influence on criminal tendencies.
2. Studies show that early _____ can significantly reduce delinquent behavior.
3. Offspring of criminal fathers are statistically more likely to _____ multiple convictions over their lifetime.
4. All too often, journalists willfully _____ the conclusions of criminal research.
5. Proponents claim that society plays an _____ role in the development of criminal tendencies.
6. A useful _____ is to imagine that the prefrontal cortex is the brain's remote control.
7. There isn't sufficient data to _____ the impact of peer pressure on criminal tendency.
8. The findings were published to _____ with the international conference on criminal behavior.

3 Work in a group. Discuss the questions.

1. What factors, aside from genetics and upbringing, do you think play an integral role in the development of criminal tendencies?
2. Why do you think news outlets often seem to distort the real findings of scientific research?

CRITICAL THINKING

Critical thinking

Strengthening an argument

To strengthen an argument, it is necessary to add support from alternative sources. These will typically be quotations from experts or research into the topic. Finding multiple sources or studies to support the same main argument further strengthens the argument. For example;

Various studies have also found a correlation between intelligence and crime. Moffitt et al. found that men with a lower IQ went on to commit two or more crimes by the age of twenty. Denno (1994) also tested the intelligence of nearly 1,000 children at different points in their life and found a consistent negative correlation between IQ and criminal behavior.

1 Read the text and answer the questions.

> There is not a strong correlation between low levels of intelligence and crime. In fact, many types of crime require significantly high levels of intelligence in order to commit the crime.

1. Why is this not a particularly strong argument?
2. What evidence would strengthen their argument?

2 Scan *Is your brain ready yet?* and find evidence to support the following opinions.

1. The decision-making power of the prefrontal cortex may be overridden by other factors.
2. In low stakes or unemotive situations teenagers make effective decisions.
3. Certain mental abilities decline by our late twenties.

3 Work with a partner. Discuss the questions.

1. What other evidence might you find to support the opinions in Exercise 2?
2. How do you think a research study differs from an expert opinion on a topic?

Writing model

WRITING

You are going to learn to use inversion for an imagined past and anaphoric and cataphoric referencing. You are then going to write an essay explaining the causes and effects of delinquent behavior in teenagers.

A Analyze

Scan the model and complete the table with the words in the box.

| disruptive behavior | genetic | home environment |
| lack of qualifications | peer group | poor concentration |

Causes	Effects

B Model

Read the model again and answer the questions.

Discuss the causes of bad behavior in teenagers and the effect it has on education.

The impact and importance of educational performance is key during teenage years, yet this coincides with one of the most challenging developmental stages. The development of the brain at this point exerts a direct influence on the behavior of teenagers, with diminished levels of fear and a heightened pursuit of risk commonplace. However, this can have a detrimental effect on educational performance and the environment as a whole.

Genetics have a direct and integral effect on teenage behavior as certain personality traits such as impulsivity and risk-taking are believed to be inherited. However, genetics is clearly not the sole cause, as people derive many of their influences from those around them. There is a correlation between an unstable home environment and those who go on to behave badly in teenage years. Jaffee et al. (2012) found that a disruptive environment at the age of nine can exert a direct influence on children aged twelve, just prior to becoming teenagers. This research suggests that had it not been for their unstable environment they would have been better able to moderate their behavior and emotions.

The effects of teenage behavior on education can be wide-reaching. In retrospect, many rational teenagers feel that had it not been for their behavior, their performance would have been significantly better. Grades and overall academic performance tend to diminish in line with increases in poor behavior. Perhaps at the lowest end of the spectrum it can simply bring about poor concentration in class and an inability to focus on the task in hand. Ultimately, but not always, this may result in a lack of qualifications and future work opportunities. However, others feel that this disruptive behavior can have a direct effect on peers and potentially limit their life chances.

1 In hindsight, what do many teenagers feel about their academic performance?
2 What personality traits are inherited?
3 What are the wide-reaching effects of teenage behavior?

Grammar

> **Inverted conditionals: unreal past**
>
> More emphasis can be placed on the result of unreal past conditionals using the following inverted construction;
>
> **had + subject + (not) + past participle**
>
> *Had upbringing been taken into account, the importance given to genetics may have been lessened.*
>
> *Had they not been raised in such an unstable environment, the twins may not have had such propensity for crime.*
>
> This can also be a useful structure for commenting on the results of someone else's research;
>
> *The research suggests that had the group received a better education, they wouldn't have gone on to exhibit criminal tendencies.*

1 Use the prompts to write inverted conditional sentences.

1. negative influence of her peers / might not develop criminal tendencies
   I'd argue that _____
2. Roberts not be labeled a criminal / he not go on to a life of crime
   Lemert would argue that _____
3. subjects raised in a more stable environment / they cause fewer problems at school
   It seems highly likely that _____
4. they grow up in a more affluent area / far less likely to turn to crime
   This implies that _____
5. the study be conducted today / results may be different
   Critics argue that _____

2 Read the extract from *Born criminal?* and write inverted conditionals about the following;

a What the research indicates about chronic offenders and their upbringing.
b How the results might have been different if the sample size had been bigger.

> Perhaps the most influential study is *The Cambridge Study in Delinquent Development* (2013), which has been following the development of 411 males since 1961. Over the fifty-year period that has elapsed since the start of the study, psychologists have interviewed the test subjects nine times, moving from a focus on their school attendance, to employment and fatherhood. It was found that a significant number of delinquent youths had criminal fathers. Under 10% of children from non-offending fathers went onto become chronic offenders, whereas just under 40% of the offspring of criminal fathers went onto regularly offend.

Writing skill

WRITING

Anaphoric and cataphoric referencing

> References using synonyms and pronouns add cohesion to writing. Anaphoric references refer back to a previous word or idea:
>
> ***The impact and importance of educational performance** is key during teenage years, yet **this** coincides with one of the most challenging developmental stages.*
>
> Cataphoric references refer forward to a later idea:
>
> *Genetics have a direct effect on teenage behavior as certain **personality traits** such as **impulsivity and risk-taking** are believed to be inherited.*

1 Complete the sentences with the words in the box.

> findings   technological developments   these   this   ways

1 Governments can intervene in many _____, such as changing the starting hours of school or delaying the age people start school.
2 The influence of peers peaks during teenager years. _____ can result in people making different decisions to maintain the social cohesion.
3 We inherit many characteristics from our parents, however; the tendency for _____ to grow or diminish in influence is shaped by our environment.
4 The original _____, which suggested that teenagers have poor decision-making skills, have been contradicted by many subsequent studies.
5 _____ have been associated with playing a role in teenage brain development. Some argue that time spent playing video games or social media has hindered brain development as people spend less time on more productive activities.
6 Although intelligence cannot be said to be a cause of crime, _____ is often a factor that shows a high level of correlation.

2 Underline the words each referent refers to.

3 Complete the sentences with an appropriate referent.

Researchers have used twin studies to show that genes play a role in influencing behavior. Though [1] _____ have found that genes do have an influence [2] _____ are still unable to separate [3] _____ from environmental factors. Although twins can have identical DNA and be raised in different environments, there can be great similarities [4] _____ places and experiences. Arguably, twins raised in identical environments can still have very different experiences, for example, their other [5] _____ such as friends and classmates can be quite different.

BEHAVIOR   UNIT 6   113

WRITING

Writing task

You are going to write a cause-and-effect essay in response to the following:
"Critically evaluate whether the cause of delinquent behavior in teenagers is mainly genetic or environmental. Analyze the effects this behavior has on society."

Brainstorm

Use the table to help you brainstorm ideas for the essay.

Genetic causes	Environmental causes	Effects on society

Plan

1 Answer the questions below.

   1 Are the genetic or environmental effects more significant?
   2 What are the most significant effects on society?

2 Find sources to include in your essay.

Write

Use your brainstorm and plan to help you write your essay. Remember to use inverted conditionals to comment on sources where appropriate and use anaphoric and cataphoric referencing. Your essay should be between 250–350 words long.

Share

Exchange your essay with a partner. Use the checklist on page 189 to help you provide feedback to your partner.

Rewrite and edit

Consider your partner's comments and write your final draft. Think about:

- whether you answered the question clearly
- whether you used inverted conditional structures appropriately
- whether you used anaphoric and cataphoric referencing appropriately.

Review

Wordlist

Vocabulary preview

counterpart (n) **	genetic (adj) **	notion (n) ***	rational (adj) **
delinquent (n)	impulse (n) *	oversimplification (n)	regulate (v) **
deviant (adj)	inherit (v) **	prominent (adj) **	systematically (adv) **
facial (adj)	neurological (adj)	propensity (n)	tendency (n) **

Vocabulary development

as a consequence of (phr)	bring about (phr v)	prompt (v) **
be influenced by (phr)	exert a direct influence on (phr)	stem from (phr v)

Academic words

accumulate (v) *	coincide (v) **	evaluate (v) **	integral (adj) *
analogy (n) *	distort (v) *	imply (v) ***	intervene (v) *

Academic words review

Complete the sentences using the correct form of the words in the box.

| coincide | commission | evaluate | implementation | imply |

1. The conference in Istanbul _____ with a vacation I am taking there, so I can spend a day at the conference while I'm in town.
2. It is difficult to _____ how much nature, versus how much nurture affects the personality and behavior of an adult.
3. The director _____ a world-famous architect to develop the hospital's new wing.
4. The results of the survey _____ that the population of the region was decreasing due to the lack of jobs and economic growth.
5. The president promised to regenerate the Rust Belt during his election campaign, but the _____ of his promises may prove to be more difficult than he envisaged.

Unit review

Reading 1	I can link in-text references and opinions.
Reading 2	I can identify cause and effect.
Study skill	I can write concise and precise texts.
Vocabulary	I can use consequence phrases.
Grammar	I can use inverted conditionals in the unreal past.
Writing	I can use anaphoric and cataphoric referencing.

7 EXPANSE

Discussion point

Discuss with a partner.

1 Look at the infographic. Which statistic(s) do you find most surprising, shocking, or worrying? Why?

2 How might these statistics be different than 100 years ago? Explain your reasoning.

3 How might statistics like these be helpful? Explain your reasoning.

If the world were a village of 100 people

Nationality of the people

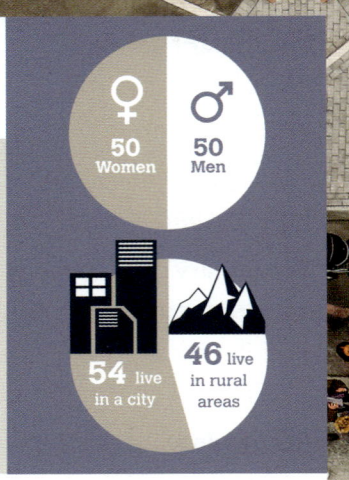

- America 14
- Europe 11
- Asia 60
- Africa 15

50 Women
50 Men

54 live in a city
46 live in rural areas

- 90 men and 82 women can read and write
- 10 men and 18 women can't read or write
- 66 men and 63 women have a secondary education
- 34 men and 37 women don't have a secondary education
- 21 people are overweight
- 63 people are healthy
- 15 people are undernourished
- 1 person doesn't have enough food

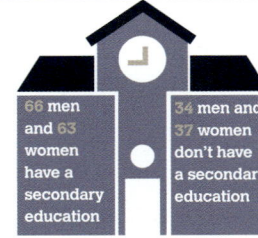

- 15 people make less than $2 a day
- 56 people make $2–10 a day
- 13 people make $10–20 a day
- 15 people make $20–90 a day
- 1 person makes more than $90 a day

One person controls 50% of the money in the village

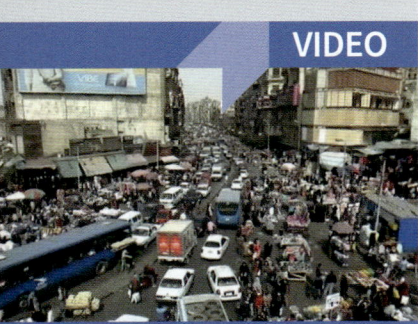

VIDEO

CAIRO'S NEW CAPITAL

Before you watch

Match the words in bold with the correct definitions.

1 **administrative** (adj)
2 **basic amenities** (phrase)
3 **driver** (n)
4 **sustain** (v)

a things considered necessary to be able to live comfortably

b provide the conditions that allows something to continue to exist

c related to the management of an institution or organization

d a factor which causes something to happen or develop

UNIT AIMS

READING 1 Identifying and inferring connections
READING 2 Identifying persuasion techniques
STUDY SKILL Emotive language and persuader words
VOCABULARY Adjective and noun collocations
GRAMMAR Nominal clauses
WRITING Paraphrasing

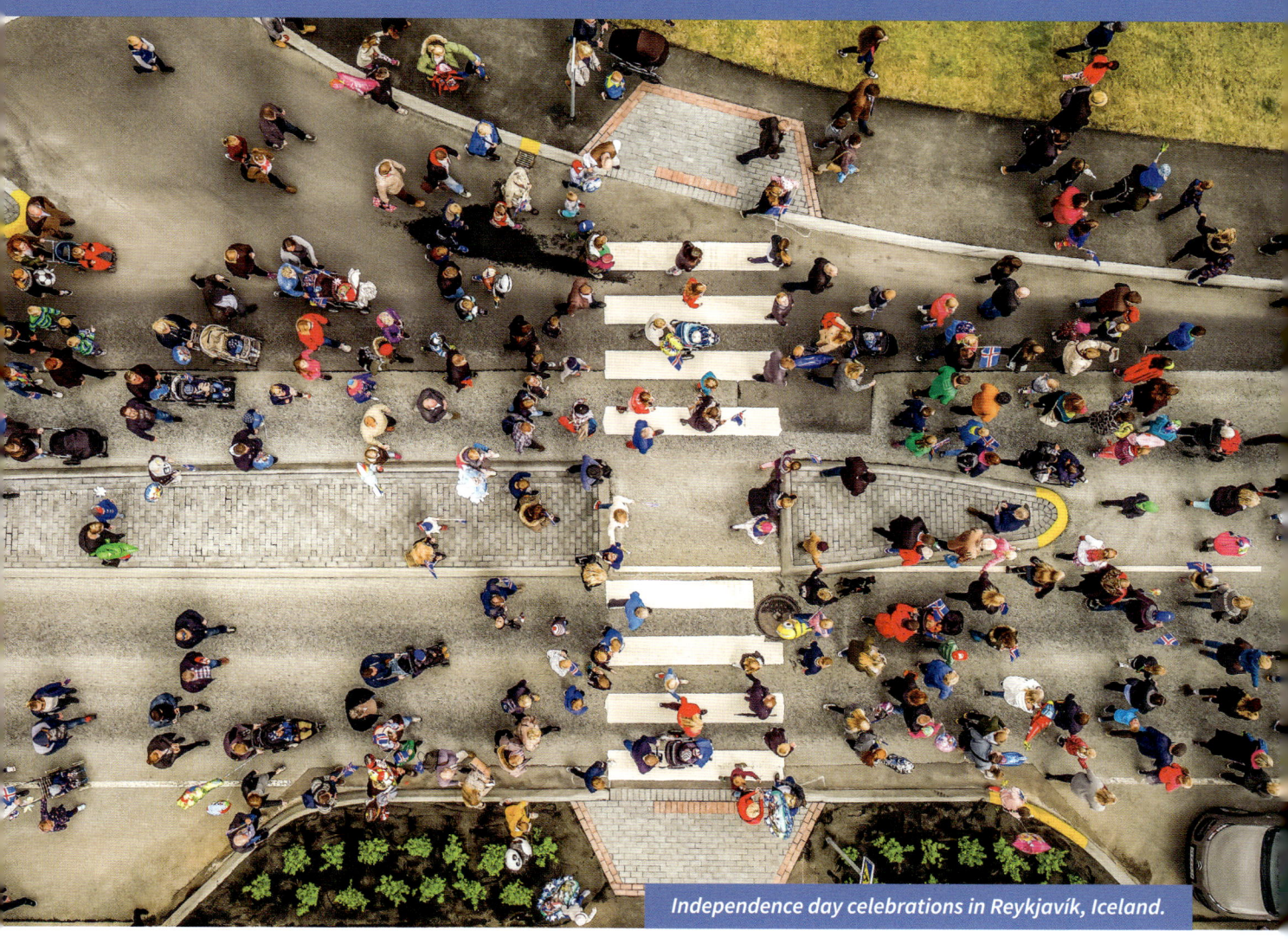

Independence day celebrations in Reykjavík, Iceland.

While you watch

Watch the video. Complete the sentences with the correct numbers.

1. The population of Cairo is set to grow by _____ over the next year.
2. The population of Egypt is _____.
3. The economic growth rate in Egypt was _____ percent in 2016.
4. The new city aims to provide housing for _____ citizens.

After you watch

Work in a group. Discuss the questions.

1. Do you think building the new city will solve the problem of overpopulation in Cairo? Why / why not?
2. What impact do you think moving the administrative and financial centers will have on both the new city and the city of Cairo? Why?
3. Do you think citizens will see the new city as an attractive place to move to? Why / why not?

EXPANSE UNIT 7

1 READING

The benefits of urbanization

A Vocabulary preview

Complete the sentences with the collocations in the box.

> carbon emissions   derive benefits   high density   housing shortages
> neglected areas   productivity growth   technological innovation   traffic congestion

1. The movement of goods across urban areas is often restricted by high volumes of _____.
2. Critics argue that urbanization has led to _____, higher levels of pollution, and poor living standards.
3. Arguably, the state can _____ many economic _____ from increased urbanization.
4. Successful urban expansion relies on the careful regeneration of _____.
5. _____ population _____ leads to increased competition for employment.
6. _____ helps urban planners increase efficiency in high density areas.
7. The findings suggest no clear correlation between a _____ in _____ and increased urbanization.
8. In a bid to reduce _____, many councils are turning to green housing projects.

B Before you read

Activating prior knowledge

You're going to read an essay titled *The benefits of urbanization*. With a partner, discuss which benefits and problems you think the writer might mention.

C Global reading

Identifying and inferring connections

> Making connections when reading helps you to engage with and understand the content better. These could be connections between ideas in the text (either explicit or implied); the text and others on a similar topic; the text and your own knowledge; and the text and the outside world.

1. Read the essay. How are the topics in each pair connected?

   1. Urbanization and development
   2. Transport and productivity
   3. Proximity and the environment
   4. Innovation and productivity
   5. Technology and the environment
   6. Urbanization and income levels

2. With a partner, discuss how the information in the text relates to you and the world around you.

The benefits of urbanization

[1] In 1950, the percentage of the world's population living in urban areas was 30%. By 2014, the figure had increased to 54% and it is predicted that, by 2050, two-thirds of us will be living in cities (World Urbanization Prospects, 2014). This means that in just 100 years, the number of urban dwellers will have more than doubled. The overwhelming majority of this urbanization is expected to occur in Asia and Africa, as people migrate to find work, housing, and gain improved access to healthcare and education. London went from a population of one million to eight million in over a century. Some Asian cities have done so in 50 years or less. While many are concerned that this surge in urban populations will lead to housing shortages and increased competition for employment, there are arguably many significant benefits in terms of development. In fact, history has shown that notable developments in a country cannot take place without urbanization. This essay will therefore argue that urbanization in developing countries should be actively encouraged.

[2] Perhaps the biggest benefit of urbanization is a growth in productivity. Rosenthal and Strange (2004) estimated that cities can increase productivity by approximately 3–8% if they double their population size—a significant number. This increase arises through economies of scale, as the growth in labor in the city allows firms to produce more output while their fixed costs remain largely the same. Essentially, more products are made with fewer resources. Transportation is also a key factor as firms are able to connect more easily and cheaply with each other when they are concentrated in clusters. These agglomeration economies, as they are known, are catalysts of economic growth. Asian cities, for example, "generate about 75 percent of a country's GDP and urban productivity surpasses 5.5 times the rural economy" (The Asia Foundation, 2016).

[3] Another benefit of urbanization is, perhaps surprisingly, related to the environment. While this may seem counterintuitive, urban life is actually more environmentally-friendly than rural life. Urban dwellers use notably less energy and fewer resources than those who live in rural areas. Buildings require less electrical heating than those in more remote places due to typically higher temperatures in urban areas and buildings which lock those temperatures in. Utility services can be offered more easily and affordably as people live in close proximity to each other. Similarly, public transportation is more viable in urban areas. It can be provided at a lower cost to a larger number of people and is more sustainable than private transportation. Public transportation has been proven to use less fuel for every passenger kilometer compared to private transportation. (Chester et al. 2010). The more public transportation is used, the smaller a city's carbon footprint. In addition to this, when urban dwellers live close to their workplace and other important facilities including schools, hospitals, and shops, there is a greater tendency towards the use of non-polluting forms of transportation, such as bicycles. This contributes to the reduction of a city's carbon footprint even further, as well as the reduction of traffic congestion.

[4] The final key advantage of urbanization is an increase in innovation. Areas of high density are known to inspire residents, entrepreneurs, and businesses to innovate more as they strive to enhance urban life. This includes local residents who work together to create better spaces for themselves and their communities, often regenerating neglected areas. Entrepreneurs look to invest in new technological innovations that create a greener environment by reducing carbon emissions, improve air quality, or develop more advanced, eco-friendly transportation systems. People within businesses innovate to improve systems or create new products with a view to both improving people's lives and making a larger profit. The sharing economy is one example of innovation that can be profitable and beneficial to people's lives and the environment. There are now companies which encourage people to share homes when they are not using them, share cars so they do not have to own one, and donate unwanted goods to those in need of them. Some local governments have schemes that allow private individuals and/or companies to use their facilities when empty (e.g., a school gym), to reduce spare capacity as much as possible.

[5] To conclude, while urbanization in substantial numbers may bring challenges, it also provides significant opportunities. Increased productivity, greater innovation, and the ability to reduce our impact on the environment are three such cases in point. As no country has ever reached middle or high income status without urbanization, it is evident that urbanization must be encouraged to allow developing countries the opportunity to derive the same benefits as developed countries, i.e., an improved standard of living. Urbanization results in progress and a decrease in poverty levels (Global Monitoring Report, 2013). Through higher productivity, people will receive higher wages and housing will become more affordable. Governments will be able to collect more taxation and therefore afford to provide better education and healthcare. Social mobility will increase for all; something that no-one can deny is a desirable goal.

References:

Chester, M.V. et al. (2010). Comparison of life-cycle energy and emissions footprints of passenger transportation in metropolitan regions. *Atmospheric Environment*. 44(8), 1071-1079

Rosenthal, S.S. and Strange, W.C. (2004). *The Micro-Empirics of Agglomeration Economies*, in *A Companion to Urban Economics* (eds Arnott, R.J. and McMillen D.P.). 1st ed. Oxford: Blackwell Publishing Ltd.

Salze-Lozac'h, V. (2016). Can Asian Cities Lead the Way to a More Sustainable Future? *The Asia Foundation*. Available: https://asiafoundation.org/2016/09/21/can-asian-cities-lead-way-sustainable-future/ [Accessed: 19th October 2017]

United Nations, Department of Economic and Social Affairs, Population Division (2014). World Urbanization Prospects: The 2014 Revision, Highlights. Available: https://esa.un.org/unpd/wup/publications/files/wup2014-highlights.Pdf [Accessed: 19th October 2017]

World Bank; International Monetary Fund (2013). Global Monitoring Report 2013: Rural-Urban Dynamics and the Millennium Development Goals. Available: https://openknowledge.worldbank.org/handle/10986/13330 [Accessed: 19th October 2017]

1 READING

Identifying and inferring connections

D Close reading

1 Read *The benefits of urbanization* again. Do the following statements match the claims of the writer? Write *Y* (Yes), *N* (No), or *NG* (Not Given).

1 Urban populations will soon be twice the size they were a century earlier. ___
2 Full employment results in increased productivity. ___
3 Denser populations stimulate economic growth. ___
4 Heat is retained more easily in rural buildings. ___
5 Congestion leads to city dwellers opting for alternative modes of transportation. ___
6 Entrepreneurs innovate for financial gain. ___
7 Some authorities encourage the full utilization of their resources. ___
8 Urbanization lowers the cost of accommodation. ___

2 Skim the text again. Complete the summary with no more than three words from the essay in each blank.

The global population living in cities is expected to be [1] _____ by the middle of this century. Such urbanization can be very beneficial. Productivity will grow due to [2] _____, as these mean that more can be produced for less. The city's [3] _____ will shrink, as people start using more public transportation and consuming lower levels of [4] _____. Innovation will allow businesses to create products and governments to create [5] _____ which improve people's lives. Urbanization should therefore be promoted in order for developing cities to enjoy the same high [6] _____ that people enjoy in developed countries.

E Critical thinking

Work with a partner. Discuss the questions.

1 As well as deriving benefits from urbanization, cities can also suffer. Make a list of counterarguments to each of the essay writer's main points.
2 Do you agree that the potential positives of urbanization outweigh the negatives? Why / why not?

Study skills: Emotive language and persuader words

Certain words can be very persuasive, and can trigger a position of trust in the reader. Which words they are will vary from subject to subject. For example, for some people the word 'experiment' summons up notions of scientific accuracy and reliability. However, the fact that an experimental approach was used does not in itself mean that the evidence is sound.

Emotive words such as 'cruel', 'unfair', 'natural', 'normal', 'commonsense', and 'unique' can prompt emotional responses that may lead the reader away from an accurate appraisal of the evidence presented.

Persuader words and phrases such as 'clearly', 'obviously', 'it is plain to see that', and 'of course' draw you in by appealing to what they claim is evident.

© Stella Cottrell (2013)

1 Read the excerpt below. What point is the writer making?

> While urbanization, in theory, promises benefits to a city, migration in such immense quantities is likely to diminish those benefits considerably. Naturally, the more people there are competing for jobs, the more companies feel they can impose unjust working practices on their employees. Those unfortunate enough not to find work live in poverty. Slums appear. Concentrated energy use leads to increased air and water pollution, and full waste disposal becomes unfeasible, often with waste abandoned on the streets. These in turn affect plant life, animal life, and the food chain for inhabitants.
>
> It is evident that all these issues have the potential to cause monumental harm to urban areas. As a result, city planners in developing cities must look to the future and plan for large migration. They must determine ways to create higher levels of employment in order to eradicate poverty; they must execute radical measures to deal with environmental issues and protect green spaces. And they must provide sufficient, affordable housing for inhabitants. Without strong city planning, there will be disastrous problems. It is unquestionably better to prevent these problems in the first place rather than have to address them at a later date.
>
> H. Thorne   March 24, 2018

2 Skim the excerpt again. Underline the adjectives used to create an emotional response and circle the persuasive words and phrases.

3 Work with a partner. Discuss the questions.

1 How effective do you think the emotive and persuasive words were in the excerpt? Did they create an emotional response in you? Were they persuasive?
2 How can you ensure you are not taken in by such language in future?

2 READING

Overpopulation: A problem or a myth?

A Vocabulary preview

Complete the sentences with the words in the box.

> biodiversity   degradation   exponential   irreparable
> irrigate   materialism   scarce   yields

1 Freshwater is _____ in many areas, partly due to competition for resources.
2 Overpopulation needs to be addressed before it causes _____ harm to the environment.
3 The global population has seen _____ growth over the past 150 years.
4 _____ in some cultures has created a higher demand for goods.
5 In order to feed more people, increased levels of water are needed to _____ farmland.
6 Recent studies indicate that crop _____ are negatively correlated with population.
7 Overpopulation has had a more significant impact on _____ than any other factor.
8 Rapid population growth and environmental _____ contribute to increased incidence of infectious disease.

B Before you read

Activating prior knowledge

With a partner, discuss the potential issues associated with a growing domestic and global population.

C Global reading

Identifying persuasion techniques

> In addition to putting forward a logical argument, academic writers use the following techniques to persuade readers to agree with their point of view:
> - repeating or paraphrasing arguments to emphasize them
> - giving future insights to highlight the consequences of an action
> - dismissing alternative arguments by providing different evidence.
>
> More informal texts such as magazine articles may also include:
> - the use of questions to involve the reader
> - language designed to engage the reader emotionally.

Read *Overpopulation: A problem or a myth?* Find at least one example of each of the techniques in the box.

READING 2

OVERPOPULATION:
A problem or a myth?

Argument A:

A problem

By ecologist Dr. Alexander J. Rice

[1] In 2011, the population of the world reached seven billion people. The UN Population Division (2015) predicts the number could be as high as 9.7 billion by 2050; that is an extra two billion people—the same number of people who currently reside in the African and American continents combined—living on Earth using its resources to survive. This is hard to conceive.

[2] Although families are getting smaller, people are living longer because medical and technical advances have lessened the impact of infectious disease. As a result, the UN's worst case scenario for 2100 is that the world population will reach almost 16 billion (UN, 2011). That is more than twice the number of people we have today. And yet already we are placing undue pressure on the Earth. The kind of pressure that, if increased, could have a profound and irreparable effect on our planet.

[3] The first fundamental issue is water. Just 2.5% of the world's water is fresh, with much of that caught up in polar ice caps (University of Michigan, 2000). Drought and poor infrastructure mean that already today water is a scarce resource. Over seven hundred million people lack access to clean water (WHO, 2013) and one in three people in every continent do not have enough water to satisfy their daily needs (WHO, 2009). Without clean drinking water, there will be an exponential increase in the incidence of diseases such as cholera and typhoid, which will undoubtedly place an excessive strain on healthcare systems. Without water for agriculture and industry, our food and manufacturing industries will be unable to satisfy demand. Already today, 10% of people consume foods which have been irrigated using waste water full of chemicals or disease (WHO, 2009). Should water become even scarcer, this is likely to grow further.

[4] The second critical issue is land. Current agricultural practices and the impact of pollution both contribute to soil erosion and a decreased level of soil fertility. It is estimated such poor quality land affects 1.5 billion people around the world (UNCCD, 2011). Deforestation and mining have had a devastating impact on our ecosystem and the biodiversity on which it thrives. The WWF (n.d.) estimates that we may be losing 10,000 species a year. All of this affects the number of crops that can be grown and produces greater food insecurity. How can we allow such environmental degradation to occur under our noses?

[5] Another prime concern is energy. Governments, such as those in Denmark and Germany, are investing in renewable energy to eliminate their reliance on oil and to tap into resources with greater sustainability. However, the number of road vehicles reached one billion in 2010 (WardsAuto, 2011), an increase of 20 million from the previous year, and is continuing to increase due to the growing wealth in developing countries. It is therefore likely that there will be an unprecedented demand for oil over the next 50 years, pushing prices to exorbitant levels. This will make it more difficult for people to afford food, heating, and other manufactured goods, placing more people into poverty.

[6] Overpopulation is not a problem for one country or continent; it is a problem for all of us. The UN (2012) estimates that by 2030 the world will need 50% more food, 30% more water, and 45% more energy than it does today. We must stop burying our heads in the sand and make a sustained effort to reduce population growth. We must develop a coherent strategy that will increase access to education for all. Not only is education a fundamental human right, it also facilitates a reduction in population growth. Large families tend to be prevalent in developing countries and yet when men, women, and children in these areas receive education, family sizes shrink. The UN estimates that in less developed countries where women are not educated, they have twice as many children as in those countries where they are educated. It is therefore this area in which we should invest time and money. Who can argue with free and equal education for all?

2 READING

Argument B:

A myth

By environmentalist Marilyn Cratchley

¹ It is true that the world's population is growing, but this is not the cause of our current and future global problems. Believing this will give rise to ignorance of the real problem and the resulting irreparable damage to our planet.

² Let me start by explaining why overpopulation is a myth. The UN Population Division regularly predicts population growth, but provides a low variant, medium variant, and high variant to factor in various likelihoods. In the 2010 revision, their high variant suggested that the world population will be almost 16 billion in 2100, but the low variant predicted it will peak at 8 billion and decrease to just over 6 billion by 2100. In most cases, it is the low variant that has come true in the past, suggesting the same will be true of their future population predictions. Furthermore, the size of families is actually decreasing. The average woman now has 2.4 children (World Bank, 2015), which is very close to the replacement level of 2.3. In many countries the fertility rate is even lower.

³ For the Earth to be overpopulated, there needs to be insufficient food, water, and space for humans to live. Indian economist Raj Krishna estimates that India alone is capable of increasing crop yields to the point of providing the entire world's food supply. The World Food Programme (n.d.) confirms that there is sufficient food grown to feed the world and there is the same amount of fresh water on the planet now as there was 10,000 years ago; it has simply been redistributed. So how is it possible that the number of people in the world is impacting on our planet?

⁴ It is not an increase in population that is a dire threat. It is an increase in consumption. Materialism and overconsumption are facts of life for everybody in the western world, as possessions reflect a person's status in society and people strive to obtain happiness through owning the latest fashionable goods. Not only that, but waste is a widespread occurrence which has a huge impact on our resources. In addition, our current consumption is imbalanced, unsustainable, and estimated to be 30% higher than the Earth can regenerate (LaTouche, n.d.). It is a sad truth that 80% of the world's resources are currently used by just 20% of the world's population (UN, 2008), which means that a fifth of us use four-fifths of the world's food and energy.

⁵ Our overconsumption must be addressed now to make our lives more sustainable and avoid continuing the abhorrent damage to the environment we appear to be causing. With more developing countries set to generate greater wealth, there is bound to be an exponential increase in overconsumption in the future, so we must be prepared today. The key is education. The more people understand about the consequences of their materialism, the fewer resources they are likely to consume. Attitudes must be changed if our consumption habits are to change. We must not let ourselves be misguided. If we focus on the wrong issue and do not work towards this, we may find ourselves living on a planet that can no longer provide for all of us, or worse, can no longer sustain human life at all.

READING 2

Identifying persuasion techniques

D Close reading

1 Read Argument A in *Overpopulation: A problem or a myth?* again. Complete the sentences with no more than two words from the article.

1 The reduced impact of _____ has increased life expectancy.
2 Water shortages are the consequence of little or no rainfall and _____.
3 Issues created by polluted water place considerable stress on _____.
4 The removal of trees brings about a significant loss of _____ each year.
5 People will experience higher levels of _____ should the demand for cars increase.
6 The solution to overpopulation is to make _____ accessible to everyone.

2 Read Argument B again and choose the correct answer (a, b, or c).

1 The writer regards population estimates as insignificant due to
   a the lack of clarity in the number of alternatives.
   b the methods used to calculate them.
   c the outcome of previous forecasts.
2 The writer suggests there is sufficient food to feed the current population as
   a one country has yet to fully exploit its natural resources.
   b the level of natural resources remains unchanged.
   c the birth rate has diminished in recent years.
3 What best describes the writer's view on high levels of consumption?
   a They exist only in a proportion of the world.
   b They are determined by a need to keep up with trends.
   c They are the result of a desire to be accepted by others.
4 The writer claims that the solution to overconsumption is the
   a targeting of consumer's purchasing practices.
   b highlighting of the destruction of our environment.
   c improved understanding of the effects of our behavior.

E Critical thinking

Work in a group. Discuss the questions.

1 Which of these two problems concerns you more—overpopulation or overconsumption? Why?
2 What can individuals, schools, governments, and business leaders do to help address the issue of overconsumption? Think of at least one action point for each group.

VOCABULARY

Vocabulary development

Adjective + noun collocations
Adjectives that are synonyms or partial synonyms often do not collocate with the same noun.
The ~~great~~ **overwhelming majority** of urbanization is expected to occur in Asia and Africa.
Services can be offered more cheaply when people live in ~~near~~ **close proximity** to each other.

1 Choose the most appropriate adjective to complete the collocations.
   1 We are already placing **undue / unjust** pressure on the natural environment.
   2 It could have a **prime / profound** effect on our planet.
   3 There will be an **abrupt / exponential** increase in the incidence of diseases.
   4 This will undoubtedly place an **excessive / extravagant** strain on healthcare systems.
   5 Deforestation and mining have had a **hazardous / devastating** impact on our ecosystem.
   6 Another **prime / severe** concern is energy.
   7 There will be an **unprecedented / insistent** demand for oil, pushing prices higher.

2 Complete the collocations with the adjectives in the boxes.

   immense   radical   underlying   widespread

   1 There is a _____ but incorrect belief that overpopulation is a developing world problem.
   2 Education is of _____ importance in fighting overpopulation.
   3 Some people say that _____ changes to our buying habits are needed.
   4 Our materialism is one of the _____ causes of environmental destruction.

   overriding   prominent   sizeable   systematic

   5 We must take an effective, _____ approach to the overpopulation problem.
   6 World leaders must play a _____ role in the fight against global issues.
   7 The _____ aim of the UN Population Division is to monitor population growth.
   8 A _____ number of people are unaware of problems caused by overconsumption.

Academic words

1 Complete the definitions with the words in bold.

1 Without an effective **infrastructure**, goods cannot be transported.
2 To be competitive, companies must produce more **output** for less money.
3 People **migrate** from the north as cities in the south are bigger.
4 A **fundamental** issue for urban planners is transportation.
5 Planners need to **conceive** a plan to deal with a growing population.
6 People and companies **innovate** to try and make life easier.
7 It is easier for **utility** companies to provide a good service in the city.
8 It is difficult for urban planners to create a **coherent** strategy.

a _____ (v) to think of a new idea, plan, or design
b _____ (v) to go to another place or country to find work
c _____ (n) a public service such as gas, water, or electricity
d _____ (n) the set of systems in a place, e.g., telephone and transportation system
e _____ (n) relating to the basic nature or character of something
f _____ (adj) reasonable and sensible
g _____ (n) the amount of something that an organization produces
h _____ (v) to invent or begin using new ideas, methods, equipment, etc.

2 Work with a partner. What other forms of the words in Exercise 1 can you think of?

3 Complete the sentences with words from Exercise 1. Change the form if necessary.

1 The city is attractive to economic _____ seeking an improved standard of living.
2 Readily available education is _____ in the fight against overpopulation.
3 The _____ of new ideas begins with motivated residents, not those in charge.
4 The confusing layout of the city indicates an _____ planning strategy.
5 There are many examples of technologically _____ practices in the city.
6 Urban dwellers produce more _____ per person than those in rural areas.
7 Poor _____ has a negative impact on communication in the city.
8 _____ companies in the region are able to meet the increased demand, but at an inflated cost.

CRITICAL THINKING

Critical thinking

> **Assessing the logic of an argument**
>
> After identifying arguments in an academic text, it is necessary to assess their logic. To test the logic of an argument, ask:
>
> - Is the argument based on a generalization (a statement that seems to be true but is not based on fact), an assumption (something you consider likely to be true but you have no proof), or speculation (something which is possible)? If so, are these reasonable?
> - Is there sufficient supporting evidence? Is the evidence relevant?
> - Do all parts of the argument follow logically from one another?

1. Skim Dr. Rice's argument in *Overpopulation: A problem or a myth?* again. Do these numbers describe a trend (a gradual change of development), a pattern (a series of repeated actions or events), or a static figure?

   a 2bn   c one in three   e 1.5bn
   b 2.5%   d 10%   f 20m

2. What point is Dr. Rice making with each trend / pattern?

3. Read the whole article again. Analyze the arguments below. Are they logical? Is there enough evidence to support them?

   A problem
   1. An increase in demand for clean drinking water will result in more disease.
   2. Farmers will risk using more waste water if fresh water becomes scarcer.
   3. Deforestation and mining affect our ecosystem and the biodiversity within it.
   4. The number of cars on our roads is increasing.
   5. Education is the solution to overpopulation.

   A myth
   6. The lowest population variant predicted by the UN usually comes true.
   7. The amount of fresh water has not changed in 10,000 years.
   8. Materialism and overconsumption are a fact of life for everyone in the western world.
   9. Waste is a common occurrence.
   10. People will change consumption habits if they are educated.

4. Which writer presented the better and more logical arguments? Why?

Writing model

You are going to learn about using nominal clauses and paraphrasing. You are then going to use these to write a persuasive essay about children's education.

A Analyze

Use ideas from the model below to complete the essay plan.

Introduction: _____
Reason 1: _____
Reason 2: _____
Reason 3: _____
Conclusion: _____

B Model

Read the model again and answer the questions.

> To conclude, education is a fundamental tool in the battle against overconsumption and we must make a considerable effort to ensure it is integrated into schools across the country. There is overwhelming evidence, as presented, that education about sustainable living at an early age can make children more conscious of the impact of their decisions on the environment. Similarly, it provides them with concrete solutions for addressing issues of materialism that may arise during their adult lives and encourages them to conceive their own, sometimes more, radical ideas. As explained, research also demonstrates that education on sustainable living does not only improve awareness, it can also have a profound impact on purchasing habits as children become teenagers. However, how schools integrate sustainable living education into lessons can determine just how successful it is. For it to be effective, it is imperative that schools adopt a coherent and systematic approach so that sustainable living features not only in one or two types of lessons, but across the whole school curriculum. This will require funding, but when allocating resources across schools, I would urge policy makers to consider whether there is anything more important than addressing the devastating impact we are having on our planet.

1 What evidence did the writer use in the main body of the essay to persuade the reader to believe in her stance? How persuasive is this type of evidence?

2 Which of the following do you think feature in a persuasive essay? Why?

> balanced viewpoint   discussion of opposing argument
> evidence   neutral language   persuasive language
> strongest argument first   thesis statement

Grammar

Nominal clauses

A nominal clause is a group of words that performs the same function as a noun. They can be the subject or object of a sentences;

Families *are getting smaller.* (= subject)
The UN estimates **that by 2030 the world will need 50% more food.** (= object)

Nominal clauses include clauses which follow *that*, *if/whether*, and *questions*.

- *That* clauses usually come after adjectives or verbs describing thoughts and opinions, and reporting verbs. The word *that* can be omitted.

  People are concerned **that oil prices are rising**.
  It is believed **we will need 50% more food in future**.

- Question clauses include question words and answer the question.

  Pollution is **what worries me the most**. (What worries you the most?)

- We use *if/whether* to place *yes/no* questions in a statement.

  We must ask ourselves **whether we can really cope**. (Can we cope?)

1 Underline the nominal clauses in the sentences below.

1. People today know they can follow fashion without spending much money.
2. People are not always aware that fast fashion affects the environment.
3. People may not be conscious of the fact that polyester is made from petroleum.
4. What may result from this is the release of harmful gases.
5. How cotton is grown varies, but pesticides may be used.
6. People should carefully consider whether they need new clothes or not.

2 Complete the nominal clauses in *italics* in the sentences with an appropriate word(s). There may be more than one possibility.

1. It is clear _____ *we have become a throw-away society.*
2. I don't think _____ *many people fix things that break anymore.*
3. _____ *authorities dispose of unwanted goods* is becoming a huge problem.
4. It is sad _____ *most things we buy only last a couple of years.*
5. _____ *most companies do these days is make products that don't last.*
6. Perhaps we should question _____ *we need so much packaging when we buy things.*

3 Work with a partner. Discuss whether you agree with the statements in Exercise 2. Explain your reasoning.

Writing skill

> To paraphrase effectively, you must significantly change the original source material. Specialized terms can remain as they are, but you should paraphrase other language by:
> 1 Changing passive verb forms to active verb forms, and vice versa.
> 2 Using synonyms or different phrases that mean the same thing.
> 3 Changing word forms.
> 4 Changing the word order.
> 5 Turning positive verbs to negative, and vice versa, where appropriate.

WRITING

Paraphrasing

1 Look at the information in the source text. Then decide which writer has paraphrased the information more effectively (a or b).

> **Education and overpopulation: A never-ending cycle**
> **(D. Hamilton, 05.23.17)**
> When education is not made available to all children, there is a greater risk of overpopulation, but overpopulation can also result in a lack of education. For example, people without qualifications who work in low-paid jobs sometimes choose to have larger families, especially in rural areas, in order to have more hands to help earn an income. This contributes to overpopulation. These parents, and often the government, then struggle to provide education for these children so they grow up without an education. This continues the cycle.

a According to Hamilton (2017), a lack of education contributes to overpopulation, but overpopulation can also contribute to a lack of education. This is because it can be difficult for parents and governments to educate all children when larger families exist, and yet a lack of education often results in the existence of larger families and overpopulation.

b Hamilton (2017) suggests there is a greater chance of overpopulation when education is not available to all children. This is because people in low-paid jobs, particularly in the country, sometimes have bigger families so they can earn more income. However, this can cause overpopulation because the parents and government cannot send them to school, so they grow up uneducated. The cycle resumes.

2 Paraphrase the language in these three sentences.
1 When education is not made available to all children, there is a greater risk of overpopulation. (Smith, 2015)
2 People without qualifications who work in low-paid jobs sometimes choose to have larger families, especially in rural areas, in order to have more hands to help earn an income. (Taylor, 2014)
3 Parents, and often the government, struggle to provide education for these children so they also grow up without an education. (Polo, 2014)

WRITING

Writing task

You are going to write a persuasive essay in response to the following:
"An international charity believes education for all children is necessary in the fight against overpopulation. What do you consider to be the major reasons for this?"

Brainstorm

How can education for all children help to overcome overpopulation? Complete the notes with your ideas.

General—70 million children do not attend school. Millions start but do not finish (World Bank, 2012). *Why? Effects?*
Health—Cutler and Lleras-Muney (2006) research—education improves health. *How? Effects?*
Poverty—UNESCO (2006), the higher the number of school years, the higher GDP per capita of the country. *Why? Effects?*

Plan

Plan your essay. Organize your ideas from the brainstorm into a logical persuasive essay structure.

Write

Use your plan and brainstorm to help you write your essay. Remember to use nominal clauses and paraphrasing where appropriate. Your essay should be between 250–350 words long.

Share

Exchange your essay with a partner. Use the checklist on page 189 to help you provide feedback to your partner.

Rewrite and edit

Consider your partner's comments and write your final draft. Think about:

- whether you organized your essay and answered the question clearly
- whether you used nominal clauses appropriately
- whether you used paraphrasing appropriately.

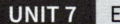

Review

Wordlist

Vocabulary preview

biodiversity (n)	emission (n) **	irreparable (adj)	productivity (n) **
congestion (n)	exponential (adj)	irrigate (v)	scarce (adj) *
degradation (n)	housing (n) ***	materialism (n)	yield (n) *
density (n) **	innovation (n) **	neglected (adj)	

Vocabulary development

devastating (adj) *	immense (adj) **	profound (adj) **	undue (adj)
excessive (adj) **	insistent (adj)	radical (adj) **	unjust (adj)
extravagant (adj)	overriding (adj)	sustained (adj)	widespread (adj) **
hazardous (adj) *	prime (adj) **	underlying (adj) **	

Academic words

coherent (adj) *	fundamental (adj) ***	innovate (v)	output (n) **
conceive (v) **	infrastructure (n) *	migrate (v) *	utility (n) **

Academic words review

Complete the sentences using the correct form of the words in the box.

| accumulate | fundamental | infrastructure | innovate | output |

1 Many developing countries suffer from a poor _____: it is difficult to transport goods from one place to another, and to move around the country.
2 Water is a(n) _____ important resource which not only supports life, but is also a basic requirement for agriculture and industry.
3 Profit margins suffer when production costs rise, but _____ and revenue remain the same.
4 Danish architect Bjarke Ingels is known for his technically _____ designs.
5 Evidence on the harmful effects of smoking have been _____ for years.

Unit review

Reading 1	I can make connections.
Reading 2	I can identify persuasion techniques.
Study skill	I can use emotive language and persuader words.
Vocabulary	I can use academic collocations.
Grammar	I can use nominal clauses.
Writing	I can paraphrase.

8 CHANGE

Discussion point

Discuss with a partner.

1 How did the companies in the infographic change their business strategies over the years?
2 Why do you think the companies changed their strategies?
2 How well do you think these companies have adapted to the changing world? Why?

Four start-ups that changed the world

Nintendo
Worth $42bn
Made $4.3bn net sales (2016)
Sold 240,000,000 Mario games
But did you know?
The company started out as a seller of playing cards in 1889 and tried its hand in the hotel and taxi industry before becoming a successful toy company in 1966 and then a games company in 1974.

Tiffany
Worth $11.8bn
Made $4bn net sales (2016)
More Jewelry accounts for 92% of the company's global net sales
But did you know?
The store opened in 1837 and sold stationery and "fancy goods" until 1853 when it started specializing in jewelry.

Instagram
Over 700 million monthly active users
Sold to Facebook for $1bn in 2012
1 million advertisers
But did you know?
It started out as a location-based app that let users check into places, make plans for meet-ups, earn points for meet-ups, and post photos of those meet-ups, but when it became too similar to Foursquare, they decided to focus solely on the photos.

Nokia
Worth $30.3bn
Made $24bn net sales (2016)
Sold over 126m Nokia 3310 phones
But did you know?
It started as a wood mill in Finland in 1865. It was also a manufacturer of rubber goods, a generator of electricity, and an owner of cable works before it moved into the telecoms industry.

VIDEO
JOINT VENTURES

Before you watch

Match the words in bold with the correct definitions.

1 **goldmine** (n)
2 **joint venture** (n)
3 **magnitude** (n)
4 **retail** (n)
5 **revive** (v)
6 **vehement** (adj)

a a business partnership between companies
b make something active, successful or popular again
c of great size or importance
d a business or activity that makes large amounts of money very easily
e showing strong feeling
f the sale of goods to the public

UNIT AIMS

READING 1 Inferring cause and effect
READING 2 Identifying concepts and theories
STUDY SKILL Checking your reading speed
VOCABULARY Academic phrases
GRAMMAR Participle clauses
WRITING Report writing

A young creative planning team strategy.

While you watch

Watch the video and choose *T* (True) or *F* (False).

1 The new government legislation is designed to help small shop owners.   T / F
2 The majority of retail transactions are made in small local shops.   T / F
3 The new legislation allows big international chains to compete with the small shops.   T / F
4 The legislation should bring huge amounts of foreign investment into the Indian economy.   T / F
5 International retail companies hope that investing in India will be equally as successful as their investments in China.   T / F

After you watch

Work in a group. Discuss the questions.

1 What positive impacts could this legislation have for both the Indian economy and local consumers?
2 Some small shop owners are understandably opposed to the legislation. What measures do you think they could take to protect their businesses?
3 How do you think we can account for the pervasiveness of international brands in today's society?

1 READING

Adapt or die

A Vocabulary preview

1 Complete the questions with the words in the box.

> dedicated   exemplify   insolvent   knowledgeable   lawsuit
> tailor   teamed up with   tech-savvy

1. Which companies do you think _____ good customer service?
2. Which companies are known for having staff _____ to their work?
3. Which companies can you name that became financially _____ and went bankrupt?
4. Do you know of any companies which have been issued with a _____? What happened?
5. Which successful products initially relied upon _____ early adopters?
6. Can you think of a company that has successfully _____ another on a project?
7. Which companies are known for having _____, customer-facing staff deal with inquiries?
8. Do you think big companies should make an effort to _____ their offering to local communities? Why / why not?

2 Answer the questions in Exercise 1 with a partner.

B Before you read

Activating prior knowledge

Work with a partner to list five reasons that companies are forced out of business. Give examples.

C Global reading

Identifying text organization

1 Read *Adapt or die*. Which of your five reasons are mentioned?

2 Six sentences have been removed from the article. Skim the text again and match sentences (a–g) with the blanks (1–6). One sentence is not needed.

   a Its main rival on the other hand, decided to take an alternative approach.
   b The brand's outlook was further darkened by the credit crunch.
   c However, in retrospect, this was too little, too late.
   d This challenging situation was not taken lightly by senior management.
   e In fact, this was likely a convenient tale used to explain the business model.
   f Yet despite this success, the company has had its fair share of failure.
   g It had also successfully expanded into several international markets.

Adapt or die

READING 1

¹Each year thousands of companies find themselves struggling to survive in an ever expanding marketplace. While the majority of these are small, local businesses, or new companies unable to get a foothold, some large, well-established companies have been known to fail. In this article, we evaluate the actions, or inaction, of three multimillion dollar companies that ended in failure, in order to assess where they went wrong.

Blockbuster

²Blockbuster—an American-based video rental chain—was founded by David Cook in 1985 and quickly established itself as a key player in the market. Two years later, Cook sold the business for $18.5 million, and by 1991, when it was sold to Viacom for $8.4bn, it had established itself as the biggest video rental chain in the world, with thousands of stores across the globe.

³A key element of Blockbuster's business model, and one that would eventually lead to its downfall, was its inflexibility on late return penalties. They accounted for around 16% of its revenue in 2000, but were hugely unpopular with customers. It is often claimed that when Reed Hastings was issued a $40 penalty for the late return of *Apollo 13* in 1997, he was inspired to found Netflix, an online DVD mail-order rental company and direct competitor of Blockbuster.¹ _____. So popular was Netflix's offering that in 2000 Hastings proposed a partnership with Blockbuster which the latter, perhaps mistakenly, declined.

⁴At the turn of the new millennium, Blockbuster began to lose its market share, with a 75% drop in market value between 2003 and 2005. Netflix's service had begun to attract attention not only among innovators, but also among early adopters of new technology whose positive word of mouth influenced less tech-savvy consumers. As confidence in the business grew, its popularity increased and it diversified into the streaming market. In 2004, Blockbuster launched its own online subscription rental service, abolishing late penalty fines the following year. ² _____. When an advertising campaign that was criticized for misleading customers on the content of the new policy led to several lawsuits, the company's collapse looked increasingly likely. After internal wrangling, the CEO was replaced in 2007 and while his successor, to his credit, looked to streaming as a new company strategy, heavy debt resulted in the company's bankruptcy in 2010.

Fresh & Easy

⁵Tesco is the leading retailer in the UK and one of the largest retailers in the world. In fact, in 2007 it was reported that £1 in every 7 spent in Britain was spent at a Tesco branch. ³ _____. Having successfully diversified into markets such as Poland, Japan, and Turkey in the early 2000s, Tesco turned its attention to the U.S., a country where consumers are used to driving to large supermarkets to do their shopping, receiving personal attention at the checkout, and getting takeout when busy. After, two years of research, the company identified the potential for a store based on the Tesco Express model in the UK, i.e., a convenience store with self-service tills located in local neighborhoods, selling fresh food and ready meals at reasonable prices.

⁶Tesco launched Fresh & Easy in 2007. Although the name was meant to represent the supermarket's green ethos—a notion exemplified by its solar-powered warehouses and electric vans—customers found it easily forgettable, and by April 2008, reports suggested that the sales were far lower than projected, something initially denied by the company. ⁴ _____. This was because the majority of its stores had been built in working class neighborhoods and sales were significantly affected by the subprime mortgage market. Consumer spending was down, and 13 outlets were forced to close due to falling populations and the outflow of migrant workers. In April 2009, Tesco announced that although sales had risen from the previous year, Fresh & Easy was operating at a trading loss of $142m. In a bid to maximize profits and cover high infrastructure costs, Tesco announced rapid expansion plans. In 2012, with losses now at $1bn, all planned store openings were canceled, and the following year, all 200 operational Fresh & Easy stores were sold.

Borders

⁷The Borders book store was founded in 1971 by brothers Tom and Louis Borders. Graduates of the University of Michigan, the brothers developed an inventory system that allowed them to tailor each store's offering to demands of the local community. The brand became known for its big stores, large variety of books, and knowledgeable, dedicated staff, and along with Barnes & Noble, came to dominate the bookstore market in the U.S. in the early nineties.

⁸Near the end of the decade, Borders attempted to diversify from its core business, investing heavily into the CD and DVD market. ⁵ _____. It focused its attention on creating a Barnes & Noble e-reader. Meanwhile, Borders, rather than developing its own online presence, chose to team up with Amazon, redirecting their own customers directly to the burgeoning, less expensive online retailer.

⁹By 2004, Borders had over 1,200 stores across the U.S. ⁶ _____. However, 2006 proved to be the company's final profitable year, and increasing losses over the next five years led to the sale or closure of all overseas operations. In an attempt to recoup sales, Borders terminated its deal with Amazon in 2007 and launched its own website the following year. In 2010, it opened an e-book store on its website, allowing customers to download books to their devices. However, by 2011 Borders had become financially insolvent and filed for bankruptcy.

1 READING

Inferring cause and effect

D Close reading

In case studies and other texts which outline problems, cause-and-effect relationships may not be explicit; you may need to infer them. To do this:

1 Look for explicit information or clues that describe the cause of the problem.
2 Look for explicit information or clues about the effects of the problems.
3 Use your existing knowledge of the world to make connections between the causes and effects.

Read *Adapt or die* again. Match the causes (1–8) with their effects (a–h).

1 A substantial percentage of the company's profits were dependent on penalizing customers. ___
2 A competitor capitalized on a demand for instant access to streamable content. ___
3 Poor communication misled customers. ___
4 The company chose a business model different than the one consumers were used to. ___
5 Problems in the housing market affected the disposable income of potential customers. ___
6 The company was operating at a substantial deficit from the outset. ___
7 The company invested heavily in physical media. ___
8 The company steered its customers toward an online collaborator. ___

a Planned expansion was abolished.
b Customers were lured away by the lower prices of a competitor.
c Stores in some areas generated less revenue.
d The company lost a considerable share of the market.
e Stores were not enticing and therefore demand was lower than anticipated.
f The company was required to pay out substantial amounts of compensation.
g Profits were negatively affected when a policy was changed.
h A competitor which had invested in a different product gained a competitive edge.

E Critical thinking

In a group, discuss what key lessons companies could learn from the case studies described in the text.

Study skills — Checking your reading speed

- Find something familiar to read.
- Set the alarm for ten minutes.
- Read for ten minutes at a speed that allows you to understand what you read.
- Count how many words you read.
- Divide this number by ten, to find out how many words you read in one minute.
- Do this using different texts. If you read fewer than 200–250 words per minute, even with material that is clear and interesting, it is worth trying to increase your speed.

© Stella Cottrell (2013)

1. Follow the instructions in the *Checking your reading speed* box using *The rise of crowdfunding* on page 10 and *Are online "friends" a threat to development?* on page 14. What is your word speed?

2. Rate the following according to how much they affect your reading speed. 1 = no effect. 5 = significant effect.
   1. You mouth the words as you say them.
   2. You re-read parts of the text.
   3. You read every word individually.
   4. You don't read advanced/academic material very often.
   5. You try to remember what you read.
   6. You read without a clear purpose.

3. With a partner, discuss how you could improve your reading speed. Use the ideas below to help you.

Tips for improving your reading speed

Keep your eyes moving forward to avoid re-reading parts of the text
Avoid moving your mouth or using your fingers to follow the lines
Read with a clear purpose to keep you motivated and on track
Practice reading academic material more often
Actively improve your reading speed through practice
Change your reading speed according to what you are reading. Slow down for sections with unknown technical words and speed up for sections with more familiar language

4. Make a plan to practice improving your reading speed over the next two weeks. Then test your reading speed again. Has it improved?

2 READING

Leadership and change management

A Vocabulary preview

1 Work with a partner. Decide if the statements about the words in italics are *T* (True) or *F* (False).

1 A *business model* is a manager who works for a fashion company. T / F
2 If someone does something and you *follow suit*, you do the same as them. T / F
3 A *transition period* describes a time when things are stable. T / F
4 If you *empower* someone, you take their power away. T / F
5 If someone feels *hostility* toward something, they support it. T / F
6 Companies try to *incentivize* their staff by giving bonuses. T / F
7 A *mentoring scheme* involves less experienced people helping more experienced people. T / F
8 If you *execute* a strategy, you end it. T / F

2 Correct the sentences which are false. Do not change the words in italics.

B Before you read

Activating prior knowledge

With a partner, make a list of five successful companies that you know. What has made them successful? How have they changed over the years?

C Global reading

Identifying concepts and theories

> Some texts present concepts rather than arguments. A concept is a general idea about something that exists or an idea about how something should be done. An argument is supported by objective reasoning.
>
> *Lewin's change model includes a three-step approach to change management known as Unfreeze, Change, Refreeze.* (= a concept)
>
> *People do not like change. In a 2013 survey, 76% of workers did not want their circumstances to change. Change should therefore be implemented carefully.* (= an argument)

Look at the headings and diagrams in *Leadership and change management*. Match the three business models in the text to the descriptions below.

a A detailed, step-by-step approach to managing change _____
b A theory of how change affects individuals within an organization _____
c A simple three-step approach to change management _____

Leadership and change management
Janelle Franklin

READING 2

¹Like a climber reaching a mountain peak, leading businesses must not spend too long standing and admiring the view or they may find themselves swiftly overtaken by leaner and more adaptable mountaineers. High-profile companies such as Apple®, Google, and Amazon are all examples of industry leaders which understand that they still have a mountain to climb; while other companies have mistakenly spent far too long looking at the scenery, not appreciating that further heights were there to be scaled.

²We are all aware that if a business wants to succeed, it has to create a culture of innovation in a fast-changing market. When one company innovates, others will quickly follow suit. Without continued creativity, a business will become stagnant, lose its competitive edge, and very quickly find itself behind the times. The need for change is blatantly obvious and yet businesses around the world fail to actively work towards change, unnecessarily suffering the consequences. Company bosses making a commitment to change is the first, and easiest, step forward. However, planning and executing a change strategy can be an uphill struggle, with organizations often withdrawing strategies at the first sign of difficulty. Fortunately, there is a lot of support for businesses in the academic field of change management, with several business models to draw on.

Lewin's Unfreeze, Change, Refreeze model

³The need to manage change first came to prominence with a three-stage theory by Kurt Lewin (1947) known as Unfreeze, Change, Refreeze. As a physicist and social psychologist, Lewin uses a block of ice to explain his theory. He suggests that if you have a square block of ice, but you want a cone-shaped block of ice, you need to melt it (unfreeze), change it into a cone-shape (change), and then solidify the new shape (refreeze). He suggests a three-stage approach:

- People become aware of the need for change and prepare themselves for it.
- A mentoring scheme is implemented to support employees who are given the power to find their own solutions to problems during the transition period.
- The change becomes normal behavior for the organization.

It is the final stage which companies may struggle to apply in today's fast-moving world; a place where there is little time for stability. However, this model has been, and continues to be, highly influential in the business world and its impact is perceptible in more recent models.

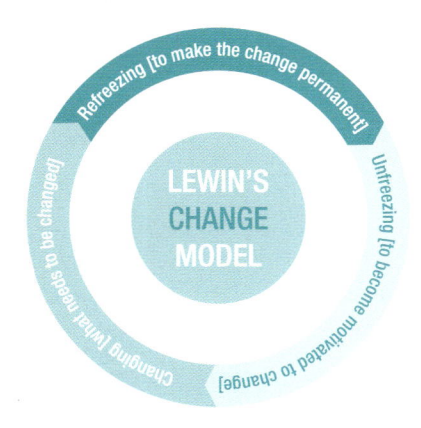

Kotter's eight-step approach to change management

Step 8: Incorporating changes into the culture
Step 7: Never letting up
Step 6: Generating short-term wins
Step 5: Empowering broad-based action
Step 4: Communicating the vision
Step 3: Developing a change vision
Step 2: Guiding the leading coalition
Step 1: Creating sense of urgency

⁴One of the more recent models of change was created by Dr. John Kotter (1995) and is an eight-step approach to change management, a more robust template for change that business leaders can follow to build a detailed plan. Having spent 30 years researching change management strategies in companies, Kotter realized that 70% of them fail and so developed this model as a means of helping those businesses to avert that situation.

⁵Kotter's first step involves creating a sense of urgency. Like Lewin's Unfreeze stage, it focuses on making the need to drive the company forward fully transparent, thereby negating hostility and creating a buzz around the company which incentivizes people to participate. The next three stages involve establishing leaders and other key people who have the expertise and respect to push change forward. They shape the vision which is simple and motivating and then communicate it to everyone in the organization, encouraging two-way communication in the process.

⁶Steps five to seven involve empowering staff through skills development and new systems of work before setting short-term goals that people can attain. By persisting with the changes and not backing down, the company can show staff that the changes are producing small, but impressive results. In the end, in step eight, the changes are accepted and incorporated into the company culture.

LEWIN'S CHANGE MODEL
Refreezing [to make the change permanent]
Unfreezing [to become motivated to change]
Changing [what needs to be changed]

2 READING

Fisher's model of personal change

[7]Kotter's model is very much a top-down process, where leaders at the top drive the changes. Yet one of the principal reasons for the high failure rate of change management strategies is the lack of understanding that systems and people go hand in hand. Focusing solely on systems and excluding people could be at the expense of success. Handling them appropriately ensures a greater chance of survival. For this reason, John M. Fisher (2005) developed a model of personal change to examine an individual's experiences of change in an organization. He likens it to crossing from one peak to another, suggesting that an individual will go through a series of emotions during the crossing. These are: anxiety, happiness, fear, threat, guilt, depression, gradual acceptance, and moving forward. How exactly a person experiences these emotions depends very much on how the change was initiated, how much autonomy that individual has, their self-image, and past experiences of change, meaning that each person's journey is dissimilar.

[8]Imagine that an accounting manager has been asked to implement new accounts systems to modernize the department. Fisher suggests this course of action will cause the manager to feel *anxiety* due to a lack of understanding of the changes; his prime concern will be about how they will affect him and whether he can cope with them. The manager will then feel *happy* because things are finally going to change, but when he realizes that he will have to change his behavior, this gives rise to *fear*. The next stage is *threat*, as the manager starts to self-reflect about his behavior and actions at work and begins to perceive himself differently. It may become apparent, for example, that he is less able to adapt to new computer software than he expected and finds members of his team are more competent than he is. This leads to *guilt* and may result in *depression* as he loses a sense of who he is. Eventually, there will be *gradual acceptance* as he starts to find his feet within the new environment and becomes more skilled at using the software. Finally, he will feel as if he can *move forward*.

[9]Fisher's model provides businesses with a comprehensive and solid understanding of how much of an impact change may have on employees across the board. This understanding can be fed into a strategic plan ensuring that these feelings are managed appropriately. He goes on further to propose ways in which this can be done.

Fisher's model of personal change

anxiety | happiness | fear | threat | guilt | depression | gradual acceptance | moving forward

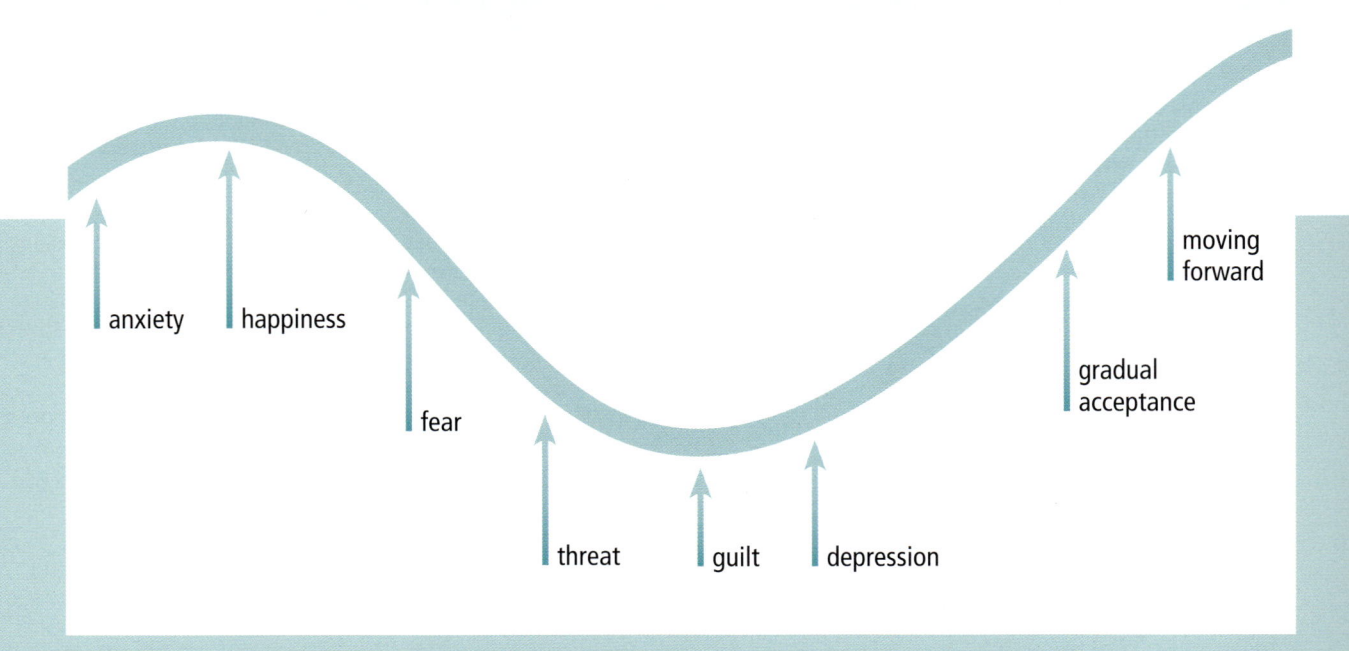

D Close reading

1 Read *Leadership and change management* again. Are these sentences T (True), F (False), or NG (Not Given)?

1 Companies should spend time celebrating their successes. ___
2 Lewin's model remains influential today. ___
3 Three-quarters of change management strategies triumph. ___
4 According to Fisher, employees experience the same emotions during change. ___

2 Read the text again and decide whether the features belong to Lewin's model (L), Kotter's model (K), or Fisher's model (F). Some features exist in more than one model.

1 It commences by raising employees' awareness that change is imperative. ___
2 It inspires staff to want to be part of the change. ___
3 It connects employees with experienced staff members for support. ___
4 It puts people and their experiences at the heart of the model. ___
5 It empowers staff. ___
6 It is based on the notion that emotions need to be managed. ___
7 A group of people are put in charge of the strategy. ___
8 The final stages come about when the changes are accepted. ___

3 Draw a Venn diagram and place the features (1–8) in Exercise 2 into the appropriate place. Which two models have the most in common?

4 What analogies does the writer use to describe the following and why?

1 How some well-known companies have been too slow to innovate.
   Admiring the view too long on a mountain without realizing there is more to climb.
2 The task of creating and implementing a change management strategy.
3 Lewin's Unfreeze, Change, Refreeze model.
4 People's individual experiences of change.

E Critical thinking

Work in a group. Discuss the questions.

1 Which of the three change models in the excerpt do you think would be most useful to a company preparing for change? Why?
2 Think about Fisher's model of personal change. What should the senior managers of a company do to reduce negative feelings experienced by staff during a period of change?

READING 2

Reading for specific information

VOCABULARY

Vocabulary development

Academic phrases

Phrases in academic texts can act like a noun, a verb, an adjective, or an adverb:

- Nominal phrases, e.g., *a sense of urgency, a fast-moving market*
- Verb phrases, e.g., *drive through the changes, become apparent*
- Adjective phrases, e.g., *blatantly obvious, aware of the need for change*
- Adverbial phrases, e.g., *behind the times, as a way of*

Note that in some less formal content, phrases may have an idiomatic meaning, e.g., *follow suit, go hand in hand, find your feet*.

1 Skim *Leadership and change management* again and find phrases with the following meanings. Use the paragraph numbers in parentheses to help you.

 1 a benefit over competitors (2) _____
 2 a difficult task (2) _____
 3 became important or well-known (3) _____
 4 very able to affect how someone thinks or behaves (3) _____
 5 one thing suffers because of another (7) _____
 6 things you choose to do in a situation (8) _____
 7 make something (often unpleasant) happen (8) _____
 8 involving everyone or everything in a place or situation (9) _____

2 Complete each question with a phrase from Exercise 1. Change the form if necessary.

 1 Two-way communication can be _____ when it comes to empowering staff.
 2 Flexibility and adaptability can give one company a _____ over another.
 3 Adopting a change in strategy can be a long, _____ for any company.
 4 When market changes occur, a company must swiftly agree on an appropriate _____.
 5 It is imperative that staff _____ be consulted prior to any drastic change in strategy.
 6 Transforming a company's culture may come _____ some staff who choose to resign.
 7 Any contentious issues with regards to a strategy will _____ during staff meetings.
 8 Even just the notion of change can _____ to feelings of panic among staff.

Academic words

VOCABULARY

1 Match the words in bold with the correct definitions.

1 **core** (adj)
2 **exclude** (v)
3 **incorporate** (v)
4 **inflexibility** (n)
5 **initiate** (v)
6 **maximize** (v)
7 **persist** (v)
8 **successor** (n)

a to include something as part of something else
b to deliberately not include something
c to make something start
d the most important or central part of something
e someone who holds an important position after someone else
f continue to do something in a determined way
g an inability to change your ideas, beliefs, or decisions
h to increase as much as is possible

2 Complete the prompts with words from Exercise 1. Change the form if necessary.

1 For a smooth transition, an outgoing employee's _____ should…
2 If a company wants to change its _____ business, it should first…
3 Should senior management be _____ when it comes to decision-making, it could result in…
4 Decision-making processes which support the _____ of staff are likely to…
5 A company which _____ with a strategy and does not give up may…
6 To ensure _____ productivity, companies must help staff…
7 Before the _____ of any change in a company, there should be…
8 All companies should _____ two-way communication into their culture because…

3 Work with partner to complete the prompts in Exercise 2 with your own ideas.

CHANGE UNIT 8 145

CRITICAL THINKING

Critical thinking

Inferring criticism

Although most academic writing strives for balance and impartiality, some authors may criticize an idea or argument that they are discussing without specifically saying they dislike it. Be aware of your own and / or an author's personal opinions on a topic, which may not be objective. For example, in the excerpt below, the underlined words suggest the author is critical of businesses that do not try to keep up with a changing market.

The need for change is <u>obvious</u> and <u>yet</u> businesses around the world <u>fail</u> to actively work toward change, <u>unnecessarily</u> <u>suffering</u> the <u>consequences</u> as a result.

1 Read the following excerpt from *Leadership and change management*. Underline the sentence which shows criticism.

Like a climber reaching a mountain peak, leading businesses must not spend too long standing and admiring the view or they may find themselves swiftly overtaken by leaner and more adaptable mountaineers. Successful companies such as Apple®, Google, and Amazon are all examples of industry leaders which understand that they still have a mountain to climb; while other companies have mistakenly spent far too long looking at the scenery, not appreciating that further heights were there to be scaled.

2 Read the full text again. Check (✓) the things below that the writer is critical of. Then explain your answers to a partner.

1 ___ The behavior of Apple®, Google, and Amazon (para. 1)
2 ___ The behavior of other companies (para. 1)
3 ___ Companies whose change management strategies fail (para. 2)
4 ___ Lewin's Unfreeze, Change, Refreeze model (para. 3)
5 ___ Kotter's eight-step model (para. 7)
6 ___ John M. Fisher's model of personal change (para. 9)

3 Work in a group. Discuss the questions.

1 Why might someone imply criticism rather than explicitly stating it?
2 What are the potential dangers of implied criticism?
3 What is the best way to criticize something in your academic writing?

Writing model

You are going to learn about participle clauses and how to structure a report. You are then going to use these to write a business report on preparing a company for change.

A Model

Read part of a report on change management within an organization. What is the purpose of the paragraph?

> In order to make certain that a change strategy is successful, it is thoroughly recommended that companies implement a clear and comprehensive plan in consultation with staff representatives from all areas of the organization. This plan should endeavour to cover both systems and personnel, allowing for a smooth transition across the board. The plan should incorporate:
> - the purchase of any equipment or software required
> - the hiring of any new staff required
> - training for all staff
> - counseling offered to support all staff through the process.
>
> After being implemented, the plan should be evaluated at regular intervals throughout the process. Inflexibility may harm the strategy, therefore planned courses of action should be revised where necessary. Dealt with swiftly, issues will be avoided and the final strategic goal can still be achieved.

B Analyze

1 Which recommendations in the model might solve the potential problems with change management strategies below?

- The decisions are all top-down.
- There is a focus on systems only.
- People's fears are not accounted for.
- Strategies are abandoned at the first hurdle.
- There is no coherent strategy in place.

2 Work with a partner. Discuss the questions.

1 What effect does the bulleted list have on the paragraph? Why?
2 In what kinds of academic texts might it be appropriate to use bulleted lists?
3 How is the bulleted list punctuated?
4 Why is the bulleted list in the model punctuated differently than the list in Exercise 1?

Grammar

Participle clauses

Participle clauses are used to make academic writing more succinct. The present participle (*-ing*) has an active meaning. The past participle (*-ed*) has a passive meaning.

- We use participle clauses to express cause, effect, and condition.
  Introduced effectively, change can be positive. (= if it is introduced)

- We can use participle clauses with *on*, *while*, *after*, and *before* to describe time.
  On/While facing reduced sales, the company implemented change.
  (= When they were facing)

- We use the present perfect participle (*having* + *-ed* verb) to say that an action finished before another action.
  Having found his feet, he accepted the change. (= because he had found his feet).

1 Rewrite the sentences using a participle clause. Use the prompts to help you.

1 Because they wanted to create a change strategy, senior managers brought in a consultant.
   Wanting _____
2 When they were reading the consultant's report, they realized they needed to organize a meeting.
   While _____
3 The meeting took place in the boardroom and was attended by all management.
   Attended _____
4 When they heard about the report, the managers had a lot of questions.
   On _____
5 Employees were known to dislike change and so managers thought they may reject the proposals.
   Known _____

2 Rewrite the sentences, replacing the underlined section with a participle clause.

1 <u>As some staff members heard about the changes, they</u> became angry.
2 Some staff members resigned <u>because they did not welcome change</u>.
3 <u>After they outlined the need for change</u>, managers received positive feedback from the staff.
4 <u>All staff received training</u> and successfully coped with the changes.
5 <u>If they are implemented appropriately</u>, change strategies can succeed.

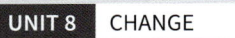

Writing skill

In business, science, and technical courses you may be required to write a report. A good report is clear, concise, and divided into sections which will always include an introduction, a main body, and a conclusion. Each section will have a heading.

A report may also include:
- an abstract/executive summary (the essential elements of the report)
- method and materials (related to an experiment or research)
- recommendations (things that arise from your conclusions)
- a bibliography (references you source in your report)
- appendices (information that is too big to go in the main body).

Report writers often use numbering or bullet points (as above) to present information simply.

WRITING

Report writing

1 The report below has been written by the HR director of a small company. What problems does the company face?

> **Buckson's supermarket**
>
> Buckson's is a long-standing family grocery store located locally. Because sales have been dropping slowly for the last ten years, research has been conducted to find out the underlying reasons for this. The research involved face-to-face interviews with 30 Buckson's customers and 30 customers of Buckson's closest rival supermarket, Shop Mart. The results of the research established that customers are purchasing less due to long lines at the check-out, no Internet presence, and no delivery service. The results also revealed that customers believe Buckson's goods to be of premium quality, especially their freshly baked goods. Several customers said, "They make the best cakes in town." Customers believe the staff to be friendly and helpful. Overall analysis of the results suggests that customers would be happy to pay Buckson's prices if they were able to benefit from faster check-out service and home delivery via their website. It is strongly recommended that Buckson's invest in faster scanners to avoid long lines at the check-out, develop a shopping app, purchase delivery vans, and implement a delivery service. In addition, a strategy should be implemented to ensure that current staff members are able to adapt to the new changes.

2 Work with a partner. Rewrite the report to make it clearer and easier to read. Include bulleted lists with appropriate punctuation, and insert the following headings:

Conclusions   Introduction   Recommendations   Research method   Results

CHANGE   UNIT 8   149

WRITING

Writing task

You're going to write the body and conclusion of a business report in response to the following:

"Write a business report about forthcoming changes to a supermarket. Make recommendations as to how the company can ensure supermarket staff are prepared for and support the changes."

Brainstorm

Read the report introduction. Then, with a partner, think of at least four practical suggestions to ensure Buckson's staff are prepared for and support the forthcoming changes.

> **Introduction**
> Buckson's supermarket has committed to modernizing its operations over the next 12 months by investing in:
> - a new, faster check-out system
> - a new website and app
> - a van delivery service.
>
> There is a concern that many long-term staff will struggle with the changes, resulting in the strategic aims of the company not being met (i.e., increased profits). As a result, Buckson's would like to implement a program to encourage staff to adopt the new system enthusiastically. The purpose of this report, written by TWC Consultancy, is to make recommendations as to what that program should comprise.

Plan

Imagine you work for TWC Consultancy. Plan the main body and conclusion of the report to Buckson's. Include your recommendations.

Write

Use your brainstorm and plan to help you write your report. Remember to use participle clauses and to structure your report appropriately. Your report should be between 250–300 words long.

Share

Exchange your report with a partner. Use the checklist on page 189 to help you provide feedback to your partner.

Rewrite and edit

Consider your partner's comments and write your final draft. Think about:

- whether you made relevant recommendations
- whether you used participle clauses appropriately
- whether you used an appropriate structure for your report.

Review
Wordlist

MACMILLAN DICTIONARY

Vocabulary preview

business model (n)	exemplify (v)	insolvent (adj)	tailor (v)
dedicated (adj) *	follow suit (phr)	knowledgeable (adj)	teamed up with (phr v)
empower (v)	hostility (n) **	lawsuit (n) *	tech-savvy (adj)
execute (v) **	incentivize (v)	mentoring scheme (n)	transition period (n)

Vocabulary development

across the board (phr)	come to prominence (phr)	course of action (phr)	uphill struggle (idiom)
at the expense of (phr)	competitive edge (n)	give rise to (phr)	

Academic words

core (adj) **	incorporate (v) **	initiate (v) **	persist (v) **
exclude (v) ***	inflexibility (n)	maximize (v)	successor (n) **

Academic words review

Complete the sentences using the correct form of the words in the box.

coherent	incorporate	maximize	successor	utility

1 _____ companies supply gas, electricity, and water to consumers.
2 To be efficient, manufacturers need to _____ productivity, and at the same time maintain quality and contain costs.
3 The CEO of the company was forced to resign and his _____ has not yet been appointed.
4 When writing essays, it is important to follow a well-thought-out plan so that your work is clear and _____.
5 Staff reluctantly _____ the management's changes into their working practices.

Unit review

Reading 1	☐	I can infer cause and effect.
Reading 2	☐	I can infer criticism.
Study skill	☐	I can improve my reading speed.
Vocabulary	☐	I can use academic phrases.
Grammar	☐	I can use participle clauses.
Writing	☐	I can write reports.

CHANGE UNIT 8

9 FLOW

Discussion point

Discuss with a partner.

1. Of the threats listed in the infographic, which do you think poses the greatest challenge? Why?
2. Which sectors do you think will be most affected by increased automation?
3. What practical measures could be implemented to address the growing economic divide?

Top 5 challenges facing humanity.

1 Lack of freshwater
Globally, the agricultural sector consumes over 70% of the planet's accessible freshwater.

2 Food production
It is estimated that farmers will have to produce 70% more food by 2050 to meet the demands of the projected 9-billion-strong population.

3 Invasive technology
Nearly 40% of U.S. jobs are at risk of automation by the early 2030s.

4 Increasing economic divide
In the 34 members states of the OECD, the richest 10% of the population earns 9.6 times the income of the poorest 10%.

5 Climate change
The IPCC recently recommended reducing carbon emissions by 40 to 70% by 2050 in order to prevent irreparable damage to the environment.

VIDEO: THE CO_2 FOREST

Before you watch

Match the words in bold with the correct definitions.

1. **array** (n)
2. **indefinitely** (adv)
3. **installation** (n)
4. **mitigate** (v)
5. **nutrient** (n)

a. a system or piece of equipment
b. a number of pieces of equipment of the same type, connected together to do a particular job
c. reduce the harmful effects of something
d. a substance that plants, animals, and people need to live and grow
e. for a period of time with no fixed ending

UNIT AIMS	READING 1 Using headings to understand main ideas	VOCABULARY Verb and noun collocations
	READING 2 Identifying commentary on evidence	GRAMMAR Verb patterns
	STUDY SKILL Planning your assignments spatially	WRITING Critically commenting on sources

An isolated polar bear in Hudson Bay, Canada.

While you watch

Read the sentences. Watch the video and choose the correct option for each sentence.

1 The experiment has been designed to investigate how well the forest can cope with increased levels of CO_2 **now** / **in the future**.
2 According to estimates, 20–30% of the additional CO_2 caused by human activity **can** / **cannot** be absorbed by forest ecosystems.
3 Introducing more CO_2 into forests is not difficult because it is a **main** / **secondary** nutrient for trees.
4 The experiment in the UK is **unique** / **similar to other experiments in Europe**.

After you watch

Work in a group. Discuss the questions.

1 What would you predict the results of the experiment to be? Why?
2 Do you think conducting research experiments such as this one is a good use of money? Why / why not?
3 Implementing global policies to reduce CO_2 emissions is often difficult and controversial. Why do you think this is still the case?

1 READING

Climate change 101

A Vocabulary preview

Complete the sentences with the words in the box.

> adaptation   attributable   cyclical   drought   fluctuate
> greenhouse gases   phenomenon   unprecedented

1. The severe _____ that plagued Kenya has driven up food prices.
2. Rising sea levels are a natural _____, yet the rate of increase is significantly affected by global warming.
3. Research suggests that our planet is warming at an _____ pace.
4. The state recently committed to a 40% reduction in _____ by 2030.
5. _____ to the adverse effects of climate change is key to the survival of our species.
6. Increased levels of CO_2 in the atmosphere are directly _____ to human activity.
7. _____ ice ages have only been observed for the past 2.5 million years.
8. Climate change deniers argue that temperatures naturally _____, willfully ignoring long-term increases.

B Before you read

Activating prior knowledge

In a group, discuss how each of the following is affected by climate change: oceans, polar regions, and weather patterns.

C Global reading

Using headings to predict content

> Before reading a text in detail, look quickly at the heading, subheadings, and any images to predict what the content might be. This can help you to decide whether to read a text or not, and which sections to focus in on.

1. Look at the headings, subheadings, and images in *Climate change 101*. Predict which section (1–7) will contain the information (a–g).

   a Historical examples of climate change occurring naturally ___
   b Data linking CO_2 emissions to increased temperatures ___
   c Data on rising sea levels and increased acidification ___
   d Evidence of glacial retreat ___
   e The predicted impact of an immediate emissions cap ___
   f Data on average global temperature increase ___
   g Examples of increased flooding and drought ___

2. Read *Climate change 101* and check your predictions in Exercise 1.

Climate change 101

READING 1

Multiple studies published in peer-reviewed journals show that 97% of scientists agree that the effects of climate change are due to human activity. Yet in a recent survey conducted by the PEW Research Center, less than 50% of U.S. adults agree with the scientific consensus. So is this half of the population justifiably skeptical or does the research support the experts? To help you decide for yourself, we've used the latest evidence to address the big questions.

1 Is there any evidence for global warming?

In short, yes. Since global temperature records began in the late 19th century, the planet's average surface temperature has risen by approximately 2.0° F (1.1° C), with 16 of the 17 hottest years on record occurring over the last 35 years. Eighty percent of this additional heat is absorbed by the world's oceans, the surface of which has increased in temperature by 0.13 degrees Fahrenheit per decade since 1901. (NASA, n.d.)

2 Hasn't the Earth's climate always fluctuated?

Yes. Changes in the Earth's climate are a natural and frequent phenomenon. Ice ages—driven by slow variations in the Earth's orbit that alter distribution of the sun's energy—have occurred, on average, every 100,000 years. These climatic events have led to mass extinction, the migration of populations, and dramatic changes in the landscape, so why is modern climate change such an issue? While ice ages are cyclical, the pace at which the planet has warmed since the end of the last ice age is unprecedented—making adaptation virtually impossible. According to the Royal Society, the increase in the Earth's temperature over the 7,000–18,000-year period since the end of the last ice age is approximately 4° C, 25% of which occurred in the last 200 years.

3 Is human activity the primary cause?

A blanket of greenhouse gases—carbon dioxide, water vapor, nitrous oxide, and methane—in the Earth's atmosphere absorb heat and warm the planet's surface, a natural phenomenon known as the greenhouse effect. Measurements of the atmosphere and air in ice indicate a 40% increase in CO_2 levels in the 200-year period to 2012 (The Royal Society and the U.S. National Academy of Sciences, 2014). This rapid increase is almost certainly a consequence of human activity. Over the last century, burning of finite resources such as coal and oil, deforestation for agriculture, and industrial expansion have all greatly increased the concentration of CO_2 in the Earth's atmosphere. Increased levels of other greenhouse gases are also directly attributable to human activity. The cultivation of domestic livestock and the expansion of landfills have increased levels of methane, while nitrous oxide is largely generated by soil cultivation. The bottom line is that while the greenhouse effect is a natural phenomenon, its expansion (and global warming by extension) is largely due to human activity.

4 How does climate change affect our oceans?

The Earth's oceans absorb about 80% of the additional heat generated by global warming. When water heats up, it expands, causing sea levels to rise. Over the past century, global sea levels have risen by 4 to 8 inches (10 to 20 centimeters), and approximately 50% of this increase is directly attributable to thermal expansion. As with the greenhouse effect, this is a natural phenomenon. However, recent data suggests that over the past 20 years, sea levels have risen by 0.13 inches (3.2 millimeters) a year—roughly twice the speed of the preceding 80 years. Such a rapid increase can have devastating consequences for coastal inhabitants such as erosion, flooding, and soil contamination. Not only are sea levels rising, but their chemical composition is also changing. Carbon dioxide is not only released into the Earth's atmosphere, but it is also dissolved into our oceans, causing higher levels of acidity. Since the early 1800s, ocean acidity has increased by around 25%, depressing the metabolic rates of some species, lowering the immune responses of others, destabilizing marine ecosystems, and causing the bleaching, and possibly the eventual death of, the world's coral reefs.

5 How have the polar ice caps been affected?

Data from NASA's Gravity Recovery and Climate Experiment (n.d.) show Greenland and Antarctica lost a combined 300 to 450 cubic kilometers of ice annually between 2002 and 2006. One hundred and eighteen billion metric tons of ice is lost from Antarctica alone each year. Over the past 20 years, Arctic sea ice has declined rapidly. Glaciers from the Andes to the Alps lose approximately 400 billion tons of ice every year. Events that typically happen in geologic time are happening in the human lifespan. The disappearance of Himalayan glaciers is forecast within the next two decades. Not only do global ice sheets help to counteract the greenhouse effect, but their disappearance is also a primary contributor to rising sea levels.

6 Can it be blamed for the rise in extreme weather events?

According to research conducted at the University of Illinois, a rise in sea level of 5–10 centimeters could double the frequency and intensity of coastal flooding, potentially having devastating effects on major global cities. In addition, rising temperatures have increased the amount of water vapor in the Earth's lower atmosphere, creating favorable conditions for more intense rain and snowstorms; both of which have been occurring with greater regularity in the U.S. over the past 50 years. Other extreme weather events, such as drought, are caused by changes in planetary waves—patterns of wind that encircle the northern hemisphere from the tropics to the poles. Under certain temperature conditions, movement of the wave can be halted, effectively prolonging periods of hot weather that may result in drought. However, while scientists have long suspected this event is a direct result of increased emissions of greenhouse gases, their relative infrequency make them difficult to evaluate reliably and we therefore cannot conclusively state that climate change is the cause.

7 Can we reverse the damage?

Unfortunately, no. Although the recent resolution reached in Paris is hugely significant, many claim it is too little, too late. Even if legislation were introduced to immediately stop the emission of greenhouse gases, the CO_2 that has already been absorbed by the atmosphere and oceans would take thousands of years to be reabsorbed by deep ocean sediments. Sea levels would continue to rise, ice caps would continue to melt, and extreme weather would occur at an increasingly devastating rate. The damage to our planet is irreparable. The only question is … can we adapt?

1 READING

Reading for specific information

D Close reading

Read *Climate change 101* again. Are these sentences *T* (True), *F* (False), or *NG* (Not Given)?

1 NASA data indicate that 2016 was the warmest year on record. ___
2 If the pattern of cyclical ice ages continues, the next glacial period will begin in 10,000 years' time. ___
3 Carbon emissions have increased significantly since humans learned to harness fossil fuels. ___
4 Rapid global population growth is the primary cause of global warming. ___
5 Carbon dioxide absorbed by our oceans has a direct negative impact on marine life. ___
6 Loss of the polar ice caps contributes to the expansion of the greenhouse effect. ___
7 There is evidence to suggest that changes in planetary waves result in a lack of rainfall. ___
8 An immediate ban on carbon emissions would reverse the effects of climate change. ___

E Critical thinking

Work with a partner. Discuss the questions.

1 How compelling do you find the evidence that human activity is the main cause of climate change? Explain your reasoning.
2 Is there any point changing our behavior if it will take thousands of years to reverse the damage caused by climate change? Why / why not?

Study skills — Planning your writing assignments spatially

It can sometimes be difficult to gain a sense of what the word limit means in terms of how much you will actually write.
- Work out roughly how many words you type on one page of A4 / letter size.
- Check the overall word limit for your assignment.
- Draw out in pencil how much space you will give to each section, item, or topic. How many words can you allocate to each section?

© Stella Cottrell (2013)

1 Read the essay prompt and answer the questions.

> **Global warming is one of the biggest threats to our environment. What problems are associated with global warming and how could they be tackled by individuals?**
> Word limit: 500 words

1 What are the key elements that must be discussed in the essay?
2 What topics might you cover in each paragraph?

2 Look at the information about essay extent and complete the task below.

> Five hundred words is approximately two sides of A4 / letter size typed in a 12-point font size with double spacing. Many tutors require double spacing to allow for their feedback.
> 1 Take two sheets of A4 / letter size.
> 2 Draw boxes for the amount of space you have for each topic you identified in Exercise 1.
> 3 Write an approximate word count in each box.

3 Work with a partner. Discuss the questions.

1 Does your planned content fit the word-count limit?
2 Have you covered the same topics as your partner?
3 Do you have similar word counts for each part?
4 How might you lose points for going over or under the word count?

2 READING

Thirstier than ever

A Vocabulary preview

Complete the sentences with the words in the box.

> exacerbate gallons modification particles
> purification scarcity stable viable

1. Securing a _____ supply of freshwater is one of the greatest challenges we face as a species.
2. Water _____ affects over 40% of the global population.
3. Improved _____ techniques could be key to solving the global freshwater crisis.
4. Critics argue that desalination simply isn't a _____ solution for most countries.
5. At 11,000 feet the aircraft releases _____ of silver iodide that help freeze existing water in the clouds.
6. It's estimated that the average hamburger takes 650 _____ of water to produce.
7. The report aims to assess the efficacy of current weather _____ techniques.
8. Arguably, the effects of climate change will further _____ the freshwater crisis.

B Before you read

Activating prior knowledge

With a partner, discuss how the following might relate to solving global water shortages: vegetarianism, salt water, clouds, and manufacturing.

C Global reading

Identifying main ideas

Read *Thirstier than ever*. Match the headings (a–f) to paragraphs (1–6).

a Wealthy regions can utilize the sea
b Functionality and feasibility of cloud seeding
c Lessening the impact of manufacturing
d Water consumption and scarcity
e The ramifications of not changing our current usage
f Altering our food consumption

Thirstier than ever

READING 2

[1]Water covers approximately 75% of the Earth's surface, yet only 3% of it is drinkable; the rest is salt water. Of the little that is fresh, a staggering 99% is inaccessible, buried deep beneath the world's glaciers. According to Kummu et al. (2010), roughly a third of the world's population is at risk from water scarcity, and population growth is only exacerbating the issue. Not only does our species need water to survive, we also rely heavily on it to water our crops and sustain our livestock—people typically drink around five liters of water per day, while agriculture accounts for the majority of global freshwater consumption. In some parts of the world, water scarcity severely limits food production capabilities. Coumou and Rahmstorf (2012) have also forecast that climate change will increase precipitation variability (i.e., the frequency of rain) raising the risk of flooding and drought that blight food production. So, what solutions are available to ensure a consistent and stable freshwater supply?

[2]The agricultural sector accounts for approximately 70% of global freshwater consumption—double that of industrial and domestic use combined. While more efficient irrigation practices could reduce this volume by an estimated 30–70%, cutting consumption of animal products for less water-intensive crops would also have a perhaps unexpectedly significant impact. Some people advocate a switch to a vegetarian or vegan diet on the basis that the production of meat is much more water intensive than the production of grains and vegetables. Mekonnen and Hoekstra (2012) estimated that on average, 10,412 liters of water are required for the production of one kilo of lamb. Goat requires around 5,521 liters per kilo, poultry 4,325 liters per kilo, and beef approximately 15,400 liters per kilo. The variations in water consumption are largely due to the animal feed required. Different animals are much more water intensive to produce and thus their water footprint is higher. When we compare these meats to a range of vegetables we can see that, in general, cultivation of vegetables is far less water intensive—bananas require approximately 790 liters per kilo, cabbage 237 liters per kilo, and tomatoes a mere 214 liters per kilo. Based on this evidence, it is clear that a switch to a vegetarian or even vegan diet would dramatically reduce the amount of water consumed by agriculture. However, in virtually every country apart from India, the percentage of vegetarians equates to less than 10% of the total population. This casts some doubt as to whether this solution could work as there would need to be huge cultural shifts in dietary attitude.

[3]In areas regularly stricken by water shortages, but wealthy enough to address the issue, desalination—the removal of salt from seawater—offers a viable solution. The most common method of desalination is reverse osmosis. Salt water is forced through an ultrathin, semi-permeable membrane, trapping salt molecules and other toxins on one side. The result is fresh, drinkable water, yet the sheer volume of pressure required makes it an energy-intensive process. In addition, despite claims to the contrary, desalination is fairly inefficient. According to the International Desalination Association, 18,426 desalination plants produced a mere 86.8 million cubic meters of water per day in June 2015; only enough water to meet the needs of 1% of the world's population. Desalinated water also comes at a high price. At $3 per cubic meter, it costs around double that of traditional purification methods such as sedimentation. However, according to

2 READING

Professor Raphael Semiat, the costs vary greatly depending on location (Johnston, C., 2015). For example, it can be far more expensive and energy-intensive to pump freshwater 200 kilometers, than it would be to desalinate and use water on the coast. While desalination is arguably a necessary solution in some countries, in others, such as northern Europe it would make much more sense to focus on reducing the volume of wastewater. As droughts are rarely an issue in these regions, such an expensive and energy-intensive method of water purification makes little sense.

[4]Another new, and perhaps more controversial, solution to the freshwater crisis is a form of weather-modification known as cloud seeding; a technique that aims to boost rainfall by stimulating production of ice crystals in clouds. Essentially, particles of potassium chloride, sodium chloride, or silver iodide are fired into passing clouds where they attract existing water vapor. The vapor bonds with the chemical particles to form ice crystals, which increase in size until they are too heavy to remain suspended and fall, often melting on the way to form rain. Cloud seeding can also be used to dissipate clouds—in fact, the technique was famously employed by the Chinese government during the 2008 Beijing Olympics to prevent rainfall during the opening ceremony.

Proponents argue that cloud seeding offers an inexpensive and energy-efficient alternative to desalination. Chinese officials claim to have triggered artificial snowstorms in drought-stricken regions of northern China, and in the U.A.E., Dr. Habib of the National Center of Meteorology and Seismology recently argued that studies suggest rain enhancement programs could increase rainfall by 10–30% (Pennington, 2017).

However, while research into cloud seeding is ongoing, the technique has garnered its fair share of criticism. In fact, the United States National Academy of Sciences (2003) stated that 30 years of research showed no convincing evidence that it worked. This is primarily because you cannot use the technique to actually generate clouds and it is impossible to conclusively demonstrate that the clouds that have been treated wouldn't have produced rainfall anyway. Essentially, you cannot extract moisture from the air if it isn't there to begin with, meaning the technique simply isn't viable on cloudless days or during periods of drought.

[5]One final solution is to reduce water consumption in the manufacturing sector. In the U.S., just under 5% of freshwater is used in the production of consumer goods, usually as a coolant or cleaning agent. This may sound like a fairly insignificant percentage, but the volume of water it equates to is staggering—for example, the United States Environmental Protection Agency estimates that it takes 39,090 gallons of water to manufacture a single car. One way to reduce consumption is to seek alternative sterilization methods such as carbon dioxide cleaning, which uses CO_2 recycled from other industries in place of water to allow for "dry cleaning in an eco-friendly manner" (Wickstrom, 2015). While CO_2 cleaning has been used for decades in the aerospace and automotive industries, it has unfortunately not been rolled out to the manufacturing sector as a whole. Another way to reduce the industrial water footprint is to recycle more. It's estimated that recycling just one newspaper saves around 3.5 gallons of water. Buying second-hand clothes would also help because, for example, it takes over 100 gallons of water to produce a single cotton T-shirt.

[6]Global water consumption has reached unsustainable levels. If we do not modify our behavior, billions of people will be plagued by water scarcity. To put it simply, freshwater shortages are likely to cause the next great global crisis. In the words of Jean Chrétien, former Canadian prime minister and co-chair of the InterAction Council, "The future political impact of water scarcity may be devastating … using water the way we have in the past simply will not sustain humanity in future."

REFERENCES:

Coumou, D. and Rahmstorfy, S. (2012). A decade of weather extremes. *Nature Climate Change*. 2, 491-496

Kummu, M. et al. (2010). Is physical water scarcity a new phenomenon? Global assessment of water shortage over the last two millennia. *Environmental Research Letters*. 5(3)

International Desalination Association (2017). *Desalination by the Numbers*. Available: http://idadesal.org/desalination-101/desalination-by-the-numbers/ [Accessed: 20th October 2017]

Johnson, C. (2015). Desalination: the quest to quench the world's thirst for water. *Guardian* [Online] Available: https://www.theguardian.com/technology/2015/may/27/desalination-quest-quench-worlds-thirst-water [Accessed: 20th October 2017]

Mekonnen, M.M. and Hoekstra, A. Y. (2012). A Global Assessment of the Water Footprint of Farm Animal Products. *Ecosystems*. 15(3), 401-415

Pennington, R. (2017). Cloud seeding plays its part. *The National*. Available: https://www.thenational.ae/uae/environment/cloud-seeding-plays-its-part-1.34639 [Accessed: 20th October 2017]

The Guardian [Online] (2016). *How much water is needed to produce food and how much do we waste?* Available: https://www.theguardian.com/news/datablog/2013/jan/10/how-much-water-food-production-waste [Accessed: 20th October 2017]

The National Academies of Sciences, Engineering, and Medicine (2003). *U.S. Should Pursue Additional Research on Weather Modification*. Available: http://www8.nationalacademies.org/onpinews/newsitem.aspx?RecordID=10829 [Accessed: 20th October 2017]

The U.S. Geological Survey (2017). *Industrial water use*. Available: https://water.usgs.gov/edu/wuin.html [Accessed: 20th October 2017]

The U.S. Environmental Protection Agency (2016). *Water Trivia Facts*. Available: https://www3.epa.gov/safewater/kids/water_trivia_facts.html#_ednref12 [Accessed: 20th October 2017]

Wikstrom, J. (2015). 6 Solution to the Water Shortage Crisis. *Triple Pundit*. Available: http://www.triplepundit.com/2015/06/innovative-solutions-water-shortage-crisis/ [Accessed: 20th October 2017]

D Close reading

> Academic writers commonly cite information to exemplify an argument. Often just before or after the source, the author will include a line of evaluative commentary that indicates their stance on the broader topic being discussed.
>
> Identifying this commentary will help you to evaluate the strength of the argument and identify the personal opinion of the author.

Identifying commentary on evidence

1 Scan *Thirstier than ever.* Identify the source(s) used to support the topics (1–5).

1 The impact of reducing the consumption of animal products _____

2 Energy costs of desalination _____

3 The history of research into cloud seeding _____

4 Alternative cleaning methods in manufacturing _____

5 The necessity for change in habits _____

2 Read the text again. Match the opinions (a–e) to the evidence in Exercise 1.

a This method might be inefficient in some areas, but it is viable along the coast. ___

b This solution has yet to be adopted by the entire sector. ___

c Although this is a viable solution, it seems unlikely that it will appeal to the masses. ___

d This will be the cause of a major humanitarian disaster. ___

e There isn't enough evidence to support the efficacy of this solution. ___

E Critical thinking

Work with a partner. Discuss the questions.

1 Rank the methods in the text from the most to the least effective in dealing with water shortages. Compare your order with a partner.

2 Do you think personal solutions, such as changing your diet, are effective or should governments and companies solve the problem?

VOCABULARY

Vocabulary development

Verb and noun collocations

1 Match the collocations in bold with the correct definitions.

1 **accelerate change**
2 **address the issue**
3 **allocate resources**
4 **assess the impact**
5 **cast doubt**
6 **consider the role**
7 **reduce demand**
8 **slow the decline**

a to try to deal with a problem
b to give money, time, or energy to something
c to reduce the speed at which something changes or falls
d to think about the influence something has
e to increase the speed at which something becomes different
f to make something seem less certain, good, or real
g to lower the amount desired or used
h to make a judgment about the effect of something

2 Complete the questions with collocations from Exercise 1. Change the form if necessary.

1 To what extent do you think _____ for animal products could help lessen the effects of climate change?
2 What do you think is the simplest way to _____ of marine species caused by ocean acidification?
3 What factors make it difficult to _____ of human activity on climate change?
4 How might social media help _____ a _____ in people's water consumption habits?
5 Would you be prepared to change your diet _____ it plays in the freshwater crisis? Why / why not?
6 Do you think climate deniers are right to _____ on the evidence for climate change? Why / why not?
7 How could governments better _____ to tackle climate change?
8 Whose responsibility is it to _____ of high volumes of water consumption in manufacturing?

3 Work with a partner. Discuss the questions in Exercise 2.

Academic words

VOCABULARY

1 Complete the definitions with the words in the box.

advocate equate eventual finite intensity legislation ongoing resolution

1 _____ (adj) happening at the end of a process or period of time
2 _____ (adj) continuing to happen, exist, or develop
3 _____ (n) strength
4 _____ (v) to publicly support a policy or way of doing things
5 _____ (n) a law, or a set of laws
6 _____ (n) an agreement reached by a council or committee
7 _____ (v) to consider something to be the same as something else
8 _____ (adj) limited in size or extent

2 Complete the text with words from Exercise 1. Change the form if necessary.

Some people [1] _____ a switch to a vegetarian diet as an [2] _____ way of reducing their use of water. The principle is based on the idea that the [3] _____ of water usage is much lower when growing crops. Growing one kilo of meat roughly [4] _____ to the same water usage as five kilos of most vegetables. The problem is that as economies become more developed, our reliance on meat tends to increase. People rarely consider the [5] _____ product they consume and the water or energy required to produce it. One solution is to introduce [6] _____ that limits the amount of meat farmers can produce. This [7] _____ would be controversial as it would increase the cost of meat and worsen the diets of many poor people. However, the resources on our planet are [8] _____ and we need to conserve them.

3 In groups, discuss the extent to which you agree with the opinions expressed in Exercise 2. Explain your reasoning.

CRITICAL THINKING

Critical thinking

> **Evaluating supporting data: 2**
>
> Once you've established that supporting data hasn't been manipulated (see page 38), it's important to question whether any significant information has been omitted that would influence your evaluation of the argument. For example:
>
> *Research conducted at Pembrook State suggests that desalination plants could provide up to 35% of the U.A.E.'s freshwater needs.*
>
> While this may sound superficially impressive, it also raises a number of important questions such as:
>
> - What were the research parameters?
> - How many plants would be needed to provide this amount of water?
> - As "up to" implies a maximum estimate, what is the lowest estimate?
>
> Identifying what you don't know can help you evaluate the significance of the data presented.

1 Read the argument and answer the questions.

> Cloud seeding has proven to be a successful technique for generating rainfall in five different countries and is therefore one of the best solutions for dealing with drought.

   1 What is the main argument, and what data is used to support it?
   2 What other information would help you to evaluate the significance of the data?

2 Work with a partner. Discuss what data might strengthen the arguments and where it could be sourced.

   1 Carbon emissions have risen since the Industrial Revolution, clearly signifying a link between humans and climate change.
   2 Countries that desalinate water use up to five times higher the level of energy consumption than those that use other methods.
   3 A company producing new solar panels has data from a dozen countries to show that their panels are now the most efficient way of producing renewable energy.

3 Discuss these questions in a group.

   1 Outside of academic writing, when else is it important to evaluate the significance of data used to support a claim?
   2 Is it ever in the company's best interest to omit information from the data they present? Why / why not?

Writing model

WRITING

You are going to learn about verb patterns and ways to comment on sources. You are then going to use these to write a problem-and-solution essay on global warming.

A Analyze

Put these ideas into the correct column. Then add four more ideas of your own.

> dietary changes   focus on renewable energy   food shortages
> recycling   rising sea levels   unpredictable weather

Problems	Solutions

B Model

1 Read the essay prompt and an extract from the answer. Which of the ideas from Exercise 1 are covered?

> *Global warming is one of the biggest threats to our environment. What problems are associated with global warming and how could they be tackled on an individual level?*
>
> Intermittent and regional food shortages have been an ongoing problem for centuries; however, they could be greatly exacerbated by two factors unless we address the issue. According to the World Bank (2016), the world needs to produce at least 50% more food to feed nine billion people by 2050. But climate change could cut crop yields by more than 25%. Clearly, reducing demand could both secure the future of our food supply and significantly slow the decline to the damage we are causing in terms of global warming.
>
> While governments can come together to allocate resources more efficiently or to improve legislation, there are a number of changes individuals can make. Each person can assess the impact of his or her own consumption habits. For example, if we consider the role of animal products in the food change, simply reducing the amount of meat and dairy we consume would increase the overall food supply and reduce the carbon footprint while still meeting our dietary requirements. Some people cast doubt on the willingness of individuals to embrace such a change, however, the positive effects could equate to millions more tons of food being produced and water saved.

2 Work with a partner. Underline the citation used in the essay and discuss the questions.

1 Does the writer agree with the citation?
2 Does the writer use cautious or assertive language?
3 Do you agree with the writer of the essay?

Grammar

> ### Verb patterns
> Two common verb patterns used in academic English are:
>
> **verb + preposition + gerund**
>
> *It **works by adding** particles to the cloud that attract water vapor.*
>
> Verbs that usually follow this pattern include *admit to, believe in, benefit from, care about, concentrate on, cope with, decide against, depend on, disagree with,* and *object to.*
>
> **verb + object +** *to* **+ base form**
>
> *Chinese officials claim to have **used the technique to trigger** snowstorms in arid northern regions.*
>
> Verbs that usually follow this pattern include *advise, allow, ask, encourage, expect, order, permit, persuade, remind,* and *warn.*

1 Choose the correct form of the verbs to complete the sentences.

1 It's essential that we allocate resources **to support / supporting** disaster victims.
2 Limited people may be willing to make a change, but the whole of society will benefit from **make / making** these alterations.
3 In general, governments don't try to persuade people **to make / making** significant lifestyle changes.
4 Due to a lack of empirical data, the government decided against **building / build** the proposed desalination plants.
5 The company rules **don't permit / isn't permitting** employees to take their car to work.
6 Controversially, the government decided against **close / closing** the nuclear power plant.

2 Complete the sentences with the correct form of the words in parentheses. Add prepositions where necessary.

1 It's essential that we allocate _____ (resources / support) disaster victims.
2 The public will simply have to adjust _____ (pay) higher taxes.
3 Governments should concentrate _____ (encourage) more sustainable lifestyles.
4 Due to the shortage, governments have warned _____ (people / waste) water supplies.
5 Some countries permit _____ (companies / pay) less tax if they meet certain environmental standards.

Writing skill

WRITING

Commenting on sources

When you include a source in your work, you should always comment on it. You need to say how the source relates to the point you are trying to make. You can use a mixture of cautious and assertive language, but you should only use more assertive phrases when the quotation shows something clearly. For example:

Based on this evidence, **it is clear that** *a switch to a vegetarian or even vegan diet* **would dramatically reduce** *the amount of water used.*

It is also important to show the limitations of something:

However, *in* **virtually every** *country, apart from India, the percentage of vegetarians equates to under 10% of the total population.* **This casts some doubt as to whether** *this solution could work as there would need to be huge cultural shifts in the attitude to diets.*

1 Complete the table with the phrases in the box.

could mean   it is certain that   this clearly indicates
which implies   which may suggest   which means

Cautious	Assertive

2 Work with a partner. Add three more phrases to each column.

3 Underline the comment in each extract. Then add the cautious and assertive language to the table in Exercise 1.

1 There is increasing scientific evidence that the process of climate change is accelerating (Hedger, 2017). This is likely to result in a higher risk of flooding and droughts across different regions.

2 According to the National Oceanic and Atmospheric Administration (NOAA) and the World Weather Attribution Group (2016), climate change has increased the chances of flooding in areas such as Louisiana by up to 40%. While arguably only a contributory factor, it is clear that it is a significant one.

4 Imagine you want to include the following citation in the essay for this unit. Comment on the citation.

Global warming could slow economic growth and reduce worldwide individual wealth levels by 23% in 2100 (Burke, 2015).

WRITING

Writing task

You are going to write an essay in response to the following:
"Global warming is one of the biggest threats to our environment. What problems are associated with global warming and how could they be tackled at a national level?"

Brainstorm

Complete the brainstorm below.

Problems	Solutions

Plan

Find at least two sources to integrate into your essay.

What comment would you make on the sources?

Write

Use your brainstorm and plan to write your essay. Remember to use verb patterns as appropriate and to comment on your sources. Your essay should be between 250–300 words long.

Share

Exchange your essay with a partner. Use the checklist on page 189 to help you provide feedback to your partner.

Rewrite and edit

Consider your partner's comments and write your final draft. Think about:

- whether you answered the question clearly
- whether you used verb patterns appropriately
- whether you commented on your sources appropriately.

Review

Wordlist

Vocabulary preview

adaptation (n) *	exacerbate (v)	modification (n) *	scarcity (n)
attributable (adj)	fluctuate (v)	particle (n) **	stable (adj) **
cyclical (adj)	gallon (n) **	phenomenon (n) **	unprecedented (adj)
drought (n)	greenhouse gas (n)	purification (n)	viable (adj) *

Vocabulary development

accelerate change (phr)	allocate resources (phr)	cast doubt (phr)	reduce demand (phr)
address the issue (phr)	assess the impact (phr)	consider the role (phr)	slow the decline (phr)

Academic words

advocate (v) *	eventual (adj) *	intensity (n)	ongoing (adj)
equate (v)	finite (adj)	legislation (n) ***	resolution (n) *

Academic words review

Complete the sentences using the correct form of the words in the box.

| advocate | initiate | legislation | persist | resolution |

1. Management chose to _____ with its policy changes despite serious opposition from the staff.
2. A safety training program was _____ as a result of the accident at the factory in which four workers died.
3. Environmentalists have long _____ a ban on diesel and gasoline-fueled vehicles. Governments across Europe are finally taking action.
4. In the U.S., all _____ must have the approval of both the House of Representatives and Congress before it is signed by the president.
5. Although the UN passed a _____ on the conflict, the two sides have not agreed to a ceasefire.

Unit review

Reading 1	I can use headings to understand the main ideas.
Reading 2	I can identify commentary on evidence.
Study skill	I can plan my assignments spatially.
Vocabulary	I can use verb and noun collocations.
Grammar	I can use different verb patterns.
Writing	I can comment on my sources.

10 CONFLICT

Discussion point

Discuss with a partner.

1. Which of the eight causes would you say poses the greatest risk to the stability of a team?
2. What do you think "differing perceptions" means, and how would it affect the workplace?
3. Are there any other sources of conflict that aren't mentioned in the infographic?

8 causes of workplace conflict

1. Conflicting styles
2. Differing perceptions
3. Incompatible goals
4. Competing pressures
5. Opposing roles
6. Different personal beliefs
7. Unpredictable policies
8. Conflicting resources

VIDEO
ESCAPE ROOMS

Before you watch

Match the words in bold with the correct definitions.

1. **allotted** (adj)
2. **intellect** (n)
3. **opt** (v)
4. **pool** (v)
5. **standpoint** (n)

a. choose
b. share something such as ideas or knowledge with a group of people in order to work together more effectively
c. given, available
d. a person's ability to understand difficult or complicated ideas
e. a way of considering something, a perspective

UNIT AIMS	**READING 1** Identifying references	**VOCABULARY** Adverbs of stance
	READING 2 Preparing for a seminar	**GRAMMAR** Conjunctions
	STUDY SKILL Using material of suitable quality and content	**WRITING** Reference lists

Colleagues disagree about which way to turn.

While you watch

Watch the video and choose *T* (True) or *F* (False).

1 Escape room experiences have long been popular in the U.S. as a teambuilding activity.   T / F
2 The escape room is a form of problem solving activity.   T / F
3 The escape room experience works best if each individual concentrates on a different puzzle.   T / F
4 The majority of participants manage to escape the room within the allotted time.   T / F

After you watch

Work in a group. Discuss the questions.

1 What personal attributes do you think would be brought out of participants during an escape room experience?
2 Do you think teambuilding events are a worthwhile use of both the employee's and the company's time and money? Why / why not?
3 To what extent are positive working relationships more important than other factors in the overall profitability of a business?

1 READING

Groupthink

A Vocabulary preview

Complete the sentences with words in the box.

> cohesive   consensus   detrimental   hinder
> inferior   peer pressure   tactic   theoretical

1. Critics argue that groupthink is purely _____ and doesn't reflect the realities of the modern workplace.
2. Despite three days of open discussion, the group was unable to reach an acceptable _____.
3. Perhaps counter intuitively, conflict avoidance may actually _____ the progress of a group.
4. _____ discourages individuals from voicing their concerns.
5. A _____ team relies on open channels of communication throughout a project.
6. Attacking the individual, rather than their argument is a _____ employed to shut down an argument.
7. Frequent managerial intervention can be _____ to productivity.
8. Individuals cannot be successful if they consider themselves _____ to their colleagues.

B Before you read

Activating prior knowledge

Discuss these questions in a group.

1. What factors have a negative influence on a group's ability to make decisions?
2. How might a lack of conflict negatively affect a group?

C Global reading

Predicting content

1. Scan *Groupthink* and use the topic sentences to predict the content of each paragraph. Then compare your ideas with a partner.

   paragraph 1   *Why and how people try to avoid conflict*
   paragraph 2   _____
   paragraph 3   _____
   paragraph 4   _____
   paragraph 5   _____
   paragraph 6   _____
   paragraph 7   _____

2. Read the text in full and check your predictions.

Groupthink

[1]Many people consciously try to avoid conflict. Some swallow their feelings, smiling through situations that cause them pain or distress. Others steer conversation away from contentious issues, while others go out of their way to avoid discussing them in the first place. Turner and Weed (1983) described these kinds of people as "concealers," arguing that they're unwilling to take risks and say nothing as a result. All of these behaviors can lay the foundations for a psychological phenomenon defined by William H. Whyte Jr. in 1952 as "groupthink"—a state that he argues has a detrimental effect on a group's ability to make decisions.

[2]Although the term was coined by Whyte, the initial research into groupthink was pioneered by the Yale psychologist, Irving Janis. Janis stated that groupthink occurs when "concurrence-seeking becomes so dominant in a cohesive ingroup that it tends to override realistic appraisal of alternative courses of action" (Janis, 1971). Or, to put it another way, groups often become so obsessed with maintaining a harmonious relationship that they lose the ability to objectively evaluate alternative viewpoints. Individuals feel pressured to conform to the views of their peers, and this hinders the group's ability to make informed choices. To a certain extent, the better the relationships between the individual members are, the more likely the group is to make an irrational decision.

[3]In his 1972 publication, *Victims of Groupthink*, Janis prescribed three main causes of the phenomenon. As already mentioned, a strong cohesiveness can lead to groupthink. When groupthink occurs, it is as a result of conflict avoidance in favor of maintaining harmony. Groups that are not cohesive can make poor decisions, but this is different from decisions made as a consequence of groupthink. A lack of willingness to challenge the views of others will almost certainly lead to poor decision-making, and this is further exacerbated by structural issues such as isolation from other groups. Closed leadership styles—when decisions are dictated by management, not shaped by the group as a whole—also hinder the productivity of a team. High-stakes situations also often lead to groupthink because stress and anxiety are not conducive to rational thought. Decisions are made with very little discussion or disagreement because individuals are wary of the consequences of upsetting the status quo.

[4]When groupthink occurs, various behaviors become more dominant. For example, even when presented with evidence that contradicts their views or decisions, the group persuades themselves of the validity of their original course of action. Peer pressure also plays an increasingly significant role in the group dynamic. Anyone who expresses views contrary to the group consensus will be put under enormous pressure to conform. Successful, early decisions may also lead to complacency, and individuals will feel even less inclined to voice concerns. At this point, the group becomes overconfident and even hostile towards individuals or teams outside their sphere of influence. The general perception of other teams is that they are inferior and that as a result, any opinions they hold can easily be discredited.

[5]Arguably, groupthink can be avoided with effective planning of the decision-making process. An environment needs to be created in which team members feel able to challenge decisions or opinions without fear of reprisal. The group also needs to be objective in its assessment of alternatives and the risks that each carries, before making a decision. Furthermore, they should be flexible enough to reconsider the alternatives should information come to light that challenges the validity of their original decision. So what measures can be taken to avoid groupthink? According to Janis (1971), one method is to create the role of "critical evaluator" within the group. This person essentially plays the role of devil's advocate, raising objections or doubts at all points during the decision-making process. The role of the leader is also key, as rather than taking a dominant role, he or she should aim to attend fewer meetings so that the group feels free to work how it wants without fear of judgement. The leader should also, if resources allow, set up several independent groups working on the same problem because this will allow for varying perspectives to emerge. Furthermore, outside experts should be frequently consulted so the group can gain a neutral perspective on their work.

[6]Because it is difficult to artificially replicate an environment conducive to this naturally occurring phenomenon, groupthink is notoriously challenging to verify under laboratory conditions. As a result, there is little empirical data to support the concept. Park (1990) conducted a literature review of studies into groupthink and found no evidence for the claim that cohesiveness and leadership style lead to groupthink. However, when testing individual variables, some support has been found. For instance, Erdem (2003) found that high degrees of trust can lead to groupthink, and others have pointed to the concept's relationship with other psychological theories as support for its validity. Although not empirical studies, many case studies seem to have found evidence of the groupthink phenomenon. Dimitroff et al. (2005) found symptoms of groupthink in both the *Challenger* and *Columbia* space crashes. Scharff (2005) suggested that groupthink helped to explain some of the fraudulent behavior that appeared in the company Worldcom. Many others examples from decisions in war to company strategy seem to indicate the existence of groupthink.

[7]Many critics of groupthink would actually like to modify, rather than dismiss, the concept entirely. Although laboratory research is limited, there are many case studies where it appears groupthink played a role in poor decision-making. Despite the concept having limited theoretical support, it remains one of the most well-known theories in management and psychology. The fundamental question is whether groupthink is a myth or whether further research could actually validate the concept.

1 READING

Identifying reference functions

D Close reading

> Citations in academic texts serve three main functions:
>
> 1 **To support or refute a claim or argument**
>
>   *Murphy et al. claim that groupthink is a well-documented phenomenon, yet this isn't borne out by the research. "There simply isn't ample empirical data to support the idea." (Roberts, 2016)*
>
> 2 **To provide definitions of key terms**
>
>   *Lacey (2014) defines groupthink as "making group decisions often associated with unchallenged poor-quality decision-making."*
>
> 3 **To summarize theories and hypotheses**
>
>   *In her 1975 publication,* The Dangers of Working Together, *Young describes three stages of group development. The first, "Foundation," is characterized by…*

1 Read *Groupthink* again and match sources to the following statements.

  1 There is insufficient data to support the claim that group cohesion and closed leadership styles lead to groupthink. _____

  2 There is evidence to suggest that high levels of trust within a team can result in groupthink. _____

  3 A "critical evaluator" can help teams avoid groupthink by taking opposing views throughout the process. _____

  4 Broadly speaking, the three main causes of groupthink are high group cohesiveness, structural faults, and stressful situational contexts. _____

  5 It is claimed that groupthink played a role in multiple incidents in the space industry. _____

  6 Groupthink occurs when a team is so intent on maintaining unity that it fails to objectively assess alternative ideas. _____

  7 There is evidence to connect groupthink to criminal behavior. _____

  8 Those that avoid conflict and are unwilling to take risks are defined as "concealers." _____

2 Match the sources in Exercise 1 to a function from the *Identifying reference functions* box.

E Critical thinking

In a group, discuss why theories like groupthink remain so popular despite a lack of empirical data to support them.

Study skills — Using material of suitable quality and content

Only a small proportion of the vast amount of information available in print and online will be suitable for academic assignments. To help you identify good quality sources, look for:
- where they are published (e.g., in a reputable series, a peer-reviewed journal, etc.)
- the number and quality of the references they make to experts in the field
- use of original source material and data
- clear references and details of source materials.

© Stella Cottrell (2013)

1. Work with a partner. Make a list of questions under the headings that would help you to evaluate a potential resource.

   1. Currency   *When was the information published or posted?*
   2. Relevance _____
   3. Authority _____
   4. Accuracy   _____
   5. Purpose   _____

2. List the potential advantages and disadvantages of the following sources.

	Advantages	Disadvantages
Academic books		
Academic journals		
Blogs		
Newspapers		

3. In a group, discuss where else you could source information for academic writing and the potential advantages and disadvantages of each.

2 READING

Successful teams and conflict

A Vocabulary preview

Complete the sentences with the words in the box.

> assertive   collaborate   confrontation   impatience
> intolerance   leadership   mediate   optimum

1 A neutral third party is often required to _____ potentially confrontational discussion.
2 Arguably, _____ should be seen as a virtue if it drives productivity.
3 Despite claims that modern society is more accepting of other people's beliefs, _____ is still rife in the workplace.
4 Applications such as Google Docs make it easier to _____ on large-scale projects.
5 It's important to be _____, but a good manager trusts his or her team and doesn't try to control everything.
6 I much prefer her _____ style—she's always willing to take other people's ideas on board.
7 Dr. Habib further claims that _____ is a necessary evil in the modern workplace.
8 It is impossible for a team to keep achieving _____ performance without occasional conflict.

B Before you read

Activating prior knowledge

Discuss these questions with a partner.

1 To what extent do you agree that conflict is necessary in the workplace? Explain your reasoning.
2 What is the most efficient way to manage conflict? Is there only one way?

C Global reading

Identifying main ideas

Read *Successful teams and conflict*. Complete the article with the headings (a–e).

a Balancing the needs of the individual ___
b Adapting to context ___
c Utilizing conflict to reach our full potential ___
d Workplace conflict; a necessary evil? ___
e The role of conflict in team development ___

176   UNIT 10   CONFLICT

READING 2

1

We've all been there. The boardroom falls silent as two of its occupants lock horns. Some of the onlookers revel in the conflict, silently watching it unfold. Others try to pacify and mediate. Others still, strategically take sides. Although conflict in the workplace has traditionally been seen as detrimental, some modern theorists claim it is essential to productivity. An ugly, but necessary obstacle on the path to optimum performance. So, at what stage in a team's development might conflict arise and how can it be successfully navigated?

2

One of the first academics to see conflict as a necessary and inevitable part of a team's development was the psychologist, Bruce Tuckman. In his 1965 publication, *Developmental Sequence in Small Groups*, Tuckman proposed a four-stage theory of team development. The model explains the maturity, development, relationships, and performance of a group. The four stages are:

FORMING

At this stage, the group is created and learns about the opportunities and challenges available. They agree on goals and discuss how to tackle any issues present. One challenge at this stage is the fact that each team member will still largely be operating as an individual and the predominant behavior is polite and courteous, meaning people refrain from conflict. Leaders tend to play a dominant role at this stage, offering guidance and direction.

STORMING

At this stage, people start to push against any of the established boundaries and begin to form strong opinions about the other personalities and characters in the group. When people are perceived as not pulling their weight or attempting to dominate the group, then others will push back. If disagreements and conflicts of personality are not resolved at this stage, some teams may never move on, or will quickly re-enter this phase as disputes arise. Intolerance and impatience can be high. Managers frequently need to intervene in order to resolve issues.

NORMING

If a group is able to move beyond the storming stage, then agreement and consensus evolves. Leaders can take more of a facilitative role, rather than acting as autocratic leaders, as people become comfortable with their colleagues and have a much clearer appreciation of their roles and responsibilities. Teams are committed and unified towards a common goal and strive to accommodate each other's needs.

PERFORMING

The team now has a shared vision that does not require the intervention of a leader. They work in a largely autonomous manner and generally want to outperform the goals set during the group's inception. Conflict is easily resolved and the members now look to each other, rather than leadership, for help and support.

In 1977, Tuckman revised his theory to include a fifth stage:

ADJOURNING

This final stage reflects the status of a group after it has disbanded. If a strong team was formed initially, then the break-up stage can leave people feeling vulnerable and insecure about the change. A great deal of empathy is often required from management at this stage.

3

Successfully navigating the "storming" stage of Tuckman's model relies, in part, on the ability to recognize sources of conflict. A lack of shared goals or the perception of different priorities is a common cause of conflict, as are personality clashes. Significant differences in working styles, conflicting methods of communication, and differing expectations of individual output can all contribute to a hostile working environment. People often value different things or face a scarcity of resources that makes it hard to collaborate. When individuals feel that they have to compete with other team members for a share of a limited budget, it is inevitable that conflict will occur.

2 READING

4

So if conflict of varying degrees is highly likely, what's the best way to resolve the issues that arise? Given the diverse sources of conflict, it is perhaps unsurprising that successful teams are able to adapt their reactions to suit a range of contexts. According to Thomas and Kilmann, in conflict situations, an individual's behavior can be broadly described along two dimensions; assertiveness (i.e., the extent to which the individual tries to satisfy his or her own need) and cooperativeness (i.e., the extent to which the individual attempts to satisfy the needs of his or her competitor). These two basic dimensions can then be used to define five conflict management styles:

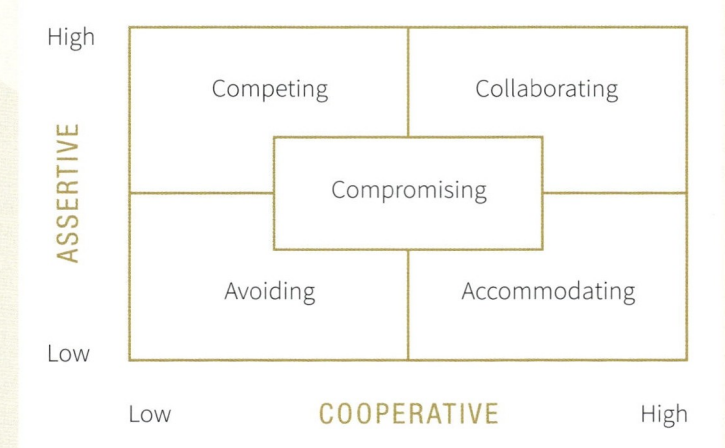

(Diagram: A 2x2 grid with ASSERTIVE on the vertical axis (Low to High) and COOPERATIVE on the horizontal axis (Low to High). Quadrants: Competing (high assertive, low cooperative), Collaborating (high assertive, high cooperative), Avoiding (low assertive, low cooperative), Accommodating (low assertive, high cooperative). Compromising is in the center.)

ACCOMMODATING

Individuals show a high degree of cooperation, often to the detriment of their own objectives. It may involve yielding to the view of someone else, even when you disagree with them. This style works well when the other person has more expertise and/or a better solution, and can also strengthen long-term relationships.

AVOIDING

Here the individual neither addresses their own concerns, nor helps others resolve theirs. Rather than confront issues head on they actively avoid them, often by diplomatically moving to another topic, postponing discussion, or retreating from discussion altogether. For minor issues this is a good way to minimize conflict and is also effective when a situation is emotionally charged or tense. However, in the long-term, this strategy can lead to conflict and failure.

COLLABORATING

Here people mutually try to achieve both sets of goals through consultation, which can be effective in complex situations. However, it requires a lot of trust, time, and effort to reach a consensus that accommodates all ideas and perspectives.

COMPETING

Individuals aggressively pursue their own interests at the expense of those around them, subsequently making little to no attempt to cooperate. Often this approach does not work well and leads to the greatest amount of conflict. However, when decisive action is needed, for example, in times of emergency, this can be an effective way to resolve conflict.

COMPROMISING

This mode presents a happy medium. Both parties aim to find a mutually acceptable solution to the issue at hand. This might mean accepting views that you don't agree with in order to have some of your own accommodated. This style could work when goals are of equal importance, but largely it leads to neither goal being reached effectively.

5

Given the diffuse sources of conflict, a successful team must learn to adapt both its working and management styles in order to optimize performance, regardless of individual beliefs and preferences. In other words, teams that are unable to accommodate and harness conflict may never achieve their full potential. However you choose to address conflict in the workplace, one thing is clear; it is an essential part of a team's development, and until we view it as such, we will consistently underperform.

D Close reading

> Prior to taking part in a seminar, you will often be expected to complete reading. You may have a formal task, such as a mini-presentation, to perform. However, more often you will simply be expected to discuss various issues around a topic. Practicing discussing these with a partner first can help to give you confidence for the seminar.

READING 2

Preparing for a seminar

1 Read paragraph 2 of *Successful teams and conflict* again. Match the stage headings (1–5) to the summary sentences (a–e).

   1 Forming ___
   2 Storming ___
   3 Norming ___
   4 Performing ___
   5 Adjourning ___

   a As team members become accustomed to their goals, managers are able to take a less-dominant role. You try to reach a win-win situation.
   b Conflict frequently occurs and some teams may even disband. Leaders constantly have to resolve conflict.
   c The team sets objectives and agrees on how best to achieve them. Behavior is polite, yet restrained, and the group is yet to fully unify.
   d Successful teams can struggle as individuals once they reach this stage.
   e Optimum performance has not quite been reached. However, people understand everyone's roles and have a single aim.

2 Discuss these questions in a group.
   1 Why might leaders need to take a dominant role during the "forming" stage?
   2 Is it always the responsibility of leaders to resolve conflict that arises during the "storming" stage? Why / why not?
   3 Although their intervention is limited during the "performing" stage, why might teams still require an overall leader?

E Critical thinking

Discuss these questions with a partner.

1 Think about when you have worked on teams. Did you develop in the manner Tuckman describes?
2 Which conflict management styles described in the text is your dominant style? What do you think are the strengths and weaknesses of this style?

Vocabulary development

Adverbs of stance

Adverbs of stance can be used to enhance or imply your attitude toward an issue, source, or line of argument. Choosing the best adverb to accurately express your opinion is an important part of academic writing.

1 Match the adverbs in bold with the correct definitions.

1 **arguably**
2 **equally**
3 **essentially**
4 **fundamentally**
5 **highly**
6 **inevitably**
7 **realistically**
8 **unquestionably**

a used to say that something cannot be avoided or prevented
b used for emphasizing what is the most important aspect of something, or fact about something
c used to say what is likely in a situation
d in a very important or basic way
e used to show that something is obvious and leaves no room for doubt
f used to introduce an idea as important as the last
g used for stating your opinion or belief, especially when you think other people may disagree
h used before some adjectives to mean "very" or "to a large degree"

2 Choose the correct adverb to complete each sentence.

1 While the theory is **unquestionably / equally** influential, it is largely unsubstantiated.
2 The idea that conflict should be avoided is **fundamentally / inevitably** flawed.
3 **Realistically / Equally**, minor disagreements are unavoidable in such a large group.
4 While many employees thrive in a collaborative environment, others are **equally / essentially** content to work alone.
5 I, for one, am **highly / broadly** skeptical about the teams' ability to perform effectively.
6 **Essentially / Inevitably**, I concur with the scientific consensus—groupthink is a purely theoretical construct.
7 High-pressured environments like these **inevitably / partially** lead to conflict within the group.
8 **Equally / Arguably**, there is insufficient data to substantiate the claim.

Academic words

VOCABULARY

1 Complete the definitions with the words in the box.

| accommodate | constrain | instruct | intervene |
| predominant | restraint | unified | utilize |

1 _____ (adj) behaving or treated as one group, country, or system
2 _____ (adj) the most common or greatest in number or amount
3 _____ (v) to consider and include something when you are deciding what to do
4 _____ (v) to limit someone's freedom to do what he or she wants
5 _____ (n) the ability to behave calmly and with self-control
6 _____ (v) to tell someone to do something, especially officially or as an employer
7 _____ (v) to become involved in a situation in order to try to stop or change it
8 _____ (v) to use something

2 Complete the sentences with words from Exercise 1. Change the form if necessary.

1 A group must be _____ in the face of opposition–in-fighting makes a team look weak.
2 Managers should aim to limit _____ in group decision-making as much as possible.
3 Good managers _____ their colleague's expertise to help them make informed decisions.
4 Managers should ask team members to repeat _____ to ensure they've understood them correctly.
5 Group conflict is _____ due to a lack of coherent leadership.
6 It's important to _____ other people's stance even when we are opposed to it.
7 When leadership _____ creativity, a company becomes ineffective.
8 Even when we disagree strongly, it is important to exercise _____ to minimize conflict.

3 Work in a group. Discuss the extent to which you agree with the statements from Exercise 2. Explain your reasoning.

CRITICAL THINKING

Critical thinking

Critical thinking review

The critical evaluation of claims and arguments, both those made by another writer and your own, is an essential part of academic study. When reading or writing a text, use the following types of questions to guide your assessment or construction of a claim or argument:

- Has sufficient evidence been provided to support the claim?
- Does the information come from credible, unbiased sources?
- Has the data been fairly represented or has it been manipulated?
- Is the writing biased or impartial?
- Does the writing contain any logical fallacies (e.g., ad hominem attacks, arguments from popularity, etc.)?
- Do the conclusions logically follow the main argument?

1 Read the text and identify the claim / argument, the supporting evidence, and the conclusion.

> Dealing with conflict fairly and directly is a fundamental skill of all effective managers. According to Hooper (2017), his extensive personal experience led him to believe that those who persistently avoid conflict will have less respect from both their team and the management of an organization. Managers who lack the respect of others due to their unwillingness to approach the situation effectively will be faced with an untenable situation.

2 Work with a partner. Use the questions in the *Critical thinking review* box to evaluate the strength of the argument from Exercise 1.

3 Construct your own argument on the topic of "Managing conflict." Find an appropriate source to support your argument.

4 Exchange your arguments with a partner. Use the checklist in the skills box to evaluate its strength.

Writing model

You are going to learn about conjunctions and writing a reference list. You are then going to use these to write an essay on successful teams.

A Analyze

Read the extract from an essay on workplace conflict and complete the mind map.

Positive — **Conflict** — *Negative*

B Model

Workplace conflict is realistically an everyday phenomenon that arises for a variety of reasons. Essentially, conflict occurs for three predominant reasons. According to Lipsky (2016), these are wherever there is the incompatibility of goals between two or more people, a serious and protracted disagreement, and structural organization features and work arrangements. This essay will argue that while conflict unquestionably has a number of negative consequences, when managed well, it can actually be positive.

Whenever conflict at work occurs, it has not only a number of negative effects on individuals, but it can also affect the company as a whole. Adkins (2015) found that over half the people surveyed had left positions at some point to escape their manager. Such poor staff retention will inevitably affect company performance. Fundamentally, the amount of time spent mediating conflict has a negative impact on the bottom line.

However, conflict also has many positive effects on performance. Broadly speaking, utilizing conflict can lead to open and honest consultation which, in turn, drives higher productivity. Baron (2001) found that such exchanges can facilitate greater flexibility and thus overall enhance performance. However, such benefits can only be achieved through clear, stable and unified leadership.

In conclusion, while there are many financial risks associated with employee conflict, effective management of the situation can actually lead to a more productive and profitable company.

References:

Adkins, A. (2016). Employee engagement in U.S. stagnant in 2015. *Gallup News*. Available at: http://news.gallup.com/poll/188144/employee-engagement-stagnant-2015.aspx [Accessed: 13th September 2017]

Baron, R. A. (1991). Positive effects of conflict: A cognitive perspective. *Employee Responsibilities and Rights Journal*. 4(1), 63–66

Lipsky, D. B., Avgar, A. C., and Lamare, R. J. (2016). Managing and resolving workplace conflict. Bingley: Emerald Group Publishing Ltd.

Scan the text again and answer the questions.

1 What extra information about each source is given in the reference list?
2 How does each source support the writer's argument?

Grammar

Conjunctions

When we add *-ever* to *wh-* words such as, *what, which, when, where,* and *who,* we change their meaning to "it doesn't matter / no matter." We use these as subordinating conjunctions to give focus and to join the clause to the rest of the sentence.

Whoever is in charge needs to utilize the skill set of their team effectively.
Whatever changes are made need to align with the budget.
Whichever option is selected, a unified team needs to be behind it.
Managers need to intervene whenever conflict arises.

1 Match the sentence halves.

1 Whatever the source of the conflict,
2 Whoever takes responsibility for this decision
3 Whichever option is given precedence,
4 An opinion voiced by a large group must be heard,
5 Wherever the company relocates to,
6 Whenever managers intervene,
7 It's unwise for team members to focus on

a it needs to accommodate as many perspectives as is feasible.
b they need to do so in a timely manner.
c however absurd it may sound at first.
d a swift resolution must be found.
e it will need to consider the cultural implications.
f whoever is to blame for their team's shortcomings.
g needs to be willing to face the consequences.

2 Rewrite the sentences using an appropriate subordinating conjunction. Delete or change the form of words as necessary.

1 Lucas and Hitomi must reach an acceptable consensus regardless of their differences.
   _____

2 We must ensure the person we appoint is experienced in conflict mediation.
   _____

3 We will not be able to appease everyone with the solution we choose.
   _____

4 Mark leading a team inevitably leads to conflict.
   _____

5 A degree of dissatisfaction is guaranteed for any location we base our head office in.
   _____

Writing skill

> All sources cited in an academic essay need to be added to a reference list at the end of the text. A common referencing system is the Harvard system. In this system, all references are listed alphabetically by the author's surname, but different information is included for books, journals, and websites:
>
> - **BOOKS:** Last name, initials. (Year published) *Title.* Edition. City: Publisher.
>
>   Janis, I. L. (1973). *Victims of Groupthink.* 2nd ed. Boston: Houghton Mifflin.
>
> - **JOURNALS:** Last name, initials. (Year published). Article title. *Journal name.* volume number (issue number), page numbers.
>
>   Leana, C. R. (1985). A Partial Test of Janis' Groupthink Model. *Journal of Management.* 11(1), 5–18
>
> - **WEBSITES:** Last name, initials. (Year published). Article title. *Website name.* Available: URL [Accessed: Date]
>
>   Cain, S. (2012). The Rise of the New Groupthink. *The New York Times.* Available: http://www.nytimes.com/2012/01/15/opinion/sunday/the-rise-of-the-new-groupthink.html?mcubz=3 [Accessed: 13th September 2017]
>
> Note, if the journal is accessed online the URL and access date should be added at the end of the reference.

1 Rewrite the references so the information is presented in the correct order.

1. *Conflict Management.* Smith, L. (2016) New York: 3rd ed. Academial Press
2. P. Johnson. *Journal of Applied Management.* Management Techniques (2017) 15 (2), 25–26
3. Dealing with Conflict. *Practical Psychology.* [Accessed: 15th October 2017] Adams, K. (2014) Available: http://www.practialpsych.com/dealingwithconflict
4. The New Groupthink. *Journal of Group Psychology.* Moore, R. (2016) [Accessed: 8th July 2014] 25 (9), 15–16. Available: http://www.journals.skillfulpub.com/home/jgp/thenewgroupthink

2 Find two mistakes in each reference. Think about the order of the information, style, and whether anything is missing.

1. Richardson, G. The Benefits of Groupthink. 3rd ed. Cambridge: Loki Press
2. Caleb, C. (2017). Styles of Conflict. 17 (4)
3. J. Rolfe. Dealing with conflict. *Business Change.* Available: http://www.businesschange.com/conflict

WRITING

Writing a reference list

WRITING

Writing task

You are going to write an essay in response to the following:

"Some people think that cooperation with others makes a successful team. Others feel that conflict is necessary for better team performance. Discuss both views and give your opinion."

Brainstorm

Complete the brainstorm.

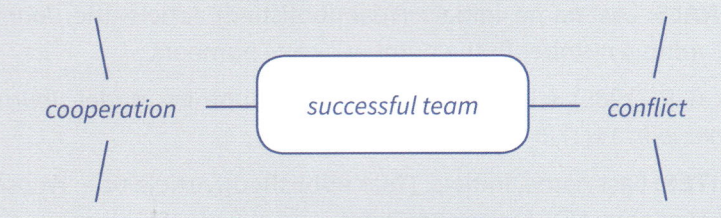

cooperation — successful team — conflict

Plan

1 Find citations to support your ideas in the brainstorm stage.

2 Plan the introduction, body, and conclusion of your essay, noting where to incorporate the citations you found in Exercise 1.

3 Add notes to your plan, explaining how the sources support your ideas.

Write

Use your plan and brainstorm to help you write your essay. Remember to use conjunctions where appropriate, and to include a reference list. Your essay should be 300 words long.

Share

Exchange your essay with a partner. Use the checklist on page 189 to help you provide feedback to your partner.

Rewrite and edit

Consider your partner's comments and write your final draft. Think about:

- whether you answered the question clearly
- whether you used conjunctions appropriately
- whether you included a reference list.

Review

Wordlist

Vocabulary preview

assertive (adj)	confrontation (n) **	inferior (adj) *	optimum (adj)
cohesive (adj)	detrimental (adj)	intolerance (n)	peer pressure (n)
collaborate (v) *	hinder (v)	leadership (n) ***	tactic (n) **
consensus (n) **	impatience (n)	mediate (v)	theoretical (adj) **

Vocabulary development

arguably (adv) *	fundamentally (adv) *	partially (adv) **	unquestionably (adv)
broadly (adv) **	inevitably (adv) **	realistically (adv)	

Academic words

accommodate (v) *	instruct (v) **	predominant (adj)	unified (adj)
constrain (v)	intervene (v) *	restraint (n) *	utilize (v)

Academic words review

Complete the sentences using the correct form of the words in the box.

| accommodate | eventual | instruct | ongoing | utilize |

1. During the Norming stage of conflict resolution, teams are asked to _____ the needs of others in the group.
2. Many staff members felt that the management did not _____ their potential, and were not willing to invest in them.
3. The groups were _____ to put aside their individual grievances and resolve their problems as a team.
4. European governments have been reluctant to tackle the _____ refugee crisis in countries such as Greece and Italy.
5. Despite persistent injury problems, the defending champion was the _____ winner of the tournament.

Unit review

Reading 1	☐	I can prepare for a seminar.
Reading 2	☐	I can identify supporting evidence.
Study skill	☐	I can use material of suitable quality and content.
Vocabulary	☐	I can use adverbs of stance.
Grammar	☐	I can use conjunctions.
Writing	☐	I can use reference lists.

FUNCTIONAL LANGUAGE

Functional language phrase bank

The phrases below give common ways of expressing useful functions. Use them to help you as you're completing the *Discussion points* and *Developing critical thinking* activities.

Asking for clarification
Sorry, can you explain that some more?
Could you say that another way?
When you say … do you mean …?
Sorry, I don't follow that.
What do you mean?

Asking for repetition
Could you repeat that, please?
I'm sorry, I didn't catch that.
Could you say that again?

When you don't know the word for something
What does … mean?
Sorry, I'm not sure what … means.

Working with a partner
Would you like to start?
Shall I go first?
Shall we do this one first?
Where do you want to begin?

Giving opinions
I think that …
It seems to me that …
In my opinion …
As I see it …

Agreeing and disagreeing
I know what you mean.
That's true.
You have a point there.
Yes. I see what you're saying, but …
I understand your point, but …
I don't think that's true.

Asking for opinions
Do you think …?
Do you feel …?
What do you think about …?
How about you, Jennifer?
What do you think?
What about you?
Does anyone have any other ideas?
Do you have any thoughts on this?

Asking for more information
In what way?
Why do you think that?
Can you give an example?

Not giving a strong preference
It doesn't matter to me.
I don't really have a strong preference.
I've never really thought about that.
Either is fine.

Expressing interest
I'd like to hear more about that.
That sounds interesting.
How interesting!
Tell me more about that.

Giving reasons
This is … because …
This has to be … because …
I think … because …

Checking understanding
Do you know what I mean?
Do you see what I'm saying?
Are you following me?

Putting things in order
This needs to come first because …
I think this is the most/least important because …
For me, this is the most/least relevant because …

Writing task peer review checklist

Use the checklist below as you read over your partner's work.

1. Does the composition have these things?
   - a title
   - a clear structure (e.g., an introduction, body, and conclusion)
   - appropriate punctuation

2. Write the thesis statement here:
   _____

3. Underline the topic sentences in each paragraph. Write the number of any paragraphs that don't have a clear topic sentence here: _____

4. Is the author's position on the issue / topic clear?

5. Have they included any vocabulary from the unit? If so, is it used appropriately?

6. Have they used any grammar from the unit? If so, is it used appropriately?

7. Underline any sentences or passages you particularly like. What do you like about them?

8. Are sources provided for factual statements?

9. Are claims or arguments supported by evidence?

10. Write one question about the content for the author:
    _____

PEER REVIEW CHECKLIST

ACADEMIC WORDS

Academic words revision

Units 1–5

Complete the sentences using the correct form of the words in the box.

> attribute deduction dispose erosion evolve
> format fund integral offset perception

1. Over the past eight years, Kickstarter has helped _____ over 130,000 projects.
2. On-demand services are _____ to the success of the television industry.
3. Inference and _____ are fundamental aspects of the scientific method.
4. The higher cost of materials will be _____ by savings in other key areas.
5. Low-level radioactive waste can be safely _____ of in landfills.
6. Over 50% of the change is directly _____ to thermal expansion.
7. After years of costal _____, Malta's famous "Azure Window" collapsed into the sea.
8. Her new book focuses on the _____ of language during the digital age.
9. There is a _____ that the company values profits over people.
10. Despite the recent global trend toward digital, many still prefer physical _____.

Units 6–10

Complete the sentences using the correct form of the words in the box.

> accumulate analogy constrain core exclude
> finite innovate intervene migrate predominant

1. Over 100,000 people have _____ to rural areas since 2008.
2. "_____ is key to the long-term success of any organization."
3. Good speakers use _____ to illustrate challenging concepts.
4. When conflict arises, managers should _____ early in order to avoid large-scale disruption.
5. Regeneration of the rust belt was the _____ message of her campaign.
6. Water droplets _____ around the silver iodide particles and freeze to form ice crystals.
7. It's important to note that this figure _____ import taxes.
8. Fossil fuels are a _____ resource that can cause irreparable damage to the environment.
9. Landing on Mars by 2030 is impossible given current budget _____.
10. Former employees _____ cite a lack of opportunity as their reason for leaving.

Citations

p11 (Reading 1) – Gaskell, A. (2016). *Social Commerce at the End of 2016*: Trends and Statistics. https://www.forbes.com/sites/adigaskell/2016/03/15/the-rise-of-investment-crowdfunding/#78fea9184d9b

p11 (Reading 1) – N/A, (N.D). Stats. https://www.kickstarter.com/help/stats.

p11 (Reading 1) – Kuppuswamy, V. et al. (2013). Crowdfunding creative ideas: The dynamics of project backers in Kickstarter. https://www.entrepreneur.com/article/234516.

p11 (Reading 1) – Ryu, S. et al. (2016). Reward versus philanthropy motivation in crowdfunding behaviour. https://www.entrepreneur.com/article/234516.

p13 (Study skills) – Mollick, E. (2016). Containing Multitudes: The Many Impacts of Kickstarter Funding. https://papers.ssrn.com/sol3/papers.cfm?abstract_id=2808000.

p16 (Reading 2) – Casey, S. (2016). 2016 Nielsen Social Media Report. http://www.nielsen.com/us/en/insights/reports/2017/2016-nielsen-social-media-report.html.

p29 (Reading 1) – Digital TV Research. (N.D). Global SVOD Forecasts. https://www.digitaltvresearch.com/products/product?id=163.

p33-34 (Reading 2) – Kühn, S. et al. (2014). Playing Super Mario induces structural brain plasticity: gray matter changes resulting from training with a commercial video game. *Molecular Psychiatry.*

p72 (Vocabulary development) – O'Neal, EE. et al. (2017). Changes in Perception-Action Tuning Over Long Time Scales: How Children and Adults Perceive and Act on Dynamic Affordances When Crossing Roads. *Journal of Experimental Pyschology, Human Perception and Performance.*

p83 (Reading 1) – Ohanian, LE. (2014). Competition and the decline of the rust belt. https://www.minneapolisfed.org/research/economic-policy-papers/competition-and-the-decline-of-the-rust-belt.

p83 (Reading 1) – Cowan, A. (2016). *A Nice Place to Visit.* Temple University Press

p83 (Reading 1) – Eyles, J. (2008). Tourism in the rust belt: using the past as an economic development strategy. *WIT Transactions on Ecology and the Environment, Vol 115.*

p83 (Reading 1) – Lacher, RG. (2011). Is tourism a low-income industry? Evidence from Three Coastal Regions. *Journal of Travel Research.*

p83 (Reading 1) – Siddiqui, N. (2013). Rising from the Ashes: economic transformation in rust belt cities. http://chicagopolicyreview.org/2013/12/16/rising-from-the-ashes-economic-transformation-in-rust-belt-cities/.

p83 (Reading 1) – Beyerlein, T. (2012). State handling millions to businesses who threaten to move. https://www.policymattersohio.org/press-room/2012/10/08/state-handing-millions-to-businesses-who-threaten-to-move.

p83 (Reading 1) – Heins, P. (2012). Embracing Smart Decline. *Agora Journal of Urban Planning and Design, 1-6.*

p83 (Reading 1) – Lee, J. and Newman, G. (2017). Forecasting Urban Vacancy Dynamics in a Shrinking City: A Land Transformation Model. *ISPRS International Journal of Geo-Information 2017, 6(4), 124.*

p83 (Reading 1) – Hackworth, J. (2016). Demolition as urban policy in the American Rust Belt. *Environment and Planning A, Vol 48, Issue 11.*

p87-88 (Reading 2) – Urban Land Institute. (2016). Housing in the Evolving American Suburb. https://uli.org/wp-content/uploads/ULI-Documents/Housing-in-the-Evolving-American-Suburb.pdf.

p93 (Writing model) – Adler, B. (2015). How suburban sprawl causes segregation and isolates the poor. http://grist.org/cities/how-suburban-sprawl-causes-segregation-and-isolates-the-poor/.

p101 (Reading 1) – Sheldon, W.H. (1954). *Atlas of men: A guide for somatotyping the adult male at all ages.* Harper & Brothers.

p101 (Reading 1) – Lemert E, M. (1951). *Social pathology: a systematic approach to the theory of sociopathic behaviour.* New York: McGraw-Hill.

p101 (Reading 1) – Becker, H. (1963). *Outsiders: Studies in the Sociology of Deviance.* New York: The Free Press.

p101 (Reading 1) – The Cambridge Study in Delinquent Development (2013). Found in: Siegel, L. J. (2016). *Criminology: Theories, Patterns and Typologies.* Cengage Learning.

p101 (Reading 1) – Intelligence and Crime. (n.d). *Encyclopedia of Crime and Justice.* The Gale Group Inc. http://www.encyclopedia.com/law/legal-and-political-magazines/intelligence-and-crime

p101 (Reading 1) – Rousewell, D. (2014). Nature beats nurture as more than 60% of a child's intelligence comes from parents. http://www.mirror.co.uk/news/technology-science/science/nature-beats-nurture-more-60-4391333.

p101 (Reading 1) – The Minnesota Twin Family Study (n.d). Found in: Siegel, L. J. (2016). *Criminology: Theories, Patterns and Typologies.* Cengage Learning.

p111 (Writing model) – Jaffee, S. R. et al. (2012). Chaotic homes and children's disruptive behaviour: A longitudinal cross-lagged twin study. *Psychological Science.*

p116 (Infographic) – 100 People: A World Portrait (2016). http://www.100people.org/statistics_detailed_statistics.php.

p116 (Infographic) – Pew Researc h Center (2015). World Population by Income. http://www.pewglobal.org/interactives/global-population-by-income/.

p123-124 (Reading 2) – United Nations (2015). World population projected to reach 9.7 billion by 2050. http://www.un.org/en/development/desa/news/population/2015-report.html.

p123-124 (Reading 2) – UN Water (2013). Water cooperation - Facts and Figures. http://unwater-archive.stage.gsdh.org/UN-Water/www.unwater.org/water-cooperation-2013//water-cooperation/facts-and-figures/en/.

p123-124 (Reading 2) – Beddington, J. et al. (2011). Achieving food security in the face of climate change. https://cgspace.cgiar.org/rest/bitstreams/15409/retrieve.

p123-124 (Reading 2) – Fertility rate, total (births per woman). https://data.worldbank.org/indicator/SP.DYN.TFRT.IN.

p152 (Infographic) – Reuben, A. (2015). Gap between rich and poor 'keeps growing'. http://www.bbc.co.uk/news/business-32824770.

p152 (Infographic) – Dion, S. (2015). A World Price for Carbon. http://hir.harvard.edu/article/?a=11255.

p155 (Reading 1) – Funk, C. and Kennedy, B. (2016). 1. Public views on climate change and climate scientists. http://www.pewinternet.org/2016/10/04/public-views-on-climate-change-and-climate-scientists/.

p155 (Reading 1) – NASA. (n.d.) Climate change: How do we know? https://climate.nasa.gov/evidence/.

p155 (Reading 1) – United States Environmental Protection Agency. (n.d.) Climate Change Indicators: Sea Surface Temperature. (n.d). https://www.epa.gov/climate-indicators/climate-change-indicators-sea-surface-temperature.

p155 (Reading 1) – The Royal Society. (n.d.) 6. Climate is always changing. Why is climate change of concern now? (n.d). https://royalsociety.org/topics-policy/projects/climate-change-evidence-causes/question-6/.

p155 (Reading 1) – Sea Level Rise. (n.d). http://www.nationalgeographic.com/environment/global-warming/sea-level-rise/.

p155 (Reading 1) – Carrington, D. (2017). Sea level rise will double coastal flood risk worldwide. https://www.theguardian.com/environment/2017/may/18/sea-level-rise-double-coastal-flood-risk-worldwide.

p159-160 (Reading 2) – McKie, R. (2015). Why fresh water shortages will cause the next great global crisis. https://www.theguardian.com/environment/2015/mar/08/how-water-shortages-lead-food-crises-conflicts.

p173 (Reading 1) – Tuckman, B. W. et al. (1977). Stages of Small-Group Development Revisited. *Group & Organization Management.* GROUP ORGAN MANAGE. 2. 419-427. 10.1177/105960117700200404.

p173 (Reading 1) – Turner, S. P. & Weed, F. (1983). Conflict in organizations: *Practical solutions any manager can use.* NJ: Prentice-Hall

p173 (Reading 1) – Janis, I. L. (1971). Groupthink. *Psychology Today*, 5 (6): 43–46, 74–76.

p173 (Reading 1) – Janis, I. L. (1972). *Victims of Groupthink: a Psychological Study of Foreign-Policy Decisions and Fiascoes.* Boston: Houghton Mifflin

p173 (Reading 1) – Park, W. W. (1990). A review of research on Group think. *Journal of Behavioral Decision-Making*, 3 (4): 229–245. doi:10.1002/bdm.3960030402.

p173 (Reading 1) – Erdem, F. (2003). Optimal trust and teamwork: from group think to teamthink. *Work Study*, 52(5), 229–233.

p173 (Reading 1) – Dimitroff, R. D. et al. (2005). Organizational behavior and disaster: A study of conflict at NASA. *Project Management Journal.* https://www.pmi.org/learning/library/organizational-behavior-disaster-5532

p173 (Reading 1) – Scharff, M. M. (2005). Understanding Worldcom's accounting fraud: Did group think play a role? *Journal of Leadership and Organizational Studies.* http://journals.sagepub.com/doi/abs/10.1177/107179190501100309

p177-178 (Reading 2) – Johnson, C. A. et al. (2014). Technical brief for the Thomas-Kilmann Conflict Mode Instrument. http://www.kilmanndiagnostics.com/system/files/TKI_TranslationsStudy.pdf.

Macmillan Education Limited
4 Crinan Street
London N1 9XW

Companies and representatives throughout the world

ISBN 978-1-380-00600-4

Text, design and illustration © Macmillan Education Limited 2018

Written by Lindsay Warwick and Louis Rogers
Series Consultant Dorothy E. Zemach

The author has asserted their right to be identified as the author of this work in accordance with the Copyright, Designs and Patents Act 1988.

This edition published 2018
First edition entitled "Skillful" published 2012 by Macmillan Education Limited

All rights reserved. No part of this publication may be reproduced, stored in a retrieval system, or transmitted in any form or by any means, electronic, mechanical, photocopying, recording, or otherwise, without the prior written permission of the publishers.

Designed by emc design ltd
Illustrated by Carl Morris (Beehive Illustration) pp51, 57, 58 and 60.
Cover design by emc design ltd
Cover illustration/photograph by Getty Images/Moment Open/Alicia Llop
Picture research by Emily Taylor

The publishers would like to thank the following for their thoughtful insights and perceptive comments during the development of the material: Dalal Al Hitty University of Bahrain, Bahrain; Karin Heuert Galvao, i-Study Interactive Learning, São Paulo, Brazil; Ohanes Sakris Australian College of Kuwait, Kuwait; Eoin Jordan, Xi'an Jiaotong Liverpool University, Suzhou, China; Aaron Rotsinger, Xi'an Jiaotong-Liverpool University, Suzhou, China; Dr. Osman Z. Barnawi, Royal Commission Colleges and Institutes, Yanbu, Saudi Arabia; Andrew Lasher, SUNY Korea, Incheon, South Korea; Fatoş Ugur Eskicirak (Fatoş Uğur Eskiçırak) Bahçeşehir University, Istanbul, Turkey; Dr. Asmaa Awad, University of Sharjah, Sharjah, United Arab Emirates; Amy Holtby, Khalifa University of Science and Technology, Abu Dhabi, United Arab Emirates, Dr. Christina Gitsaki, Zayed University, Dubai, United Arab Emirates.

The authors and publishers would like to thank the following for permission to reproduce their photographs:

Alamy/Jeff Greenberg p123-124; **Getty Images** p69, Getty Images/AFP/Frederic J. Brown p163, Getty Images/Age footstock p173, Getty Images/Andresr p134-135, Getty Images/Arctic-Images p116-117, Getty Images/Blackstation p121, Getty Images/Bloomberg/Andrey Rudakov p26-27, Getty Images/Sam Bloomberg-Rissman p84, Getty Images/Caiaimage p181, Getty Images/Corbis p152-153, Getty Images/Cultura p47, Getty Images/d3sign p8-9, Getty Images/Michael Duerinckx p73, Getty Images/Tim Graham p94, Getty Images/Bartosz Hadyniak p131, Getty Images/Hulton Archive p110, Getty Images/ilbusca p105, Getty Images/Image Bank p62-63, Getty Images/Harold M. Lambert p90, Getty Images/Rich LaSalle p56, Getty Images/LA Times p137, Getty Images/Lester Lefkowitz p175, Getty Images/Lonely Planet Images/Matthew Micah Wright p54, Getty Images/Alexandros Maragos p155, Getty Images/Kelvin Murray p11, Getty Images/PeopleImages.com p21, Getty Images/Querbeet p156, Getty Images/Sascha Schuermann p33, Getty Images/Tomas Sereda p44-45, Getty Images/Don Smith p15, Getty Images/Taxi p109, Getty Images/Todor Tsvetkov p16, Getty Images/Universal Images Group p102, Getty Images/Tom Werner p145, Getty Images/Ted Wood p81-82; **PlainPicture**/Maskot p170-171; **Rex Features**/KeystoneUSA-ZUM/REX/Shutterstock p87; **Shutterstock**/B Calkins p13, Shutterstock/Paul Cowan p164, Shutterstock/idiz p159-160, Shutterstock/Image Source Trading Ltd p19, Shutterstock/iMoStudio p127, Shutterstock/Peter Kotoff p31, Shutterstock/LianeM p48, Shutterstock/Sayan Moongklang p83, Shutterstock/Palo_ok p130, Shutterstock/Vitstudio p98-99; **Thomson Reuters** pp8(bl), 26(bl), 44(bl), 62(bl), 81(bl), 98(bl), 116(bl), 134(bl), 152(bl), 170(bl).

The author and publisher would like to thank the following for permission to reproduce the following material:

p29, 36. Infographic from 'Global Music Report: State of the Industry Overview 2016' © IFPI 2016. Reprinted with permission. www.ifpi.org

These materials may contain links for third party websites. We have no control over, and are not responsible for, the contents of such third party websites. Please use care when accessing them.

Printed and bound in Poland by CGS

2025 2024 2023 2022 2021
24 123 22 21 20 19 18 17

PALGRAVE STUDY SKILLS

by bestselling author, **Stella Cottrell**

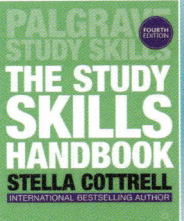

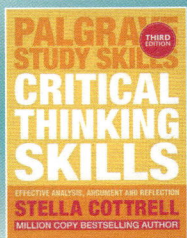

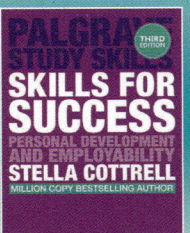

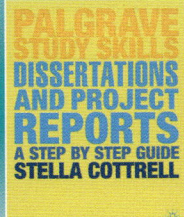

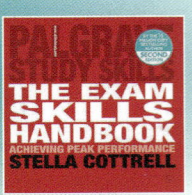

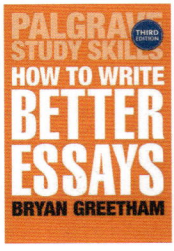

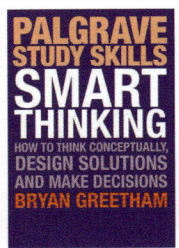

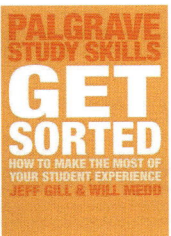

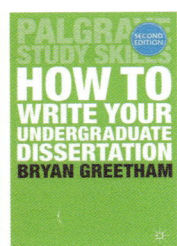

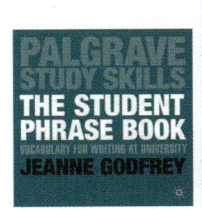

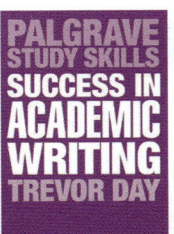

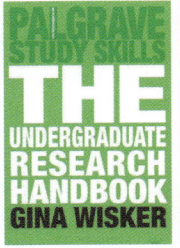

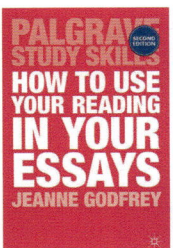

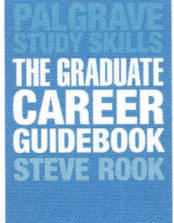

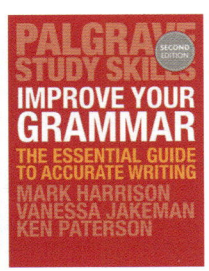

- The Study Skills Handbook — Stella Cottrell
- Critical Thinking Skills: Effective Analysis, Argument and Reflection — Stella Cottrell
- Skills for Success: Personal Development and Employability — Stella Cottrell
- Dissertations and Project Reports: A Step by Step Guide — Stella Cottrell
- The Exam Skills Handbook: Achieving Peak Performance — Stella Cottrell

- Cite Them Right: The Essential Referencing Guide — Richard Pears & Graham Shields
- How to Write Better Essays — Bryan Greetham
- Smart Thinking: How to Think Conceptually, Design Solutions and Make Decisions — Bryan Greetham
- Presentation Skills for Students — Joan van Emden & Lucinda Becker
- Get Sorted: How to Make the Most of Your Student Experience — Jeff Gill & Will Medd
- How to Write Your Undergraduate Dissertation — Bryan Greetham

- The Student Phrase Book: Vocabulary for Writing at University — Jeanne Godfrey
- Success in Academic Writing — Trevor Day
- The Undergraduate Research Handbook — Gina Wisker
- How to Use Your Reading in Your Essays — Jeanne Godfrey
- The Graduate Career Guidebook — Steve Rook
- Improve Your Grammar: The Essential Guide to Accurate Writing — Mark Harrison, Vanessa Jakeman, Ken Paterson

palgravestudyskills.com

facebook.com/skills4study

twitter.com/skills4study